Social Protest and Contentious Authoritarianism in China

Xi Chen explores the question of why there has been a dramatic rise in and routinization of social protests in China since the early 1990s. Drawing on case studies, in-depth interviews, and a unique data set of about 1,000 government records of collective petitions, this book examines how the political structure in Reform China has encouraged Chinese farmers, workers, pensioners, disabled people, and demobilized soldiers to pursue their interests and claim their rights by staging collective protests. Chen also suggests that routinized contentious bargaining between the government and ordinary people has remedied the weaknesses of the Chinese political system and contributed to the regime's resilience. *Social Protest and Contentious Authoritarianism in China* challenges the conventional wisdom that authoritarian regimes always repress popular collective protest and that popular collective action tends to destabilize authoritarian regimes.

Xi Chen is an assistant professor of political science at the University of North Carolina at Chapel Hill. His articles have appeared in *Comparative Politics* and *The China Quarterly*. He has contributed to three books: *Contemporary Chinese Politics: New Sources, Methods, and Field Strategies* (Cambridge, 2010, edited by Allen Carlson et al.); *Popular Protest in China* (2008, edited by Kevin O'Brien); and *Grassroots Political Reform in Contemporary China* (2007, edited by Elizabeth Perry and Merle Goldman).

Social Protest and Contentious Authoritarianism in China

XI CHEN

University of North Carolina, Chapel Hill

CAMBRIDGE
UNIVERSITY PRESS

CAMBRIDGE UNIVERSITY PRESS
Cambridge, New York, Melbourne, Madrid, Cape Town,
Singapore, São Paulo, Delhi, Tokyo, Mexico City

Cambridge University Press
32 Avenue of the Americas, New York, NY 10013-2473, USA

www.cambridge.org
Information on this title: www.cambridge.org/9781107014862

First published 2012

Printed in the United States of America

A catalog record for this publication is available from the British Library.

Library of Congress Cataloging in Publication data
Chen, Xi, 1972 Sept. 6–
    Social protest and contentious authoritarianism in China / Xi Chen.
        p.   cm.
    Includes bibliographical references and index.
    ISBN 978-1-107-01486-2
    1. Social conflict – China.   2. Protest movements – China.
    3. China – Politics and government – 1976–2002.   4. China – Politics
    and government – 2002–   I. Title.
    HN740.Z9.S62.C44   2011
    322.40951–dc23   2011023045

ISBN 978-1-107-01486-2 Hardback

To my parents
Chen Guorong and Yang Shuangmei

Contents

List of Figures and Tables   *page* viii
Acknowledgments   xi

PART I   A CONTENTIOUS SOCIETY

1. Introduction   3
2. The Surge in Social Protests from a Historical Perspective   27

PART II   POLITICAL OPPORTUNITY STRUCTURE

3. Market Reforms and State Strategies   59
4. The Xinfang System and Political Opportunity   87

PART III   PROTEST STRATEGIES AND TACTICS

5. Between Defiance and Obedience   135
6. "Troublemaking" Tactics and Their Efficacy   159

PART IV   CONCLUSION

7. Reflections and Speculations   189

Appendix   213
Bibliography   221
Index   235

Figures and Tables

Figures

2.1. Number of collective petitioners per million people
in Hunan and Henan Provinces, 1991–2000   *page* 30
2.2. Number of participants in individual visits and
collective visits, and number of letters in Hunan,
1991–2001   31
2.3. Participants/letters in Henan Province, 1978–1998   32
2.4. Petitions to the General Office of the State Council,
1952–1981   41
3.1. State strategies when responding to popular
claim making   66
6.1. Three routes of popular claim making in the PRC   166

Tables

2.1. Number of Collective Petitions on Several Main
Issues in Hunan Province, 1994–2001   34
2.2. Issues of Collective Petitioning in Hunan Province,
1985–1986, 1994–1995, 2000–2001   38
2.3. Number of Petitions Delivered to Some Selected
Central and Local Governmental Agencies, 1979–1981   42
4.1. Government Agencies Investigating Xinfang Cases
in County H, 1991–2001   98
4.2. The Highest Levels of Leaders Issuing Written
Instructions in County H, 1990–2001   103
4.3. Levels of Government Agencies Investigating Xinfang
Cases in County H, 1990–2001   106

4.4. Relations between Levels of Investigators and
    Investigation Results in County H, 1990–2001   107
4.5. Relations between Levels of Instructions and
    Investigation Results in County H, 1990–2001   108
5.1. Relations between the Duration of Petitioning Activities
    and the Level of Confrontation in City Y, 1992–2002   157
6.1. Incidence of Petitions with "Troublemaking" Tactics in
    City Y, 1992–2002   170
6.2. Logit Coefficients for Regression of the Presence of
    Substantial Government Responses to Petitioning
    Tactics in City Y, 1992–2002   183

Acknowledgments

During the long journey of writing this book, I have accumulated many debts of gratitude. Because the book began as a doctoral dissertation at Columbia University, I want to thank – first and foremost – the three teachers in the committee: Thomas Bernstein, Andrew Nathan, and Charles Tilly. As devoted mentors, Thomas Bernstein and Andrew Nathan provided encouragement and invaluable guidance at all stages of the project. I am profoundly indebted to Charles Tilly not just for his teaching and inspiration, but also for his incredible generosity. Even when he was battling cancer, he never failed to provide truly insightful comments promptly – usually within several hours after a draft was e-mailed to him. This book is a special tribute to him. Benjamin Liebman and Xiaobo Lü read an early version of the manuscript and gave me many important comments. I also want to thank Ira Katznelson because some ideas in this book were developed during his inspiring courses on historical institutionalism.

I would like to acknowledge the kindness shown to me by several scholars who work on contentious politics. Kevin O'Brien provided guidance and encouragement from the beginning of the project, and almost every chapter benefited from his thoughtful comments. Elizabeth Perry, Sidney Tarrow, and Andrew Walder read the entire manuscript and provided very perceptive suggestions and critiques. For helpful comments and suggestions, I also want to thank Calvin Chen, Martin Dimitrov, Merle Goldman, Baogang He, William Hurst, Lianjiang Li, Michael Lienesch, Roderick MacFarquhar, Jean Oi, Dorothy Solinger, John Stephens, Patricia Thornton, Ying Xing, and Dingxin Zhao. I am grateful as well to the participants of the Workshop on Contentious Politics at

Columbia, especially Mingshu Ho, Paul Ingram, Sun-Chul Kim, Adrienne Lebas, Roy Licklider, Francesca Polletta, and Graeme Robertson. More than half of the chapters were presented at this workshop, from which I received helpful feedback.

Like anyone who studies popular contention in contemporary China, I was faced with a formidable challenge in data collection. I therefore want to thank Jiang Ming'an, one of my former teachers at Peking University, for providing me with a temporary affiliation at the Pubic Law Center at PKU. Yi Jiming at the law school of the Central China University of Science and Technology also provided important support. I also deeply appreciate the indispensable help from several government officials in Hunan Province whose names I unfortunately cannot reveal here. From a standpoint slightly different from mine, they were also concerned with the surge of popular collective action. They not only shared their thoughts with me, but also gave me unusual access to valuable government archival materials.

The Fairbank Center for East Asian Research at Harvard University and the Departments of Political Science at Louisiana State University and the University of North Carolina at Chapel Hill provided me with warm and supportive academic environments. Financial support also came from the Weatherhead East Asian Institute at Columbia University, The Council on Research at LSU, and the Carolina Asia Center. For research assistance, I want to thank Lindsay Horn, David Iles III, Sarah Shair-Rosenfield, Zachery Smith, and Ping Xu. Martin Rivlin also generously offered his help in proofreading and editing early versions of the manuscript. At Cambridge University Press I thank Eric Crahan for shepherding my manuscript from the review process to final production and Abigail Zorbaugh for her effective support.

Some of the analysis presented here draws from previously published work. Part of Chapter 4 is adapted from "Institutional Conversion and Collective Petitioning in China," in *Popular Protest in China*, edited by Kevin O'Brien, pp. 54–70, Cambridge, MA: Harvard University Press, Copyright © 2008 by the President and Fellows of Harvard College. Chapter 5 is reprinted in slightly modified form from *Grassroots Political Reform in Contemporary China*, edited by Elizabeth Perry and Merle Goldman, pp. 253–281, Cambridge, MA: Harvard University Press, Copyright © 2007 by the President and Fellows of Harvard College. Chapter 6 is reprinted in slightly modified form from *Comparative Politics*, July 2009: 451–471. I am grateful to the publishers' permission to quote or reprint from these works.

Lastly, I want to express several thanks of a more personal nature. My parents-in-law, Zhong Zhihe and Li Yue'e, and my brother and sister-in-law, Chen Li and Yang Yinghua, provided me with a second home during my field trips. My wife, Hong, made sacrifices for this book more than anyone else, but she may find my acknowledgments to her unnecessary because she co-owns almost everything with me: success or failure, happiness or frustration. The book is no exception. Caroline and Max also deserve special recognition. While they certainly preferred me to spend more time playing with them than working on the book, they refrained from any "troublemaking." Finally, I am forever indebted to my parents, Chen Guorong and Yang Shuangmei, who have always selflessly supported me. They care about my life and my work even more than I do. I dedicate this book to them with deepest love and respect.

PART I

A CONTENTIOUS SOCIETY

1

Introduction

ROUTINIZED SOCIAL PROTESTS

On the early morning of July 8, 2002, more than one hundred pensioners quietly gathered around the municipal government compound in City Y, Hunan Province. They laid wood planks and bricks at the entrance, and then several of them sat down; most others remained standing near the area. Although they did not shout anything, they displayed two huge banners of slogans, one of which requested, "Implement the central and provincial policy, and distribute the subsidy of 51 RMB." They were pensioners from a bankrupt state-owned textile mill who suffered pension arrears, which was a common problem not only in Hunan Province but also in most other provinces in China. Not being particularly noisy, they nonetheless severely disrupted the operation of the government. Because they blocked the main entrance, no vehicle could enter or exit the government compound. Although some officials tried to persuade them to stop the blockade, no security guard or police officer was called to disperse them. The entrance remained essentially closed for five to six hours. Only after a "dialogue" between protest organizers and the municipal governmental officials did those gathered around the compound gate begin to disperse.

The protest in City Y is not an exceptional event. At the local government level, China has experienced a notable increase in social protests since the early 1990s. In Hunan Province in 2001, for instance, 9,213 collective petitioning events, defined as petitions delivered by five or more participants, took place in county-level governments or above. There were twenty-four participants on average in each event.[1] In a number of such collective

---

[1] Data from HNPXB.

petition events, petitioners employed a variety of "troublemaking" tactics, such as demonstrations, sit-downs, and highway blockades.[2]

The dramatic rise of social protests in China since the 1990s has caught much attention from both the media and academia. In the international media, it is not hard to find such passages as "Chinese Protests Grow More Frequent, Violent."[3] Many academic works have also underscored the growing frequency of such incidents as well as "increasingly open disgruntlement" on the part of protesters.[4]

Observers have also noticed that social protest has not only increased, but has also begun to be normalized. As Perry and Selden remark, "Under the reforms, economic protests have become increasingly routinized."[5] Recent media coverage effectively captures what is an increasingly common phenomenon:

> From striking cab drivers to disgruntled farmers, more and more people are taking their economic frustrations to the streets of China.... Instead of beating and arresting protesters as they might have some years ago, officials seem more willing these days to accommodate, negotiate or simply pay them off. As long as demonstrators don't make personal attacks against top leaders or demand political change, they are often free to vent their anger.[6]

The experience of the above group of textile mill pensioners illustrates how collective petitioning had become a routine practice for many ordinary people. From their first collective action in June 1994 until 2002, they staged at least twenty social protests in the district or municipal governments, some using moderate tactics and others being more disruptive. Their requests also evolved over time, sometimes because their demands had been partly met and sometimes because new issues emerged. In the long process of their collective struggle, the pensioners engaged in a sustained bargaining relationship with local authorities. In a give-and-take

---

[2] "Troublemaking" is a technical term and does not carry any negative connotation.

[3] This is the title of an article in the *Wall Street Journal*, May 11, 2004. Other examples include Howard French, "Land of 74,000 Protests (But Little Is Ever Fixed)," *New York Times*, August 24, 2005; Joseph Kahn, "Pace and Scope of Protests in China Accelerated in '05," *New York Times*, January 20, 2006.

[4] For a survey essay, see Kevin O'Brien "Collective Action in the Chinese Countryside," *The China Journal* 48 (July 2002), 139–154.

[5] Elizabeth Perry and Mark Selden (eds.), *Chinese Society: Change, Conflict and Resistance* (London: Routledge, 2000), p. 17.

[6] *Baltimore Sun*, November 20, 1998, p. 34A. Cited from Perry and Selden, *Chinese Society: Change, Conflict and Resistance*, p. 16–17.

style, petitioners gradually improved their economic situation, while local governments maintained a relatively stable social order.

Pensioners are certainly not the only group to engage in contentious bargaining. A vast array of other social groups, even though their struggles might not always have lasted as long, had also engaged in contentious bargaining. Peasants have protested against corrupt grassroots cadres, irregularities in village committee elections, or illegitimate taxes and fees; urban and rural residents have complained about insufficient compensation for house demolition or land expropriation; victims of natural disasters have complained about local officials' embezzlement of governmental funds; handicapped people have protested against local policy that banned their use of special vehicles for passenger transport; and demobilized army officers have demanded jobs. And these are just a few of the examples.

Although contentious bargaining has become a primary form of interest articulation for a large segment of the population, its efficacy has often been underestimated. This is mainly because most social protests in China operate by appropriating the official channel for petitions and appeals (the xinfang system). Because petitions and appeals, as an authorized or even prescribed form of political participation, have a connotation of moderation and submissiveness, they are generally (and correctly) perceived as ineffectual. Social protesters, however, while framing their action as petitions and appeals, have often employed a variety of "troublemaking" tactics. Protesters have thus often obtained considerable bargaining power, although it is rare for their demands to be thoroughly met in the short term. More often, their efficacy lies in the fact that they can maintain the status of de facto pressure groups in local politics so that their interests and opinions become a factor that affects policy making and implementation.

When most disgruntled social groups can find a space for interest articulation, the whole system is much more sustainable. Although the institutions for political representation are conspicuously inadequate in China, the existence of pervasive and routinized popular contention serves as an indicator of the remarkably elastic character of the Chinese system. Therefore one observes a unique political order in China: Beneath the surface of noise and anxiety, the whole political system remains stable.

THE PUZZLE OF CONTENTIOUS AUTHORITARIANISM

The central puzzle tackled by this book is why there has been a dramatic rise in, and routinization of, social protests in China since the early 1990s.

Most existing theories on popular mobilization would hardly expect such a surge to begin during this period, shortly after the Chinese Communist Party (CCP), by a high-handed crackdown of the student movement in 1989, sent a chilling message to potential activists about its capacity and determination to dampen popular contention.

Moreover, according to current theories, pervasive and routinized popular contention in an authoritarian regime is highly "unlikely." Juan Linz notes that low and limited political mobilization is a common characteristic of authoritarian regimes.[7] Sidney Tarrow also points out that by definition, authoritarian regimes are hostile to collective action.[8] Likewise, Adam Przeworski stresses that preventing collective challenges is a major strategy by which authoritarian regimes maintain political stability.[9]

China is an example of a rare phenomenon, which I call contentious authoritarianism, of a strong authoritarian regime having accommodated or facilitated widespread and routinized popular collective action for a relatively long period of time. Of course, under certain circumstances, waves of popular contention are not unusual within authoritarian regimes. Like in a democracy, ordinary people may sometimes find political opportunities to stage collective action in the context of authoritarianism. For example, they can do so when the capacity or propensity of the authoritarian rulers for repression has declined, or when there is significant division among elites. However, the window of opportunity will usually be closed in just a short period of time. This is especially true for popular movements with political goals, which have actually brought down many authoritarian regimes in history. Few such movements lasted for a long period of time, because soon after their founding, they either succeed in changing the system or get put down. Obviously, because of their political nature, they are unlikely to become regularized in a strong authoritarian regime.

Waves of protest movements focused on social and economic demands tend to have a short life span as well. For example, thanks to the political liberalization and divisions between hard-liners and soft-liners, the military regime in Brazil witnessed impressive waves of strikes and

---

[7] Juan Linz, *Totalitarian and Authoritarian Regimes* (Boulder, CO: Lynn Rienner, 2000), p. 269.
[8] Sidney Tarrow, *Power in Movement: Social Movements and Contentious Politics* (New York: Cambridge University Press, 1994).
[9] Adam Przeworski, *Democracy and the Market: Political and Economic Reforms in Eastern Europe and Latin America* (Cambridge: Cambridge University Press, 1991), pp. 58–59.

protests from 1978 to 1980. Workers played a major role in the struggle, but protest waves also spread to other social groups such as neighborhood organizations and feminist groups. Their demands "ranged from the right to strike and better work conditions to the right to land and urban services."[10] For about two years, popular contention was very vigorous. For instance, there were more than 400 strikes between January and October of 1979.[11] However, the window of opportunity soon closed as the economy got worse, the state stepped up their repression, and the installation of collective bargaining mechanisms between employers and workers also reduced workers' incentive to go on strike or protest. Consequently, strike activities sharply declined in 1980, and other protest groups soon lost momentum, too.[12] Thus Patricia L. Hipsher commented, "Although protest under authoritarian governments is not unheard of, it is much more likely to occur during transitional periods."[13]

Although contentious authoritarianism has been quite rare, there has been a trend toward routinization of social movements in Western countries. David Meyer and Sidney Tarrow call it the emergence of "social movement societies," and John McCarthy and Clark McPhail refer to it as "the institutionalization of protest."[14] However, a comparison with the situation in Western societies makes contentious authoritarianism in China appear even more puzzling. This is because China's case seems to lack all the main conditions for a "social movement society" extant in Western countries. First, a democratic system seems to be an indispensable institutional condition for the development of a "social movement society." Such a special pattern of government-citizen interaction has come into being only under well-established legal and political structures and after centuries of evolution from more confrontational interactions. In China, however, legal and political institutions for regulating

[10] Scott Mainwaring, "Grassroots Popular movements and the Struggle for Democracy: Nova Iguacu," in Alfred Stepan (ed.), *Democratizing Brazil: Problems of Transition and Consolidation* (New York and Oxford: Oxford University Press, 1989), p. 196.

[11] Thomas E. Skidmore, *The Politics of Military Rule in Brazil, 1964–85* (New York and Oxford: Oxford University Press, 1988), p. 214.

[12] Patricia L. Hipsher, "Democratic Transitions as Protest Cycles: Social Movement Dynamics in Democratizing Latin America," in David Meyer and Sidney Tarrow (eds.), *The Social Movement Society: Contentious Politics for a New Century* (Lanham, MD: Rowman & Littlefield, 1998), p. 166.

[13] Ibid., p. 155.

[14] David Meyer and Sidney Tarrow (eds.), *The Social Movement Society: Contentious Politics for a New Century* (Lanham, MD: Rowman & Littlefield, 1998); John D. McCarthy and Clark McPhail, "The Institutionalization of Protest in the United States," in David Meyer and Sidney Tarrow, ibid, pp. 83–110.

popular claim making are severely underdeveloped. Second, the trend toward a "social movement society" is closely associated with the professionalization of social movement organizations (SMO) and a decline in disruption and violence caused by the movements. By contrast, in China, professionalization of SMOs is far from feasible and the level of disruption in popular contention has increased rather than declined in recent years. Although the development of "social movement societies" in liberal democracies is certainly impressive, the emergence of a contentious society in a powerful authoritarian regime is more puzzling.

AVAILABLE EXPLANATIONS

To account for the emergence of contentious authoritarianism in China, we need to explain not only the dynamics of popular mobilization, but also the particular strategic orientations of popular protests. Indeed, in this case, the question of mobilization and that of strategic orientation are inseparable, for the upsurge we have seen consists primarily of an increase in particular types of popular contention – localized, nonpolitical, and opportunistic claim-making activities.

Most available studies are focused on the process of mobilization and have been deeply influenced by social movement theories in Western countries. In the last several decades, the dominant theoretical paradigm of popular contention has largely shifted twice. In the 1970s and 1980s, *grievances-centered* analysis, exemplified by Ted Gurr's "relative deprivation" and James Davies's "J – Curve," was severely challenged by resource mobilization theory, which emphasizes *organizational bases* of popular contention. The latter theory highlights the importance of preexisting social networks as a mobilizing structure. Yet this approach soon evolved into political process theory, which emphasizes the role of *state-centered* political opportunity structures in establishing dynamics of popular contention.

All three theoretical paradigms have been applied to China's case. However, compared to uses of grievance-centered analysis and political process analysis, relatively few scholars concentrate on the organizational bases for popular collective action. This is mainly due to the fact that independent formal organizations are evidently underdeveloped in China.

Mobilizing Structure-Based Explanations

In the China field, mobilizing structure-based explanations tend to focus on three organizational bases of mobilization: civil society, grassroots elites, and communal networks. The rise of civil society has often been used to explain the student movement of 1989.[15] However, such explanations have been challenged, given that independent organizations in China are often too weak to play a significant role in mobilization.[16] Perry even casts doubt on the applicability of the concept of civil society in China.[17] Most social protesters since the 1990s have deliberately avoided sophisticated organizations. Some of them have formed ad hoc organizations such as "association of pensioners" or "peasants' association for reducing burdens," which are usually loosely organized and also limited to a factory or a village. A few special groups, such as demobilized army officers or disabled people, have sometimes relied on their own pre-existing underground networks. However, a vast majority of protesters have relied on communal ties rather than autonomous organizations.

Another type of organization-centered analysis examines activists as a key condition for collective action. Bernstein and Lü highlighted the role of "burden-reduction heroes" in peasant resistance in the countryside.[18] Hurst and O'Brien underscore the organizational capacity of retirees who learned from their previous experience of state-sponsored collective action.[19] Ying Xing not only emphasized the role of petitioning leaders, but also raised the question of how their personal interests, as distinguished from those of ordinary petitioners, have influenced the multi-party game in collective petitioning.[20]

Finally, some scholars have paid serious attention to communal ties. When associational ties are weak, communal ties seem to play an important role as the mobilizing structure. For example, C. K. Lee observes, "The industrial workplace and the dormitory or the residential quarter organized around it can be inadvertently turned into sites of rebellion."[21]

---

[15] For example, see David Strand, "Protest in Beijing: Civil Society and Public Sphere in China," *Problems of Communism* 39, pp. 1–19; Lawrence R. Sullivan, "The Emergence of Civil Society in China, Spring 1989," in Tony Saich (ed.) *The Chinese People's Movement, Perspectives on Spring 1989* (Armonk, NY: M.E. Sharpe, 1990), pp. 126–144.

[16] For example, see Zhou, Xueguang, "Unorganized Interests and Collective Action in Communist China," *American Sociological Review*, 58/1 (Feb. 1993), pp. 54–73; Zhao Dingxin, *The Power of Tiananmen* (Chicago: University of Chicago Press, 2000).

[17] Elizabeth Perry, "Trends in the Study of Chinese Politics: State-Society Relations," *China Quarterly* 139 (September 1994), pp. 704–713.

[18] Thomas Bernstein & Xiaobo Lü, *Taxation without Representation in Contemporary Rural China* (New York: Cambridge University Press, 2003), chapter 5.

[19] William Hurst & Kevin O'Brien, "Chinese Contentious Pensioners," *The China Quarterly* 170 (June 2002), pp. 345–358.

[20] Ying Xing, *Dahe Yimin Shangfang de Gushi* (the story of the petitioning of the migrants in Dahe town) (Beijing: Sanlian Press, 2002).

[21] C. K. Lee, *Against the Law: Labor Protests in China's Rustbelt and Sunbelt* (Berkeley: University of California Press, 2007), p. 201.

This is because "dormitories have facilitated communication, coordination, and the aggregation of interest and demands."[22] Similarly, the ecology of the college campus has been used by Zhao to explain the student movement in 1989.[23]

Whereas these organizationally based explanations of the dynamics of popular grievances have proven useful in explaining a few instances of popular protest in China, such arguments are not as successful in offering an explanation for the more general surge of social protests since the 1990s. Such mobilizing structures are not particularly strong. As Xueguang Zhou remarks, "If the success of collective action depends on the strategy adopted, the extent to which interests are organized or on a social movement 'industry,' China is a puzzle. The absence of organized interests makes it impossible to identify stable interest groups or to find some systematic distribution of rewards or sanctions that would motivate individuals to join in collective action."[24] In addition, such an organizational basis has existed all the time and has not been strengthened substantially during or prior to the surge.

Grievance-Based Explanations

Large-scale social change is often followed by political instability and social disorder. This is especially true during the transition to a market economy. The rise of capitalism in Western countries together with some closely related social processes, such as urbanization, industrialization, and substantial increases in literacy and education, have traditionally been used by many modernization theorists to explain the rise of collective action.

Reform Era China seems to have provided another example of "modernization": It has witnessed the rise of a market economy, industrialization, urbanization, and social mobility, among other things, in the last two and a half decades. Therefore, the Durkheimian vein of explanations is still very attractive to many researchers on contemporary China.

Indeed the transition to market socialism in China has brought about deep changes and disorientation for many segments of the population. It

---

[22] Ibid. p. 192.

[23] Zhao Dingxin, "Ecologies of Social Movements: Student Mobilization during the 1989 Prodemocracy Movement in Beijing," *American Journal of Sociology* 103/6 (May 1998), pp. 1493–1529.

[24] Zhou Xueguang, "Unorganized Interests and Collective Action in Communist China," *American Sociological Review* 58/1 (February 1993), p. 55.

is not a process without losers.[25] On the contrary, the extensive reforms have adversely affected the life of many segments of the population: For instance, pensioners and workers have been deprived of varying degrees of socialist welfare; peasants' living conditions have often relatively or even absolutely deteriorated; many urban and rural residents have lost their houses or land with inadequate compensation. A focus on grievances has occupied a great deal of the literature on Chinese contentious politics. Some scholars are more explicit than others. For example, when analyzing pensioners' protests, Hurst and O'Brien write, "Once considered an important aspect of research on social movements, the analysis of grievances has been nudged out of the spotlight since the 'resource mobilization' and 'political process' approaches emerged in the 1970s and 1980s. To understand why Chinese retirees protest, however, the study of grievances must be pushed back towards centre stage."[26]

Most of the current studies focus on a specific social group. For each group, analysts can find political economy and public policy causes for their specific grievances. However, this line of explanation has difficulty in accounting for the rise and routinization of social protests as a *cross-sector* phenomenon. Chapter 2 will show that a variety of social groups have simultaneously become much more assertive since the 1990s. If each protest group seems to have been motivated by their particular grievances, why have so many different groups with distinctive and largely unrelated grievances become assertive during the same period?

Some scholars, therefore, search for common structures that account for discontents across different social groups. For example, Minxin Pei's discussion of the rise of the "predatory state" attributes rural and urban discontent to declining state monitoring capacity and the reduced appeal of the ruling party.[27] Likewise, C. K. Lee's discussion of the contradiction between local governments' imperative for accumulation and the central government's concern with legitimation can create grievances not only for workers, but also for peasants and urban property owners. Even if such structural conditions go a long way toward explaining cross-group grievances, grievances-centered approaches still face some

[25] Martin King Whyte, "The Changing Role of Workers," in Merle Goldman and Roderick MacFarquhar (eds.) *The Paradox of China's Post-Mao Reforms* (Cambridge, MA: Harvard University Press, 1999), pp. 173–196.

[26] William Hurst and Kevin O'Brien, "Chinese Contentious Pensioners," p. 359. It should be noted that neither of them has consistently advocated this perspective in other works.

[27] Minxin Pei, *China's Trapped Transition: The Limits of Developmental Autocracy* (Cambridge, MA: Harvard University Press, 2006).

severe challenges. Most importantly, they can hardly shed light on the forms and political orientations of popular protests, even though they are not entirely irrelevant to these questions. In fact, the most puzzling aspect of the upsurge is not why so many social groups have become so disgruntled and therefore have had strong claims to make to the state. Rather, it is why they have overwhelmingly preferred collective action in particular forms – localized collective petitions with the use of a variety of "troublemaking" tactics that can keep a balance between defiance and obedience.

As will be elaborated in Chapter 2, for almost all forms in which ordinary people can voice their grievances besides collective protests, there is no substantial increase of cases addressed to the authorities. For example, whereas social protests have increased dramatically since the 1990s, there has been no evident increase of moderate petitions and appeals. Likewise, civil litigation cases in China even decreased slightly from 1996 to 2005.[28] Another important channel, people's mediation committees, also witnessed a significant decrease in their caseload since the 1990s. The contrast between the growth of collective petitions and the stagnation or decreases in other forms of claim making is not due to the nature of popular grievances. Indeed, most issues of social protests can possibly be addressed through other forms of claim making. A group of pensioners who staged confrontational protests could address their problem to the government via mail, or by having one or two representatives deliver the petition, as prescribed by the regulations. What the upsurge indicates is, therefore, less an explosion of popular grievances and social conflicts than a dramatic change in popular behavior patterns. Even though we can learn a lot about protesters' motivations by analyzing popular grievances, it is more important to look into the political structure when accounting for such change in popular behavior patterns.

Political Opportunity Structure-Based Explanations

Given that political process theory now dominates the study of contentious politics, it comes as no surprise that many scholars resort to the concept of political opportunity structures to explain the rise and routinization of social protests. Clearly, the political environment in China has changed significantly during the Reform Era and has become more favorable to popular contention. Specifically, the withdrawing of the Party-state from

[28] See Benjamin Liebman, "China's Courts: Restricted Reform," *China Quarterly*, 191 (September 2007), pp. 620–638.

many social and economic areas and the decline of its social control has created political opportunities for social protests.

The Party-state's decline in its capacity for disciplining state agents is accompanied by its decreased control over the general population. For example, Lucien Bianco attributed the resurgence of rural disturbances during the Reform Era to the decline of the Party-state's ability to exercise control over local society.[29] Most of these changes consist of the "unraveling of many of the state-imposed controls of the Maoist era."[30] The Party-state has withdrawn from social and economic areas on which it used to exert a tremendous degree of penetration and control. It has also ended such practices as class labeling and political campaigns, which made the regime especially repressive. In addition, the reform of legal institutions and development of the media seem to have offered more protection to ordinary people.

In addition to the decline of social control, another element of administrative change that has been emphasized by many scholars is the interest divisions between central and local governments, which I will analyze in detail later. Although such explanations certainly identify meaningful changes in the political opportunity structure, they alone are not sufficient to fully explain the strong incentives provided by the political system for popular contention. In a sense, the changes of the Party-state system in the Reform Era can be understood as a "transition from totalitarianism to a classic authoritarian regime."[31] However, it is still not clear how a classic authoritarian regime can create such favorable conditions for popular contention. A closer examination of contentious interactions reveals a much more important role for the state than imposing social control. Similarly, in addition to the tensions between central and local governments, we can find other important divisions and contradictions within the state institutions and ideology, many of which have facilitated popular contention.

A STATE-CENTERED MODEL OF POLITICAL OPPORTUNITY STRUCTURE

In this book I argue that the rise and routinization of social protests is mainly due to the direct facilitation of such activities by the Party-state.

---

[29] Lucien Bianco, *Peasants without the Party: Grass-roots Movements in Twentieth-Century China* (Armonk, NY: M.E. Shape, 2001), p. 245.

[30] Elizabeth Perry, *Challenging the Mandate of Heaven: Social Protest and State Power in China* (Armonk: NY: M.E. Sharpe, 2002), p. xxx.

[31] Andrew Nathan, "Authoritarian Resilience in China," *Journal of Democracy* 14/1 (Jan. 2003), p. 16.

This explanation, however, is itself a puzzle: Why would the Party-state facilitate popular contention? The CCP leaders are actually very concerned about rampant social protests. For example, Premier Zhu Rongji claimed that the work of handling social protests is a life-or-death task for the Party-state.[32] Preventing or limiting collective petitioning with "troublemaking" tactics has been one of the top priorities for every level of government.

This book, therefore, offers a model of political opportunity structure as a solution to this puzzle. This model first underscores inherent contradictions and ambiguities found in state ideologies and institutions. For example, as required by the mass line – one of the primary principles by which the CCP regime deals with state-society relations – political power should be concentrated in Party leaders. At the same time, however, consultation of the masses is indispensable for policy making and implementation. The tension between power centralization and political consultation has created a variety of contradictions and ambiguities that have provided incentives and favorable conditions for popular collective action. As will be revealed in the detailed analysis of the xinfang system in Chapter 4, when the Chinese government invites citizens to bring their complaints to government offices, it often in fact encourages them to band together to present petitions accompanied by collective protests with "troublemaking" tactics.

Of course, contradictions and ambiguities by themselves do not provide adequate political opportunity for mass mobilization. Their potential can only be realized under certain circumstances and through certain processes. The book will, therefore, also identify a special institutional configuration in the Reform Era that has contributed to the dynamics and strategic orientation of popular collective action. One of most dramatic changes of the Chinese polity is that it has shifted away from an earlier system based on "work units" and "organized dependence." A number of social groups have thus begun to make claims directly to the government rather than to unit leaders. At the same time, divisions and functional differentiation in the state structure have also substantially increased in the Reform Era. These structural conditions have worked together in facilitating and shaping Chinese citizens' behavior patterns. In addition to specifying such conditions, the book also identifies the

---

[32] See "Comrade Zhu Rongji's Opening Speech in the Fourth National Conference on Xinfang Work in 1996," a document kept by the xinfang bureau of County H in Hunan Province. This document was probably distributed to every xinfang bureau in China.

processes and mechanisms, such as social appropriation for the transformation of popular behaviors.

Like other works that rely on a political process approach, this book also provides a state-centered model of political opportunity structures. However, it differs from most available explanations in three aspects. First, it highlights the proactive role of the Party-state in facilitating popular contention. Second, it underscores the contradictions, conflicts, and ambiguities within the state rather than the decline of its capacity. Third, it emphasizes not only changes but also the continuity of the political system in creating political opportunity, and also proposes mechanisms and processes for the formation of the political opportunity structure.

CONTRADICTORY STATE AND MASS LINE POLITICS

Clearly, the model employed in this book is centered on the state. Unlike social theories on industrialized societies, China studies have never lost the focus on the state. There is no need to "bring the state back in." Few China scholars would deny the importance of the Party-state in explaining social change. Therefore Dingxin Zhao remarks, "In fact, for those who know China, it is very hard not to think of Chinese politics in terms of the state and of state-society relations."[33]

The Party-state has not only shaped the mobilizing structures, identities, and grievances of social protesters, but also affected the costs and benefits of mobilization. A stereotypical concept of the PRC as a monolithic authoritarian regime has impeded our understanding of political opportunity structures because it ignores the divisions and contradictions of the Chinese state. In recent years, however, students of contentious politics in China have begun to pay attention to divisions of the Party-state. Perry reminds us of the danger of assuming a unitary concept of the Chinese state.[34] O'Brien and Li argue that the multilayered structure of the state is one key condition for the rise of "rightful resistance" and "boundary-spanning contention" in China.[35]

In fact, popular contention is affected not only by vertical divisions within the Party-state – that is, the divisions between the central

---

[33] Dingxin Zhao, *The Power of Tiananmen*, p. 10.

[34] Elizabeth Perry, "Trends in the Study of Chinese Politics: State-Society Relations," *China Quarterly* 139 (September 1994), pp. 704–713.

[35] Kevin O'Brien, "Rightful Resistance," *World Politics* 49 (1996), pp. 31–56; "Neither Transgressive nor Contained: Boundary-spanning Contention in China," *Mobilization* 8/1 (2003), pp. 51–64

government and local government; horizontal divisions, such as those among different Party-state agencies at the same level, can also facilitate mass mobilization. In the Reform Era, many public agencies have begun to seek a somewhat independent identity and are acquiring distinct institutional interests. To obtain either institutional power (such as in the case of the People's congresses and mass organizations) or commercial interests (such as in the case of the media), these agencies often take a position somewhat inconsistent with that of the Party and government leaders.[36] Coordination among different agencies has thus become increasingly problematic. This differentiation has to some extent created the multiplicity of quasi-independent centers of power within the regime. Therefore, such divisions and differentiations not only help create grievances, but more importantly, they also produce multiple allies and advocates for petitioners and therefore offer invaluable resources and protection to them.

Divisions among elites have long been regarded by political process theory as an essential element of political opportunity structures. This book recognizes the importance of divisions within the state, but will also highlight another source of political opportunity: contradictions and ambiguities between state institutions and ideology. Scholars focusing on this issue have identified a variety of ambiguities and contradictions in the practice, ideology, and institutions of state socialism. Officially authorized ceremonies provide rare openings for popular collective action.[37] The ideological claims and rhetoric of the CCP also offer opportunities for ordinary people to challenge the state in the name of "taking the state at its word."[38] Likewise, many political institutions are "amphibious" in that they can be used for purposes contrary to those they are supposed to fulfill, and "the same institution can simultaneously serve conflicting purposes."[39] One example is the All-China Federation of Trade Unions,

---

[36] As to the definition of major leaders, I resort to a sort of political convention in the PRC and include all members of the standing committee of local party committees, heads and vice heads of government, and the secretary-general of both the party committee and the government at each level. Unless specified, this concept in this book is not confined to leaders in central authorities.

[37] Steven Pfaff and Guobin Yang, "Double-edged Ritual and the Symbolic Resources of Collective Action: Political Commemorations and the Mobilization of Protest in 1989," *Theory and Society* 30 (2001), p. 550.

[38] Kevin O'Brien and Lianjiang Li, 2006; Jeremy Brooke Straughn, "'Take the State at Its Word': The Arts of Consentful Contention in the German Democratic Republic," *American Journal of Sociology* 110/6 (May 2005), pp. 1598–1650.

[39] X. L. Ding, "Institutional Amphibiousness and the Transition from Communism: The Case of China," *British Journal of Political Science* 24 (1994), p. 298.

the official labor union. Set up as a corporatist mass organization under the Party-state, the ACFTU nevertheless played a significant part in facilitating contention in the student movement in 1989.[40] These double-edged swords not only create a gray area or free space for popular contention, but also often provide much-needed resources for mass mobilization.

The contradictions within the Party-state have been most explicitly explored by C. K. Lee in *Against the Law*. In her book, she rejects the view that the state is a singular and insulated engine of change, and she advocates "a dialectical view of the state, pursuing the contradictory interests and tendencies between different levels and units of the state."[41] She describes the Party-state in the Reform Era as a form of decentralized legal authoritarianism wherein two important contradictions exist: one between (capital) accumulation and legitimation, and the other between economic liberalization and political monopoly. Such contradictions have significant consequences for labor politics: The gap between central regulations and local implementation has undermined working conditions in the Sunbelt and collective consumption in the Rustbelt; the state structure also "generates popular activism by furnishing the aggrieved groups with both a vocabulary and an institutional mechanism to express their demands and seek redress."[42]

Such a dialectical view of the state is certainly illuminating. However, Lee's explanations are largely confined to the production of popular grievances. For her, the primary role of contradictions is that they have created grievances for workers and provided them with tools for framing such grievances. Moreover, she treats the contradictions as "new" and fails to notice that they may actually reflect more enduring contradictions. Although the contradictions she has underscored seem to have been brought out by decentralization and legal reform in the Reform Era, they may not be as new as they appear. For instance, the contradiction between the local imperative for accumulation and the central authorities' concern with legitimacy can be found in other periods, such as during the Great Leap Forward Campaign.

Likewise, the contradiction between the development of legal institutions and the Party's monopoly of political power reflects a long-existing

---

[40] Elizabeth Perry, "Casting a 'Democracy' Movement: The Roles of Students, Workers, and Entrepreneurs," in Jeffery N. Wasserstrom and Elizabeth J. Perry (eds.), *Popular Protest and Political Culture in Modern China* (Boulder, CO: Westview, 1992), p. 159.

[41] Ching Kwan Lee, *Against the Law: Labor Protests in China's Rustbelt and Sunbelt.* (Los Angeles and London: University of California Press, 2007), p. 17.

[42] Ibid, p. 20.

tension between power concentration and functional differentiations in the system. Despite the rhetoric of the rule of law, legal institutions are regarded by Chinese leaders as but one of many functional departments of the Party-state.[43] In terms of its functions for social control, conflict resolution, and political accountability, the legal system is not substantially distinct from the xinfang system. Although legal institutions are supposed to function effectively and somewhat independently in their designated area, the Party and government leaders retain the ultimate authority for decision making. Given that it is often necessary to specialize and rationalize the agencies for the sake of efficiency, such tendencies tend to be at odds with the ultimate authority of the power center.

Compared to contradictions related to legalization, the tensions in the xinfang system have a more direct impact on popular contention as this is the primary system through which the Party-state deals with claim-making activities. The xinfang system is part of mass line politics, which features nonbinding direct political consultation in a centralized power structure, and its contradictions reflect some of the inherent tensions of mass line politics. When direct political consultation is conducted in a large and centralized system, popular input tends to overwhelm the power center. Thus specialized and local agencies need to be designed to assume most of the work in dealing with popular consultation. The rules and procedures of petitions should also be formalized to impose order and ensure efficiency.

However, because mass line ideology greatly values direct communication between leaders and the masses, the leaders need to retain the power to deal with a few important petitions, and are supposed to handle petitions and appeals regularly. Similarly, upper-level authorities need to keep the door open for a few skip-level petitioners who bypass the appropriate local agencies. The rules and procedures thus need to maintain enough flexibility for a few petitions to reach the power center. In mass line politics, inherent tensions therefore exist between bureaucratic specialization and power concentration, between formalized rules and procedural flexibility, and between local responsibility and top-down supervision and intervention.

Such contradictions create incentives and favorable conditions for popular contention. As a vast majority of petitions have no chance to reach the power center, many petitioners are motivated to employ "troublemaking" tactics to distinguish themselves from a large number of

---

[43] Benjamin Liebman, "China's Courts: Restricted Reform," *China Quarterly* 191 (September 2007), pp. 620–638.

ordinary cases. Such tactics often prove effective as government officials need to differentiate petitions according to the forms of delivery. Petitions delivered with "troublemaking" tactics are usually believed to be more urgent and legitimate. For example, if a petitioner spent several years and traveled thousands of miles to persistently deliver his or her petition to the capital, he or she was more likely to have a legitimate claim to make. In addition, in this centralized system, such protest tactics can generate top-down pressure, which is the key factor to ensure prompt and proper handling of petitions by local officials. Finally, because the system needs to maintain flexibility for a few important petitions to reach the power center, norms on claim-making activities are often ambiguous and therefore provide "troublemaking" activities with quasi-legitimacy.

Such contradictions have significantly constrained the state's ability to adopt strategies or create institutions for coping with rampant protests. Because contradictions in the xinfang system are deeply entrenched in the broad ideological and institutional framework of mass line politics, they are also extremely difficult to remove. With the surge of social protests since the early 1990s, the CCP has made many efforts to reform the system to make it less likely to motivate and facilitate popular contention. However, most such efforts have been either futile or counterproductive. For example, although the Chinese government has promulgated regulations to formalize the norm that group petitions should be delivered by no more than five representatives, this rule has seldom been strictly enforced. Likewise, the Chinese government's increased emphasis on local responsibility for preventing or dissolving skip-level collective petitioning has often resulted in strong pressure for local governments to make concessions, thus inadvertently encouraging more skip-level petitions.

By focusing on mass line politics, this study underlines the continuities between the organizational structure of the current Party-state and that in Mao's Era. Although the Chinese system has departed from a model close to totalitarianism, it has not become – and probably is not going to become – just an ordinary authoritarian regime. The inherent contradictions within the system of political authority account for a significant part of the incentives for popular contention today.

HISTORICAL CONSTRUCTION OF POLITICAL OPPORTUNITY STRUCTURES

The previously mentioned state contradictions are only a part of political opportunity structures. By themselves they cannot explain the rise and routinization of popular contention since the 1990s. After all, even in a system with significant contradictions (and divisions), ordinary people engage in collective action only under certain circumstances. The case of the xinfang system suggests that amphibious institutions can be converted into instruments for popular contention through two mechanisms: (1) changes in institutional configurations; and (2) the appropriation-reaction mechanism.

Changes in Institutional Configurations

An institution may function differently when situated in different institutional configurations. The xinfang system has been operating in a dramatically different institutional setting since the 1990s. The decline of the work unit system for a large segment of the population has been particularly influential in contributing to the changed setting for claim making. Work units in urban areas, like people's communes and their subunits in the countryside, used to constitute a primary venue for state-society interactions. Andrew Nathan therefore uses the term "unit system" to describe the grassroots structure in both urban and rural China. He remarks, "The 'unit' system tied both rural and urban residents to a work or residential unit that controlled virtually all functions of their lives."[44] The unit system has long provided one of the most important institutional settings for political participation in the PRC. As Tianjian Shi points out,

> Most governmental functions in China, such as administrating welfare programs, distributing apartments, providing education, and even maintaining social order, are the responsibility of work units rather than of functional and residential systems as in many other societies.... This arrangement shifts the pivotal point of decision making for low politics from the central government to grassroots organizations. As the decision-making center descends to the grassroots level, people's strategy for pursuing their interests changes fundamentally.[45]

This situation, however, has changed substantially since the 1990s. The decline of the unit system caused two important changes to claim-making activities. First, ordinary people have often begun to make claims directly to the government rather than work unit leaders. Their claims therefore tend to be based on categorical identities and general norms such as laws and regulations. Second, the decline of the unit system has changed the

---

[44] Andrew Nathan, *China's Transition* (New York: Columbia University Press, 1997), p. 55.
[45] Tianjian Shi, *Political Participation in Beijing* (Cambridge, MA: Harvard University Press, 1997), p. 15.

linkages between ordinary people and the state and affected the resources for protesters and the authorities. As state agents at the grassroots level, work unit cadres fulfilled the function of surveillance, sanction, and containment. Because work units featured long and dense interactions between ordinary people and state agents within a very limited space, surveillance and persuasion was usually prevalent and effective. Also, the "organized dependence" of ordinary people on their work or residential units made sanctions formidable. With the unit system, the Party-state effectively prevented most defiant activities. In this particular institutional context, the contradictions and ambiguities of mass line politics only reinforced the arbitrary power of grassroots state agents.

When working alongside the unit system, therefore, the xinfang system tends to promote controlled participation rather than contentious bargaining. A few other institutions helped the unit system fulfill this function: the food rationing system in urban areas, the system of custody and repatriation, and the railway system, to name just a few. All these apparatus served to limit social mobility, especially population flow from rural to urban areas. None of them were instituted specifically to constrain petitioning activities, but all of them worked very effectively for this purpose. Like the unit system, such institutions have also severely declined, or have even been abolished in the 1990s. Chapter 6 examines how the changes in the institutional setting of the xinfang system have forced the state to adopt a new repertoire of strategies for handling petitions and protests.

The Appropriation-Response Mechanism

Although this study relies on political opportunity structures to explain popular mobilization, it avoids a structural bias by paying considerable attention to agency and processes. For institutional contradictions and ambiguities to work as political opportunity structure, protesters have to assume a particularly active role. In short, they must make opportunities by appropriating existing channels and institutions. Chapter 5 shows how Chinese protesters strike the balance between defiance and obedience so that they can maximize the effectiveness of collective action within a limited space. Chapter 6 gives a detailed discussion on the specific tactics used by Chinese protesters to enhance their bargaining power. They have not only resorted to disruption, but also to persuasion, publicity, and elite advocacy. Most of these "troublemaking" tactics constitute a gray area for the Party-state: They are tolerable but undesirable from the standpoint of the authorities. By exploiting this particular attitude toward "troublemaking" tactics, protesters have often worked the system to their own advantage.

Of course, this study of the xinfang system indicates that the process is more complicated than social appropriation. Appropriation is just one part of the mechanism of appropriation-response. The response of the state has also significantly contributed to the conversion. In response to the pervasive appropriation of the xinfang channel by protesters, the state has strengthened its control of local response, exerted higher pressure on local officials to pacify petitioners with bargaining, and generally restrained the ability of local officials to use force. The state responds in this way because it is constrained by the general ideological and institutional framework of mass line politics, which stresses centralized measures to meet tough challenges. Such efforts encourage further social appropriation, which in turn provokes state response along the same lines.

In sum, the particular characteristics of the Chinese state have contributed to its proactive role in facilitating popular contention. It features not only multilayered structures, but also multidimensional contradictions and ambiguities, some of which are nonetheless very stable. These contradictions and ambiguities have provided a relatively safe space and much-needed resources for mass mobilization, all while significantly constraining state strategies and adaptations. Under a distinctive historical configuration, and through the appropriation-response mechanism, the amphibious institutions of mass line politics have often been converted into instruments for contentious bargaining.

PREVIEW OF THE BOOK

The main task of this book is to describe and explain a dramatic change in government-citizen interactions in Reform Era China – in particular, why has there been an upsurge of collective protests in China since the early 1990s? Most of these protests have involved some kind of group petitioning activity, and they usually target the government with a goal to pressure government officials to address their concerns. In fact, the concept of collective petitioning in contemporary China is very broad, including a wide range of activities, some of which are considered "normal" petitioning whereas others are actually labeled by the government as "abnormal" and "unlawful" protest activities. I have therefore often used "social protest" and "collective petitioning" interchangeably in this book.

Chapter 2 starts with a description of the surge of collective petitioning activities and then compares it to the levels of change in other forms of claim making or conflict resolution. The study concludes that there was no comparable rise of claim-making activities in other forms – a finding that challenges the common assumption that the recent surge belongs to a general rise in claim-making activities. Rather, what the surge indicates is primarily a shift in the preferred forms of claim making. To understand what have motivated collective protests, the chapter also includes an examination of the main demands of collective petitions during the surge and shows that between 1994 and 2001, the number of protests in Hunan Province increased substantially across almost all clusters of demands. This finding suggests that the cross-sector surge can hardly be explained by group-specific grievances of one or two population sectors, which have often been emphasized by available studies. We thus need to look into broad social change to understand petitioners' motivation. In fact, the analysis of demands of collective petitions suggests that the deepening of structural reform in the Chinese economy in the early 1990s have profoundly affected a number of population sectors and led to a variety of grievances that have stimulated collective protests. Of course, an analysis of petitioners' demands can tell us why they needed to make claims to the state authorities, but can hardly shed light on how they made claims. Chapters 3 and 4 thus focus on the political structure in China that has shaped popular behavior patterns.

In addition to describing the surge, another main goal of Chapter 2 is to situate this recent trend in a historical context. Throughout the history of the PRC, the rise and fall of petitioning activities has been deeply affected by the political atmosphere. However, overall, popular contention in the Reform Era has become more autonomous and less dependent on state initiatives or campaigns. Although there have been at least three previous surges of collective petitions since the founding of the PRC, none of them has been as enduring as the current one.

A brief survey of petitioning activities in pre-PRC history indicates that petitions and appeals have long been part of the repertoire of popular claim making. Elites sometimes staged collective petition movements on national or local political issues, but such activities tended to be highly risky. In comparison, submissive petitions and appeals by individuals were more or less institutionalized and involved much lower risk. The history of petition movements and government response has provided a cultural framework for today's protesters and government to interpret their interactions, but no similar wave of routinized collective protests can be found in imperial eras. The historical comparisons highlight the distinctiveness of the surge of collective protests in the Reform Era.

The two chapters of Part II analyze the particular institutional configuration in the Reform Era that helps account for the upsurge of collective protests. Chapter 3 discusses how the transition from a planned economy to a market economy has brought about two important changes in the political system: first, the linkages between ordinary people and the Party-state have shifted from the unit system model to the government-citizen model; and second, divisions and functional differentiations among state agencies have substantially increased. The chapter goes on to analyze how these two changes have pushed the state to develop a new strategic repertoire, which combines preventive repression, expedient concessions, practical persuasion, and procrastination. The chapter concludes that such a repertoire of state strategies has actually encouraged popular protests with "opportunistic troublemaking" tactics.

Chapter 4 is focused on another dimension of the political opportunity structure – contradictions and ambiguities within state institutions and ideology. Specifically, it explains how the evolution of socialist political institutions in general and the xinfang system in particular has provided strong incentives and facilitating conditions for popular contention. As a part of mass line politics, the xinfang system intended for controlled participation has largely been converted into an instrument for popular contention. This chapter suggests the conditions and mechanisms for such a process of institutional conversion. It illustrates how the xinfang system is amphibious and has an inherent tendency to facilitate "opportunistic troublemaking" tactics. Although widespread popular attempts to appropriate the system for social protests have triggered state responses, such as the adjustment of procedures and organization, the xinfang system has proved difficult to change. Most adjustments have often been futile or even counterproductive because they were essentially reproducing the contradictions and ambiguities that facilitated popular protests.

The two chapters in Part III explain how the institutional configuration discussed in Part II shaped Chinese petitioners' strategies and tactics. The focus has thus shifted from structure to agency. Chapter 5 discusses an essential strategic orientation of social protest in China, "protest opportunism," and illustrates how Chinese petitioners shift between defiant and submissive tactics so that they can exert an appropriate level of pressure on the government without incurring too high a risk. The findings in this chapter indicate that protesters in China may not necessarily choose moderate tactics, but they always balance defiance with actions or statements that show their obedience. Both defiance and obedience are important for protest success. Without defiance as exhibited through collective action with the use of "troublemaking" tactics, protesters cannot obtain bargaining power. However, protesters also commonly employ obedient tactics because it is these tactics that sustain their struggle and help define their behavior as reasonable and legitimate, even in instances when they may have broken some laws.

Chapter 6 probes into the range and variety of "troublemaking" tactics, and also provides a statistical test to assess their efficacy. The chapter first discusses the three basic routes through which ordinary people in China deliver petitions and then provides a descriptive taxonomy of "troublemaking" tactics that petitioners have employed to enhance their bargaining power. These nineteen tactics have been classified into four types according to the mechanisms through which they incur a government response: disruption, persuasion, elite engaging, and publicity. The quantitative study confirms that disruption, publicity, and larger event sizes all positively affect the likelihood of a substantial government response. Elite advocacy also gives some limited advantages to petitioners. This chapter thus shows an important way in which the Chinese political system has facilitated collective protests – it provides protesters with higher actual and perceived efficacy than moderate petitions.

The last chapter reflects on the implications of this study for general theories on contentious politics and regime stability. In particular, it discusses how the findings here can modify elite power theory, which undergirds the political process model. It underscores the importance of divisions, contradictions, and ambiguities within elites' practice, ideology, and institutions, which can create a space for relatively low-cost (but still limited) access to power by relatively powerless people, although they will not substantially challenge the power inequality between power elites and the underclasses.

This chapter also discusses how current theories of political opportunity structures (POS) can be improved by introducing a historical institutional approach. It suggests POS should not be conceptualized as either stable or fast-shifting conditions. Instead, they tend to be a combination of changes and enduring continuities. To understand how POS are constructed in certain historical junctures, it would be most helpful to identify specific mechanisms and processes.

Finally, the chapter challenges the conventional wisdom on the relationship between authoritarian regimes and popular contention, and
reflects on how an authoritarian state may facilitate popular contention
and popular contention can help maintain authoritarian stability. It also
suggests that current popular contention in China is unlikely to significantly enhance the chances for democratization, although some progress
on citizenship rights can be expected.

2

The Surge in Social Protests from a Historical Perspective

A variety of evidence from different sources and perspectives confirms the trend that, since the 1990s, social protest in China has risen dramatically. Some of the most frequently cited data come from the Public Security Ministry about "collective incidents" (*quntixing shijian*). According to this source, 87,000 collective incidents took place in 2005, as compared to 74,000 in 2004, 58,000 in 2003, and about 10,000 in 1994.[1] Although this data is relatively reliable, it offers too little information for us to properly analyze the trend of social protest. For example, it is not clear how the Public Security Ministry defines "collective incidents." It is quite possible that this term is broader than social protests, encompassing other social disturbances such as intervillage strife, but we cannot know for sure.[2]

This book will rely mainly on data collected from the xinfang (letters and visits) system. Such data have two significant advantages. First, although xinfang data are generally regarded as sensitive, they are more accessible than similarly sensitive data from public safety bureaus.[3] Many local xinfang bureaus have published part of their data, and xinfang officials are more willing to talk to interviewers. Consequently, we can know

---

[1] Howard French, "Land of 74,000 Protests (but Little Is Ever Fixed)," *New York Times*, August 24, 2005; Howard French, "Citizens' Groups Take Root across China," *New York Times*, February 15, 2007.

[2] Chen Jinsheng, *Quntixing Shijian Yanjiu Baogao* (Research Report on Mass Incidents) (Beijing: Qunzhong Chubanshe, 2004).

[3] Xi Chen, "State-generated Data and the Study of Contentious Politics in China," in Allen Carlson et al. (eds.), *Chinese Politics: New Methods, Sources and Field strategies* (New York: Cambridge University Press, 2010), pp. 15–32.

not only the contents of their reports and findings but also get a better idea of how such data have been collected and processed.

Second, xinfang data include the most complete information about ordinary people's claim-making activities. The xinfang system is the primary state institution for dealing with citizens' complaints and petitions. Because the CCP has a strong interest in public opinion, the xinfang system has diligently collected data on popular claims. Such data usually covers an impressive range of activities, from very disruptive ones, which are called "abnormal petitioning" (*yichang shangfang*), to very moderate activities, such as letter writing.

Although as part of the terminology of the CCP's mass line the words "letters" (*xin*) and "visits" (*fang*) suggest moderation and legitimacy, contentious popular collective action has nevertheless often been referred to using the language of "visits." The reason for this is twofold. First, most social protests in China target the government. Second, both protesters and the government want to describe their interactions as nonantagonistic and therefore prefer the term "visits" (*shangfang*) or "petitions" to "resistance" (*kangzheng*) or "protest" (*kangyi*). Indeed, a majority of social protests in contemporary China have been regarded as collective petitions (*jiti shangfang*), and are therefore included in xinfang data.[4]

For the study of social protests, the fact that the information about moderate petitions is also included is actually advantageous to researchers. As radical protest activities and moderate petitions exist on the same continuum, such data are particularly useful for explaining how different forms of action have been chosen by petitioners, and how some forms of protest tactics may shift to others.

This chapter starts with a description of the upsurge in social protests since the 1990s. To gain a better understanding of this trend, I will then examine it from three different perspectives. First, the rise of collective petitions will be compared with the trends during the same period for other forms of claim making such as moderate petitions, litigations, and

---

[4] Some local studies, based on incomplete local data, estimated that collective petitions account for about 60% to 80% of all incidents of unrest. See Chen Jinsheng, *Quntixing Shijian Yanjiu Baogao* (Research Report on Mass Incidents) (Beijing: Qunzhong Chubanshe, 2004). The actual percentage is probably even higher because in those studies, incidents that were classified not as collective petitions, but as demonstrations, gatherings, sit-in protests, and riots, are very likely some special forms of collective petitions. In the xinfang system, those incidents are often classified as "abnormal petitions."

meditation. Somewhat surprisingly, those claim-making activities did not experience a similarly sharp increase. Second, I will take a close look at the claims and participants of recent social protests. Knowledge of who participated in protests and what demands they made can provide important information for us in explaining the upsurge and routinization of social protests. Finally, this rise in social protests will be placed in a historical perspective. Contemporary petitioners and government officials have often used the history of petitions and protests during the imperial era to interpret contemporary popular action. At the same time, the significance and distinctiveness of the recent surge of collective petitions are often underestimated because of numerous contentious events in Chinese history, many of which were massive and dramatic. Historical comparisons will reveal the linkage between present-day and imperial-era popular petitions/protests, and also underscore the distinctiveness of the recent waves of collective protests.

THE SURGE OF COLLECTIVE PETITIONS

Most provinces have disclosed basic facts about petitions in their year-books since the 1980s. Of all provincial yearbooks, Henan provincial yearbooks have provided the most detailed information. Therefore, I supplement the data collected by the Hunan provincial government with the data from Henan provincial yearbooks.

From Figure 2.1, we find a similar pattern in Henan and Hunan Provinces: There has been a steady and significant increase in the population (per million) participating in collective petitioning since the early 1990s. In Hunan Province, the participants (per million) of collective petitioning in 2000 was 13.59 times that in 1991. Collective petitions in Henan province also dramatically increased during the same period: The number of people participating in collective petitioning in 2000 is 4.16 times greater than in 1991. Of course, there are some differences between these two provinces. For example, whereas the rising trend in Hunan was almost linear, Henan showed a decrease from 1998 to 2000. Also, judging by participants per million people in the two provinces, Henanese people appear to be more contentious. Unfortunately, the available data does not allow a systematic analysis of such differences. Despite some differences, both provinces have clearly witnessed a surge in social protests, confirming the trend indicated in the national data from the Ministry of Public Security.

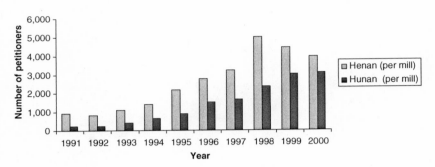

FIGURE 2.1. Number of collective petitioners per million people in Hunan and Henan Provinces, 1991–2000.

Sources: Data for Henan Province comes from Henan Nanjian (Henan Yearbook) (Zhengzhou: Henan Nianjian Chubanshe, 1990–2001). Data for Hunan Province are collected from HNPXB.

Popular collective action has become not only more common, but also routinized. Many of the collective petitions were actually part of protracted struggles. Although it is often assumed that social protests in China tend to be brief, the data from City Y indicates that a considerable portion of petitions were part of struggles that lasted at least six months. Of the 902 events in the dataset, 43 percent (385 events) belong to long struggles. As will be discussed in detail in Chapter 5, paradoxically, the more confrontational collective petitioning events are even more likely to be part of protracted protests. The frequency and durability of collective petitions have made them a "normal" phenomenon in China.

To better understand the surge of collective petitions, we can compare it with the trends of other forms of claim making.

THE TRENDS FOR OTHER FORMS OF CLAIM MAKING

A common explanation attributes this surge of collective petitions to an explosion of popular grievances and social conflicts in the Reform Era, which appeared to have stimulated a general surge of a variety of claim-making activities. However, a comparison between collective protests and other claim-making activities such as moderate petitions, litigations, and meditation presents a more complicated picture.

The Chinese government identifies three main forms of petitions and appeals: letters (*xin*), individual visits (*getifang*), and collective visits

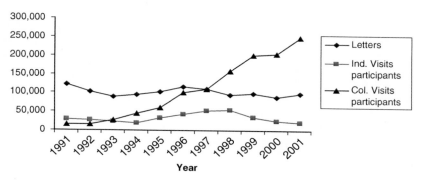

FIGURE 2.2. Number of participants in individual visits and collective visits, and number of letters in Hunan, 1991–2001.
Source: HNPXB.

(*jitifang*). Letters are counted separately when they are delivered by mail or fax. If petition letters are delivered personally, such events are treated as visits, and the letters are not counted separately. Petition delivery by one to four people is defined as an individual visit, whereas delivery by five or more people constitutes a collective visit.[5] When calculating the total of all three categories, government officials count each letter as one unit no matter how many people have signed it. For individual visits and collective visits, they count participants, so in most cases the total number (*renci*) of petitions and appeals is a combination of the number of letters that the government has received and the number of the participants in petitioning events.

Figures 2.2 and 2.3 show the trend of the three forms of claim-making activities in Hunan and Henan. Although the time periods in this data set are not identical for these two provinces, we can observe some similarities between them in the period since 1991. First, petitioning via mail has consistently been more popular than individual visits, because mail petitions incur lower costs while achieving a similar effect on government

---

[5] Many local governments once treated petition delivery events by one to two people as individual visits, and those by three or more people as collective visits. Since the 1990s, most, if not all, local governments started to count events in which five or more people participated as collective visits. Occasionally, some local governments use another term, "group visits (*quntifang*)." Group visits refer to the events in which three or four people participate. As such, they are smaller than collective visits yet larger than individual visits. In most official statistical data, however, group visits are not distinguished from individual visits.

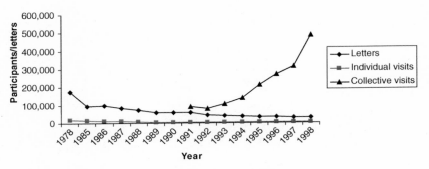

FIGURE 2.3. Participants/letters in Henan Province, 1978–1998. The data between 1978 and 1985 is not available.

Source: HNNJ.

responses. Second, from the early to late 1990s, the frequency of collective visits increased substantially, becoming the biggest category by a large margin. Third, the frequency of petition via mail or individual visits fluctuated over time and does not indicate a rising trend. In Henan, both petitions via mail and individual visits actually declined somewhat in the 1990s.

This analysis suggests a shift in behavioral patterns in China: Collective action has gained popularity in comparison to moderate petitioning. In interpreting the differences among the three forms of claim making, it should be noted that these categories are not mutually exclusive, and petitioners can combine them in a variety of ways in their struggle. Indeed, collective petitioners commonly use individual visits and letter writing to supplement their collective action. In addition, these statistics do not reflect the fact that among mailed petitioning there has been a substantial rise in letters signed jointly by multiple petitioners.

Data from other channels for conflict resolution did not witness a substantial rise in the number of cases during this period. For example, the number of first-instance cases in the court system in China increased briefly from 3,943,095 in 1994 to 5,285,171 in 1996, and then basically remained at consistent levels. There were 5,139,888 such cases in 2005. Another important channel for conflict resolution, people's mediation committees, even witnessed a decrease of cases. There were 6,123,729 mediation cases handled by such committees in 1994; the number of mediation cases then gradually decreased to 4,486,825 in 2005.

The lack of growth in the number of moderate petitions, litigations, and mediation cases indicates that the surge of collective petitions represents less of a general rise in claim-making activities than a shift in the preferred form of claim making.

PARTICIPANTS AND DEMANDS OF COLLECTIVE PETITIONS

To understand protests and social movements, two questions are usually asked: Who participated in them, and what claim did they want to make? However, it is not an easy task to classify and summarize the demands of social protesters in China. In recent years, ordinary people in China have staged social protests on a bewildering array of issues, which have changed remarkably over time.

Fortunately, we can take advantage of the statistical data collected by the xinfang system. The Chinese government has a strong interest in keeping track of demands voiced through social protests. Therefore, xinfang bureaus at each level are required to fill out a form that records the frequency in which key issues are the subject of social protests each month. They typically identify about a dozen issues that are most common across collective petitions and individual petitions in each period. These issues usually account for about 85 percent of all petitions. However, the bureau's categorization of each issue is often vague and confusing, and the use of official jargon also makes such data difficult to use. For purposes of clarity, I rearranged these issues by merging some of them and identifying six clusters of issues that were most prominent among collective petitions from 1994 to 2001 in Hunan province (ranked in order of prevalence of each issue in 2001). I also draw examples from the event catalog in City Y to illustrate these issues.

Workers' welfare and enterprise restructuring (zhigong fuli, qiye gaizhi). In 2001, there were 3,113 collective petitions focusing on this cluster of issues. They account for 33.8 percent of all collective petitions. This cluster includes demands by pensioners, laid-off workers, and workers in restructuring enterprises. The demands of these groups cover the following issues: (1) pensions or a living fee, and/or health insurance; (2) jobs for laid-off workers; (3) supply of utilities such as water and electricity; (4) workers' participation and/or government monitoring of the process of restructuring state-owned enterprises (SOEs) and collective firms to avoid illicit asset stripping; and (5) punishing corrupt officials who strip assets of enterprises illicitly. Examples include:

- On May 18, 1998, approximately 200 workers from a bankrupt chemical factory marched to the city government to complain about

TABLE 2.1. *Number of Collective Petitions on Several Main Issues in Hunan Province, 1994–2001*

	1994	1995	1996	1998	1999	2000	2001
Workers' welfare and enterprise restructuring	464	797	1,020	1,613	2,512	2,757	3,113
Societal disputes	335	388	504	1,118	1,367	1,594	1,896
Land expropriation, house demolition, and migration	238	314	533	549	657	917	1,068
Urban affairs management	N/A	N/A	N/A	446	445	604	721
Peasant's burden and villagers' self-governance	223	313	768	764	870	668	670
Job and placement	N/A	N/A	N/A	135	209	253	291
Others	255	321	618	951	1,069	1,332	1,454
Total	1,515	2,133	3,443	5,576	7,129	8,125	9,213

Source: HNPXB.

the city electricity company, which had stopped the supply of electricity when the factory could no longer afford the fees.

- On September 21, 1999, approximately seventy-five pensioners from a collective factory came to the city government in two buses to protest against pension arrears.
- On January 7, 2002, forty workers from a collective enterprise came to the city government in a truck to demand transparency during the process of bankruptcy.

Societal disputes (jiufen). In 2001, there were 1,896 collective petitions on this cluster of issues. They account for 20.6 percent of all collective petitions. They include disputes about economic and other contracts, damages such as environmental pollution, and property rights in mountains, forests, waters, cultivated land, and so forth. In these disputes, the state or state agents usually do not act as one of the disputing parties. Parties often resort to government leaders to resolve their disputes, as they can influence other parties or the courts, or may have the authority to dispose of the disputed object. The parties in economic disputes demand respectively that the government: (1) protect or recognize their rights to property or use of property; (2) pressure other parties to pay damages; (3) pressure the court to give and/or enforce (or not enforce) certain decisions; or (4) order the police to pursue specific criminal cases. Examples include:

- On August 14, 1995, seventy-six villagers petitioned the district government to complain about pollution from a nearby factory.
- On September 29, 2001, more than 100 relatives and friends of a murdered taxi driver demonstrated at the city government to demand a prompt and thorough investigation.
- On January 21, 2002, a manager accompanied by fifteen workers and friends petitioned the annual meeting of local People's Congress to complain about a government decision regarding the ownership of the enterprise.
- On March 2, 2002, eighty-nine workers from a collective enterprise petitioned to the city government to protest against a local court's failure to enforce a decision on a contract dispute.

Land expropriation, house demolition, and organized migration (zhengdi chaiqian yu yimin). In 2001, there were 1,068 collective petitions on this cluster of issues, which account for 11.6 percent of all collective petitions. They include demands by either peasants or urban residents to the government: (1) to stop illicit land expropriation when possible; (2) to provide sufficient compensation for peasants who have lost land or urban residents whose houses have been demolished; (3) to make arrangements for organized migrants to return to their homeland; or (4) to punish corrupt officials responsible for illicit land expropriation processes, who have taken bribes in land expropriation or embezzled funds for land expropriation compensation. Examples include:

- On June 8, 1994, more than 100 government-organized migrants attempted to petition the provincial government to arrange for them to return to their home village.
- On January 12, 2000, thirty-five urban residents whose houses had been demolished petitioned the annual meeting of the local People's Congress to complain about inadequate compensation.
- On July 2, 2001, when the Governor came to inspect a new district school, sixty-five villagers whose land had been expropriated delivered to him a petition letter signed by 220 villagers to complain about inadequate compensation.

Urban affairs management (shizheng guanli). In 2001, there were 721 collective petitions, which account for 7.8 percent of all collective petitions. These were mostly protests by self-employed laborers against the following: (1) regulations that are presumed to unreasonably restrict their business; or (2) excessive fees collected by government agents. Examples include:

- On March 28, 1995, more than eighty self-employed minibus drivers went on strike and blocked a highway to protest excessive government fees and government-mandated low ticket prices.
- On November 7, 2000, 150 tricycle drivers petitioned the district government to protest a policy banning tricycles as passenger transport.

Peasant burden and villagers' self-governance (nongmin fudan yu cunmin zizhi). In 2001, there were 670 collective petitions on this cluster, which account for 7.3 percent of all collective petitions. They include demands by peasants for the following state actions: (1) reductions of taxes and fees; (2) guarantees of villagers' rights to audit village budgets (*qingli caiwu*); (3) guarantees of free and fair elections for Villagers' Committees; (4) investigation and punishment of cadres' misdeeds, including corruption, election manipulation, and the infringement on peasants' rights of persons and property in the process of enforcement of state policies; or (5) poverty relief and production aid in the event of natural calamities. Examples include:

- On December 5, 1997, forty villagers blocked the entrance to the provincial government to complain about excessively high taxes and corruption of village cadres.
- On March 24, 2000, forty-six villagers petitioned the city government to complain about their village Party secretary's embezzlement of disaster relief funds.
- On January 5, 2001, fifty-four villagers petitioned the city government about the corruption of the village Party secretary and demanded to audit the village budget.

Jobs and placements (gongzuo anzhi). In 2001, there were 291 collective petitions on this cluster, which account for 3.2 percent of all collective petitions. These include demands by college students and demobilized army officers for jobs or placements. Examples include:

- On April 9, 2002, fifty-nine cadres from a county Bureau of Industry and Commerce occupied the bureau chief's office to protest against the bureau's decision to assign them to a nongovernment agency.
- On June 18, 2002, seventeen demobilized army officers working in a bankrupt collective enterprise petitioned the city government, demanding placement in new positions.

Most of these clusters of demands are focused on social and economic rights. While peasants' claims regarding self-governance are of a political nature, they were often made together with complaints about excessive taxes and fees. It should be noted, however, that there are two prominent themes in petitions delivered by a variety of groups: corruption and political representation. Whatever rights or benefits petitioners tried to claim, they often emphatically protested against corruption of government officials or grassroots cadres (SOE managers included). Similarly, they often complained how their lack of voice on public issues affected their rights and welfare.

Another striking finding from Table 2.1 is that almost all six clusters grew substantially and continuously from 1994 to 2001. Only the demands about peasant burdens and villager self-governance have decreased slightly since 1998. Collective petitions on workers' welfare and enterprise restructuring increased from 464 in 1994 to 3,113 in 2001. In other words, the number of collective petitions in this cluster in 2001 is 6.71 times of that in 1994. Dramatic growth can be found in all the other clusters as well. For example, the number of collective petitions on disputes in 2001 is 5.66 times that in 1994. For issues on land expropriation and migration, the ratio is 4.49 to 1. For issues on peasant burden and villagers' self-governance, the ratio is 3 to 1. In 1994, there were so few collective petitions on urban affairs management that the xinfang system did not treat this cluster of issues as a major category. However, in 2001, there were 721 collective petitions in this category. Similarly, there were no statistics on collective petitions about job and placement in the mid-1990s. There were 135 such cases in 1998 and the number increased to 291 in 2001.

The fact that there was a remarkable rise in all six clusters of issues suggests a trend that extends beyond specific policies or status changes in one or two social groups. Because these issues are so diverse and also largely unrelated, the surge in collective petitioning events can hardly be explained by the grievances of some small set of social groups. We need therefore to search for structural factors that have transformed all these groups' behavior patterns.

Demands in the 1985–1986 Surge vs. Those in the Current Surge

Considering the similarities between the surge in 1985–1986 and the current one, a comparison of demands in these two surges can be helpful for our interpretation of the current wave of collective petitioning events.

TABLE 2.2. *Issues of Collective Petitioning in Hunan Province, 1985–1986, 1994–1995, 2000–2001*

	1985–1986*	1994–1995	2000–2001
Workers' welfare and enterprise restructuring	7.0%	34.6%	33.9%
Disputes	36.6%	19.8%	20.1%
Land expropriation, house demolition, and migration	9.1%	15.1%	11.4%
Urban affairs management	N/A**	N/A	7.6%
Peasant's burden and villagers' self-governance	N/A	14.7%	7.7%
Household and food-rationing status	19.0%	N/A	N/A
Jobs and placements	7.2%	N/A	3.1%
Historically leftover problems	7.8%	N/A	N/A
Others	13.3%	15.8%	16.1%
Total	100%	100.0%	100.0%
Total number of petitions	516	3,648	17,338

* In this period, collective petitioning was defined as an event with three or more participants. In later statistics, it was defined as an event with five or more participants.
** N/A in this chart implies the proportion in this category is so small that the xinfang bureaus would not count it as a major issue.

Source: HNPXB.

Table 2.2 includes the proportion of each main issue in collective petitioning for three different periods: 1985–1986, 1994–1995, and 2000–2001. I used two-year periods to reduce the possibility of a large deviation. When comparing the changes in the prevalence of each category of protest, one must analyze the different meanings ascribed to each issue, because the same category may consist of quite different claims in the 1980s and in the 1990s. For example, most demands about land expropriation and organized migration in the 1980s focused on illicit occupation of cultivated land by local cadres, whereas demands in the 1990s tended to focus on problems arising from land expropriation due to construction projects sponsored or permitted by the government.

In Table 2.2, we can see two types of demands in the 1980s that disappeared in the 1990s. In the 1980s, the demands about household and food rationing status were made by peasants who did not produce food crops, such as fishermen, peasants cultivating economic crops, peasants with little land, and so forth. Those peasants relied on the household and food rationing system to obtain food at reasonable prices. Such demands substantially declined when the household and food rationing system was largely replaced by market mechanisms in the 1990s. Another type of demand involved "historical grievances" (*lishi yiliu wenti*) accumulated in various mass campaigns such as the Cultural Revolution and the anti-rightist campaigns. They accounted for 7.8 percent of all petitioning issues in 1985–1986. Since most such claims were resolved in the 1980s, petitions concerning these issues largely disappeared by the 1990s.

The overall proportion of two other types of demands (relative to the total number of petitions) also decreased from the 1980s to the 1990s. The first type is societal disputes. Petitions about various disputes between non-state groups account for 36.6 percent of all petitions in 1985–1986, but only about 20 percent in the 1990s. However, according to Table 2.2, the number of such petitions did not decrease, but in fact increased. Thus the reason for the decreased proportion lies in the fact that the number of the other types of petitions grew much faster than those concerning societal disputes.

The overall proportion of collective petitions concerning job and placement also decreased from the 1980s to the 1990s. This shift is partly due to the fact that the government was responsible for assigning jobs to students in colleges and technical schools before the early 1990s, but no longer assumed the responsibility later on. Since 1998, there has been a rise in collective petitions on these issues, mainly because when many enterprises were restructured or went bankrupt, some laid-off workers and demobilized army officers began to demand placement.

Four issues were either quite new or increased substantially in the 1990s: (1) workers' welfare and enterprise; (2) peasant burdens and villagers' self-governance; (3) urban affairs management; and (4) land expropriation, house demolition, and organized migration.

These changes highlight the impact of the structural shift from a command economy to a market economy, and the fact that political campaigns characterized by Mao's era were no longer a source of collective petitions in the 1990s. In a sense, all major types of collective petitions can be interpreted as reactions to or resistance against the social injustice caused by economic reforms. However, social transformations in the Reform Era have contributed to the surge of collective protest not just by generating grievances among many social groups. More importantly, as elaborated in Chapters 3 and 4, the social transformations created a favorable political opportunity structure for collective protests with certain political orientations.

The remainder of this chapter will focus on historical comparisons to examine the extent to which the recent surge of collective protests is distinctive in Chinese history.

PETITIONS IN PRE-1990 PRC

China has a long history of popular contention. Is the current surge of social protest simply a repetition of history? Let us first examine the history of the PRC. In Mao's era, waves of collective petitioning were extremely rare, although state-sponsored mass mobilization was very common. Most petitions were individual, and letter writing was the main form of petitioning. The number of petitions changed remarkably across time. As Ying Xing remarks, petitioning was actually part of the politics of mass campaigns.[6] Mao's politics featured cycles of mass campaigns. In the initial stage, ordinary people were encouraged to write letters to testify against other people. When the campaigns went too far (as they often did), victims petitioned to rectify decisions against them.

Because most petitions in this period were about administrative, party, or legal sanctions, the Party-state's willingness to rectify some problems had a significant impact on petitioning behavior over time. When the regime sent signals that it would reconsider previous policies, numerous petitioners would flood the authorities with their appeals.

From Figure 2.4 we can see a pattern in which the number of petitions rises and falls at regular intervals. Aside from this fluctuation, the overall number of petitions increased gradually, mainly as a result of the cumulative effect of mass campaigns. Millions of potential petitioners were created each year, and few of them had their demands met until the end of Mao's reign.

Anyone with enough knowledge of Chinese history during that period can offer a preliminary explanation for the cycles of petitions with reasonable accuracy. The rise and fall of petitions were consistent with the general "political atmosphere," which conveyed two pieces of information to potential petitioners: the safety and efficacy of petitioning. During some periods, even very peaceful petitions might incur ruthless repression. For example, during the Great Leap Forward, when cadres at every level were trying to distort or hide information,

---

[6] Ying Xing, "*Zuowei Teshu Xingzheng Jiuji de Xinfang Jiuji*" (The Xinfang Remedy: A Special Form of Administrative Relief), *Faxue Yanjiu* (Jurisprudence Research) 3 (2004), pp. 58–71.

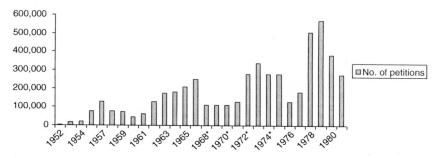

FIGURE 2.4. Petitions to the General Office of the State Council, 1952–1981.
Source: RXS. The data in 1968, 1970, 1972, and 1974 are inferred from information provided in this book.

petitioning to higher authorities via mail to expose the truth was very likely to incur persecution.[7] Therefore, from Figure 2.4 we notice that the number of petitions went down substantially during the GLF, and did not go up again until 1961, when the CCP leaders decided to extensively adjust their policies. The periods during which petitioners faced lower risks also tended to be those in which the petitions themselves were much more efficacious, thus providing even stronger incentives for petitioners.

From Figure 2.4, we identify four periods of substantial rise. The first occurred around 1956, when the CCP initiated its "rectification campaign" as well as the Hundred Flowers Campaign. Ordinary people were encouraged to speak up. The second crest occurred in 1961, as mentioned earlier. The third began in 1972, when Lin Biao had just died and Deng Xiaoping was to be restored to power shortly thereafter, sending a strong signal to the Chinese people about a possible abrupt change in policy. The fourth and the biggest rise occurred after members of the "Gang of Four" were arrested, and the CCP decided to denounce most previous campaigns and rehabilitate many of their victims.

The extraordinary peak in the number of petitions from 1978 to 1982 was by far the largest, but it still fits the same pattern as previous peaks. Table 2.3 shows the number of cases handled by the State Council as well as three provinces. In Sichuan Province alone, governments above the county level received 2.3 million cases.

[7] Diao Jiecheng, *Renmin xinfang shilue* (A Brief History of People's Letters and Visits) (Beijing: Beijing Xueyuan chubanshe, 1996), p. 121.

TABLE 2.3. *Number of Petitions Delivered to Some Selected Central and Local Government Agencies, 1979–1981 (thousands)*

	1979	1980	1981
General offices of the State Council and the CCP Central Committee	751	505	365
Anhui	1,000	430	320
Shangdong	790	370	210
Sichuan	2,300	1,380	970
Total	4,841	2,685	1,865

Source: RXS.

The trend did not last long, however, and the caseload began to drop rapidly. Table 2.3 indicates that petitions to the four authorities dropped 45 percent from 1979 to 1980 and fell an additional 31 percent from 1980 to 1981. The drop was not due to the closing of the channel of petitions, but rather to the fact that the authorities had resolved most of the issues. How could the authorities resolve so many petitions? There are two main reasons. First, most of the claims related to decisions made by the Party-state. By changing its policy, the authorities were able to solve many cases at one time. For example, when the Party decided to rehabilitate "rightists," the central authority just needed to publish the necessary standards, and local authorities could rehabilitate all petitioners who met the criteria. Secondly, the Party-state mobilized a large number of officials to supervise the process of rectifying those appeals. One of the key difficulties was that many local government officials resisted the rectification and were not willing to rehabilitate those who were perceived as their "enemies." Altogether, about 200,000 cadres in the country were sent to lower levels to supervise the campaign.

The rise and fall of petitions throughout the PRC era suggest the importance of the political environment. Most people would not voice their grievances without the presence of a favorable political environment.

Three Previous Surges of Collective Petition Movements

The PRC witnessed three surges of popular protest on socioeconomic issues before the 1990s. The first is the protest waves of 1956–1957. This surge in social protests is different from state-sponsored political campaigns in that most of protests in this period were largely bottom-up struggles, even though they were inspired by the state. Moreover, they focused on social and economic issues rather than class struggle or other political issues. As Perry's study of labor strikes in Shanghai indicates, nearly half the disputes were driven by a demand for higher income or improved welfare – usually in response to cuts imposed during the change to joint ownership. The remainder of the protests were closely connected to the newly emerging system of household registration (*hukou*).[8]

Although it was not initiated by the Party-state, this surge was closely connected to the Hundred Flowers Campaign. In particular, protesters were encouraged by Mao's speech on "handling the contradictions among the people." Like today's social protest, protesters in 1956–1957 employed a variety of tactics, such as strikes, slowdowns, forcible surrounding of cadres, and collective petition movements.

The second surge in social protests emerged during the extraordinary peak in the number of petitions in 1978–1981. Shortly after the end of the Cultural Revolution, the CCP waged an extensive campaign to correct the mistakes of previous political campaigns. Although the CCP started to abandon political campaigns as a primary instrument for achieving political, social, and economic goals, they tackled this task with another political campaign. This new campaign spurred a huge wave of petitions and appeals, as discussed earlier. Around 1980, many provinces also observed a wave of collective action in addition to moderate petitions. For example, in a speech in December 1980, a provincial leader in Hunan Province noted specifically that "there have been more than a dozen collective petitioning events in Changsha and Xiangtan."[9] Three issues were most salient. The first was job-related demands by "sent-down youth," repatriated workers, and demobilized army officers. The second involved disputes over waterworks and houses. The third issue was very specific: protest against university officials' interference with elections. The CCP started a series of reforms in 1980, usually referred to as Gengsheng reforms. In particular, local elections inspired a high degree of democratic optimism. Therefore, when university officials at Hunan Teachers' College interfered with the elections, some 2,000 students marched through the city and petitioned to the provincial party headquarters.[10]

---

[8] Elizabeth Perry, *Challenging the Mandate of Heaven: Social Protest and State Power in China* (Armonk, NY: M.E. Sharpe, 2002), p. 213.

[9] An internal document collected from the Hunan provincial government in 2002. It was entitled "Comrade Kang Zheng's Speech in a Conference on the Xinfang Work, December, 6, 1980."

[10] About the reforms and the student protests, see Richard Baum, *Burying Mao: Chinese Politics in the Age of Deng Xiaoping* (Princeton, NJ: Princeton University Press, 1994), pp. 107–108.

The third surge occurred in 1985–1986. This surge was substantially larger than the second one. From 1985 through the first eight months of 1986, the provincial government reported 423 collective petitioning events in Hunan Province; there were only 52 such events in 1984.[11]

A comparison between the waves of protests in the Reform Era and those in Mao's era indicates that popular contention has become increasingly autonomous. The first two surges were clearly inspired by grand state programs. In her study of the 1956–1957 protest wave, Perry points out, "The importance of state inspiration is undeniable. Without the chairman's explicit encouragement, it seems inconceivable that the strike wave would have assumed such massive proportions."[12] The 1980 surge was also related to the party campaign waged under the banner of "correcting the mistakes." In contrast, the two most recent surges have not been inspired by any specific political campaign. Of course, this is not to say that the Party-state has played no role in the last two surges. On the contrary, state toleration and facilitation have created the dynamics for the recent surges.

Moreover, the first two surges were also accompanied with a sharp rise in petitions via mail or individual visits. By contrast, in the two most recent surges, there was no substantial increase in petitions via mail or individual visits.

The most remarkable difference between the current surge and the previous three surges lies in the fact that all three previous surges were short-lived. None of them lasted more than two years. The current trend of rising social protests has lasted almost two decades. In this sense, the trend is unprecedented in the history of the PRC. For the first time in the PRC, popular contention has not only become pervasive, but actually been routinized.

PETITIONS AND APPEALS IN IMPERIAL CHINA

Both contemporary protesters and government officials have often interpreted their own positions and action from a historical perspective. Some Chinese protesters, especially peasant protesters, invoked memories of peasant rebellions in imperial China in their statements. For instance,

---

[11] Data from HNPXB. It should be noted that the measurement of collective petitioning events in the early 1990s and before was different than the current one. Petitions delivered by three or more persons were then regarded as collective petitioning, whereas the current rules define collective petitioning as an event with five or more participants.

[12] Elizabeth Perry, *Challenging the Mandate of Heaven*, p. 211.

a group of peasant protesters in Shandong Province shouted, "We are the offspring of Liangshan. It is time for us to rebel." (Liangshan was the home of legendary rebels in Shandong in the novel *Water Margin*.)[13] Likewise, Chinese leaders sometimes cited examples of ancient uprisings when urging local officials to handle protests carefully. However, today's social protests are actually remarkably different from historic peasant rebellions in that they are much more frequent and routinized, as well as more limited in their goals and scope. As Perry remarks, "Today's scattered protests obviously do not begin to approach these imperial or republican era precedents in terms of either ambition or outcome."[14] The invocation of memories of ancient rebellions tends to be more rhetorical than substantive. Few protesters or government officials would believe contemporary social protests were actually following the model of previous rebels.

By comparison, the history of petitions and appeals in imperial times is often more relevant to today's popular political action. Despite some dramatic differences in the guiding ideology and political systems between imperial China and the CCP regime, there are a lot of similarities between present-day and imperial-era patterns of interaction between petitioners or appellants and the authorities. CCP leaders adhere to the mass line ideology, and are therefore quite concerned about popular grievances and opinions. Chinese rulers in imperial times of course had no idea about mass line ideology, but they generally recognized the notion of "mandate of heaven" and believed that "to ignore the injury [to the population] was to risk catastrophe."[15] They therefore also cared about responding to popular grievances.

Many studies of Chinese legal history indicate that the right of appeal for a new trial was acknowledged quite early on in China, and ordinary people could find legal channels to deliver their petitions or appeals.[16] To be sure, petitions and appeals actually exist in every political system in human history. Petitioning was a general practice in Western societies as testified by the saying "nobody is forbidden to hand in supplications

---

[13] Cited from Thomas Bernstein & Xiaobo Lü, *Taxation without Representation in Contemporary Rural China* (New York: Cambridge University Press, 2003), p. 127.

[14] Elizabeth Perry, "Permanent Rebellion? Continuities and Discontinuities in Chinese Protest," in Kevin J O'Brien (ed.), *Popular Protest in China* (Cambridge, MA: Harvard University Press, 2008), pp. 205–215.

[15] Jonathan Ocko, "I Will Take it All the Way to Beijing: Capital Appeals in the Qing," *Journal of Asian Studies* 47/2 (May, 1988), p. 291.

[16] Ibid, p. 291.

and appeals."[17] Sidney Tarrow also remarks, "The petition was an ancient form for individuals seeking redress from patrons or Parliament. As such, it was culturally acceptable, perfectly lawful, and scarcely contentious."[18] Yet China is certainly among the earliest countries that started to institute mechanisms to accommodate and facilitate petitions. There are stories about how *Yao, Shun*, and *Yu*, three successive mythical emperors who supposedly lived around 2200 BC, set up an apparatus for collecting public opinion. *Yao* established a sort of banner before his court called "the banner for good suggestions" (*jinshanjing*). His successor *Shun* set up a drum called "the drum of remonstration" (*ganjian zhigu*).[19] Of course, no written records of that period have been found to verify such legendary stories. A similar mechanism, "lung stone" (*feishi*), was established in the Western Zhou Dynasty (1100–771 BC), and was actually recorded historically. In the Jin Dynasties (265–420 AD), a "grievances drum" (*dengwengu*) was set up for petitioners to use when delivering their claims.[20] This institution continued to work until the Qing dynasty (1644–1911).

Although there were official agencies and procedures for petitions and appeals, petitioners and appellants in imperial times, like their present-day counterparts, often ran into formidable barriers to addressing their issues effectively. In particular, local officials were often found to be indifferent, biased, or corrupt. Petitioners and appellants therefore needed to employ a variety of "troublemaking" tactics to enhance their effectiveness. The present-day repertoire of petitioning tactics is similar to those used during the imperial-era in several important respects.

For instance, one common tactic employed both today and during the imperial period is skip-level petitions or appeals, which means bypassing the designated level of government, and going directly to higher authorities, possibly even going to the authorities in the capital. In imperial China, a centralized state had existed since the Qin dynasty (221–206 BC). The hierarchical bureaucratic structure provided ordinary people

[17] Andreas Wurgler, "Voices from Among the 'Silent Masses': Humble Petitions and Social Conflicts in Early Modern Central Europe," *International Research of Social History* 46 (2001), p. 16.

[18] Sidney Tarrow, *Power in Movement: Social Movements and Contentious Politics* (New York: Cambridge University Press, 1998), p. 38.

[19] Such stories have been recorded in books written in later periods, such as *Dadaiji: Baofu* or *Huainanzi: Zhushupian*. See Zhao Yanlong, "Xixia Xinfang Gongzuo Zhidu Tanwei" (Exploration of the letters and visits system in Xixia), *Ningxia Shehui Kexue* (Ningxia Social Science) 119/4 (July 2003), pp. 50–53.

[20] Qiang Fang, "A Hot Potato: The Chinese Complaint Systems from Early Times to the Present," unpublished dissertation, University of Buffalo (2006), p. 18.

with an opportunity to seek justice by petitioning to higher authorities. For example, when appellants in the Qing dynasty had no confidence in remedies at or below the provincial level, they might go to the offices of the censorate and the capital gendarmerie (*bujun tongling yamen*) to bang the "grievance drum." If they were eager to reach the ears of the throne directly, they might even employ some transgressive tactics, such as kneeling before the palace gate or along the route of an imperial procession (*kouhun*). Of course, such tactics could lead to harsh punishment regardless of the veracity of their claims.[21] Living in an even more centralized political system, petitioners in today's China still find skip-level petition a very tempting option. Like their predecessors in the imperial era, many of them have even determined to bring their claims "all the way to Beijing."

In addition to skip-level appeals and petitions, there are a number of other "troublemaking" tactics used by imperial-era petitioners that may seem quite familiar to present-day petitioners. Examples include blocking an official procession, draping white cloths with characters on them (*yuanyi*), and self-inflicted sufferings such as self-mutilation and attempted suicide. Consciously or unconsciously, present-day petitioners have adopted quite a few traditional tactics in slightly altered form. Jonathan Ocko remarked that many political practices first developed under imperial systems of rule were "popularly, if informally, replicated" in contemporary China.[22]

Most petitions and appeals in imperial eras focused on private social and economic issues. They were delivered by all kinds of people. In his study of the capital appeal, Ocko writes:

> One can conclude that appellants were not confined to elites. The appellate record is peopled by an intriguing array of characters – Grand Canal boatmen, dismissed officials and wives of officials, peasants, monks, and landlords – with a broad range of problems such as grave robbing, border and market disputes, land seizures, sons assaulted by their widowed mothers, and widows forced by brothers-in-law to commit adultery and remarry in order to deprive them of family property.[23]

Similarly, petitions in contemporary China have been addressed by a wide segment of the population, and a vast majority of them focus on social and economic issues.

[21] Ibid, p. 294.
[22] Ocko, p. 311.
[23] Ibid, p. 309.

Of course, compared to the modern state, the government in imperial times played a much smaller role in social life, and ordinary people therefore had far fewer issues about which they sought to address the authorities. A majority of claims they made on the government were of a judicial nature. By contrast, the modern Chinese state plays a much bigger role in social life. Hence there is a wider range of issues about which ordinary people want to address the authorities, many of which relate to policy rather than judicial decisions.

There are still other aspects in which contemporary popular contention is different from imperial-era experiences. However, overall petitions and appeals were well-entrenched in imperial China and seemed to have had a profound impact on today's struggle. Was there any precedent in imperial times for the current waves of routinized collective petitioning?

Collective Petitioning in Imperial Eras

Quite a few collective petitioning events have been recorded in Chinese history. Most of them can be classified into two categories: those addressing national politics and those addressing local public issues. Petitions regarding national politics were often delivered in a form of "remonstration."[24] Remonstration refers to criticism of policy or other political issues by loyal polity members, such as official college students.[25] This tradition dates as far back as the Late Han (25–220 AD), when there was a gigantic "student movement" that tried to hold the power of the politically corrupt eunuchs in check by forming a "party" with officials within the central administration. The students used three main methods to attack eunuchs: (1) ballads, (2) joint petitions and official impeachments, and (3) the power of whatever office they happened to hold.[26] Obviously, this type of petitioning was very close to institutional politics, such as the procedure of impeachment.

Partly due to the high intensity of the struggle between students and eunuchs, and partly due to the high level of organization among petitioners,

---

[24] Andrew Nathan, *Chinese Democracy* (New York: Alfred A. Knopf, 1985), p. 24.

[25] College students in Chinese history are different from college students in the modern educational system. They were a sort of candidate for official positions, and usually focused their study on official ideology. Such imperial universities were well established since the Han Dynasty. For example, during the reign of Emperor Shangdi of the Late Han, the Imperial University consisted of 240 college compounds, 1,850 halls, and 30,000 college students. See Lin Yutang, *A History of the Press and Public Opinion in China* (Chicago: University of Chicago Press, 1936), p. 32.

[26] Lin Yutang, *A History of the Press and Public Opinion in China*, p. 28.

the response to the petitioning campaign in Late Han was a large-scale crackdown by the central government. As Lin Yutang noted, "it involved the wholesale murder of several hundred scholars, the imprisonment of over a thousand university students, the exile and sometimes murder of scholars' family relatives and the imprisonment and banishment from office of a thousand people who were connected with them."[27]

A wave of large petitioning events of this type also took place in the late Northern Song (960–1127 AD) and the early Southern Song (1127–1279 AD) periods. Like the petitioning campaign in the Late Han, this wave of petitions also took place when the dynasty was in crisis. In this instance, students from the Imperial College, led by Chen Dong, fought against what they perceived to be a vacillating, weak-kneed policy toward the Song Dynasty's external foe, the Jurchens. They demanded the death or dismissal from office of several powerful ministers whom they denounced as "traitors," sending petitions and kneeling before the palace gates collectively.[28]

As Lin Yutang commented, such petitioning "was decidedly a dangerous thing to do because the premier in the Southern Song period was the de facto ruler of the state, combining in himself the political, military and financial powers of the country. To send a petition demanding the death of the premier or try to inform the Emperor of his greed, corruption of incompetence, was tantamount to courting death itself."[29] However, such daring petitioning actions were quite successful and resulted in the dismissal from office of two ministers and the deaths of two others.

It should be noted that such movements were sometimes joined by a large number of ordinary people, sometimes degenerating into mob riots. The *History of the Song Dynasty* (*songshi*) tells the story of one of the largest petitioning events,

> In February 1127, Chen Dong together with the college students and tens of thousands of the people in the capital gathered before the palace and sent a petition asking for the restoration to power of Li Gang and Zhong Shidao, saying that Li Bangyan [the premier] was jealous and afraid that Li Gang might be successful in this policy, and that to dismiss Li Gang would be to do exactly what the enemy desired. It happened that Li Bangyan [the target of the protest] was passing the mob on his way to a court audience, and the crowd jeered at him and declaimed his crimes. An official Wu Min came out to speak to the people, but was

---

[27] Ibid. p. 28.
[28] Ibid. p. 47.
[29] Ibid. p. 47.

totally ignored. The crowd then beat the big drum and the noise of their
shouting and clamors shook the air. The captain of the guards, fearing
trouble, therefore begged the Emperor that the people's wish be com-
plied with. The Emperor approved and asked an official to announce to
the people the appointment of Li Gang. When the eunuch had finished
reading the edict, the people attacked and killed him, tearing his body to
pieces, besides murdering several dozen other eunuchs.[30]

The student leader, Chen Dong, organized several significant petitioning
events. Unsurprisingly, he was eventually executed in 1130. It is worth
noting, however, that Chen was not executed immediately after the petitioning events, but rather some time later and with another excuse. The
Emperor even expressed his condolences and granted him posthumous
honorary titles. This indicates that even though the rulers abhorred students' collective petitioning, they had to at least appear to show some
respect for public opinion.

Several observations can be drawn from the petitioning events in the
Han and Song Dynasties. First, student petitioning was very close to institutionalized politics. The student petitioners were candidates for official
positions, and often had close allies in the bureaucracy. Their demands
were also similar to impeachments and proposals raised by imperial cen-
sors and other officials. Second, they were sometimes also closely related
to mass collective action, as evidenced by petitioning events in the Song
Dynasty in which student petitioners were joined by more than 100,000
ordinary people. Nonetheless, it was highly risky for commoners to press
claims on national politics, even though such actions could be effective
under certain circumstances. Although college students belonged to official establishments, and were candidates for official positions, it was still
generally regarded as illegitimate for them to pressure the central government on national affairs. In one petitioning event led by Chen Dong,
the mayor of the capital declared that such an action by "commoners"
(*buyi*) to press for the dismissal or appointment of ministers amounted to
a crime that deserved death.[31]

The tradition of students' petitioning on national affairs continued
into the Qing Dynasty and the Republic (1911–1949). Among the most
famous events were the *Gongju Shangshu* (petitions by *juren*) campaign
in 1894, led by Kang Youwei and Liang Qichao, to demand a fundamental

---

[30] Cited from Lin Yutang, pp. 49–50.
[31] Cheng Zhaoqi, "Chen Dong He Jingkang Xuechao" (Chen Dong and Jingkang Student
Movement), *Shilin Zazhi* (Historical Review) 2 (2000), pp. 23–39.

reform of the imperial system, the May 4th movement in 1919, and the December 9th movement in 1936. Like their predecessors, some of these "high-minded" collective petitions ended in bloodshed. For example, in the peaceful March 18 incident in 1926, 47 petitioners (mostly students) were killed and more than 200 wounded. In condemning this brutal repression, the famous writer Lu Xun wrote angrily, "Petitioning is common in every country and is an action that does not result in death. But China is an exception!"[32] Lu Xun's comments underscore the high risk for collective petitioning on national political issues, which was confirmed once again in 1989.

In addition to national politics, Chinese elites sometimes petitioned about local public issues, and occasionally did so collectively. They demanded the dismissal of corrupt officials, protested overtaxation, or called for justice in criminal cases. In 1660, more than one hundred scholars in Wuxian County, Jiangsu Province, took advantage of the ceremony for mourning the Jiaqing Emperor and submitted a petition to the governor to demand the dismissal from office of the local magistrate. More than 1,000 ordinary people joined these scholars. This event resulted in the execution of eighteen scholars, including one of the most famous literary critics in Chinese history, Jin Shengtan.[33]

In Zhou Guangyuan's study of a petitioning event in the 1870s in Dongxiang County, Sichuan Province, he noted that peasants started their protest against unfair taxation mainly by sending their complaints to the county, prefectural, provincial, and central governments. When the conflict intensified, however, they also staged a public demonstration of about 3,000 people at the south gate of the city under a banner reading "clear up tax accounts and bring relief to the people."[34] Local officials accused them of being rebellious, and a crackdown led to the deaths of several hundred people.

In the late Qing, collective petitioning movements occurred more frequently, and many of their protest tactics looked similar to today's popular political action. Hence Esherick and Wasserstrom noted that a

---

[32] Lu Xun, "Kongtan" (Empty Talk), in *Huagaiji Xubian* (Beijing: Renmin Wenxue Chubanshe, 1980), p. 98.

[33] This case has been well studied. For example, see Robert B. Oxnam, "Policies and Institutions of the Oboi Regency, 1661–1669," *Journal of Asian Studies* 32/2 (1973), p. 279–280.

[34] Guangyuan Zhou, "Illusion and Reality in the Law of the Late Qing," *Modern China* 19/4 (1993), p. 431.

late-nineteenth-century account of a petition movement can "easily evoke images of modern protest repertoires."[35]

However, there are two noticeable aspects that distinguish petition movements during the imperial period from those of today. First, petition movements regarding local public affairs were usually led by elites. In Zhou Guangyuan's case, the leader of the petitioning activities, Yuan Tingjiao, was a poor and illiterate peasant; however, as Zhou points out, this was an exception, and "the leaders of Qing tax protests were usually members of the gentry's class."[36]

The active role of the elite, in particular the gentry, is not just due to their strong sense of social responsibility or public spiritedness. They actually enjoyed some important privileges and protections that encouraged them to challenge local officials. As Chang Chung-li noted, "When members of the gentry committed offenses, the magistrates had to take special procedures to effect any punishment."[37] Of course, a majority of the elite did not need to resort to collective action. They enjoyed much better access to the government than did peasants and had a very strong influence on local policy. Chang observed, "As spokesmen for their areas, the gentry sometimes persuaded the government to accept their point of view."[38] If they could exert their influence through persuasion, why should they mobilize for collective action? It was the lower rank of the elite, *shengyuan*, who were particularly contentious. During some periods, it was reported that "the lower gentry and elders often joined together to petition the yamen."[39] As Qu Tongzu has remarked, since *shengyuan* were outside the power group, their influence was lowest among the gentry. Their main power source came from their solidarity and collective action – for example, joint-signed petitions and boycott of exams.[40] The contentiousness of those lower-rank degree holders did not cause concerns just to the authorities. Even some independent intellectuals criticized them harshly. A famous scholar in the Qing dynasty, Gu Yanwu,

---

[35] Joseph Esherick and Jeffrey Wasserstrom, "Acting Out Democracy: Political Theater in Modern China," *Journal of Asian Studies* 49/4 (November 1990), p. 850.

[36] Guangyuan Zhou, "Illusion and Reality in the Law of the Late Qing," p. 430.

[37] Chang, Chung-li. *The Chinese Gentry: Studies on Their Role in Nineteenth Century Chinese Society* (Seattle: University of Washington Press, 1955), p. 36.

[38] Ibid., p. 55.

[39] Frederick Wakeman, "Introduction: The Evolution of Local Control in Late Imperial China," in Frederick Wakeman & Carolyn Grant (eds.), *Conflict and Control in Late Imperial China* (Berkeley and Los Angeles: University of California, 1975), p. 15.

[40] Tongzu Qu, *Qingdai Difang Zhengfu* (Local Governments in the Qing Dynasty) (Beijing: Falu Chubanshe, 2003), pp. 300–301.

castigated *shengyuan* as "arising in flocks to struggle against any prefectural government which acts contrary to their wishes."[41]

The second distinctive feature of imperial era petitioning is that punishment for collective petitioning tended to be quite harsh. Absent systematic data, it is hard to assess accurately the repressiveness of imperial rulers, but clearly punishment at that time was substantially harsher than today. Of course, government officials in imperial times occasionally tended to tolerate collective petitions staged by the gentry's members. For example, during an exam boycott in the Qing, a provincial official who was in charge of education was castigated by the Emperor for "attempting to gain a reputation of leniency."[42] More often than not, however, disruptive collective action resulted in punishment, which could be as harsh as mass execution. The severity of some of these punishments would be inconceivable today. A related tendency was for local officials to accuse the leaders of collective petition movements of attempting rebellion. Such accusations were also sometimes self-fulfilling, as some petitioning leaders might decide to rebel to avoid a punishment based on the false accusations. By comparison, present-day local officials are unlikely to make such accusations. Harsh punishment and the tendency for petitions to escalate into rebellions made collective petition movements difficult to sustain in imperial eras.

Today's petitioners have continued to seek inspiration from petitions and appeals in imperial eras and have even adopted some tactics from the imperial-era repertoire. Despite some striking similarities between present-day petitioning activities and ancient ones, however, the recent wave of collective protests is still quite distinctive in Chinese history.

CONCLUSION

This chapter has described an impressive surge of collective petitioning events in China since the early 1990s. It also shows that such a trend of widespread and routinized collective protests is a relatively new phenomenon in Chinese history. In the history of the PRC, although there have been three previous waves of collective petitioning movements, none of them lasted as long as the current one. Also, in Mao's China, waves of petitioning movements were deeply affected by state-sponsored political

---

[41] Cited from Frederick Wakeman & Carolyn Grant (eds.), *Conflict and Control in Late Imperial China*, p. 15.

[42] Li Guorong. *Qingchao Shida Kechang An* (Ten Major Criminal Cases Related to the Imperial Exams) (Beijing: Renmin Chubanshe, 2007), p. 95.

campaigns. In contrast, the surges of social protests in the Reform Era were much more autonomous. No single state initiative has spurred prevalent collective petitioning. This is not to deny the important role of the state. Indeed, throughout the PRC era, the state has exerted very strong influence on petitioning activities. But unlike in Mao's era, the state's facilitation of current popular contention is mainly due to its special configuration of political institutions, as analyzed in Chapters 3 and 4.

Of course, petitions and appeals by individuals were well entrenched in the claim-making repertoire employed in imperial China. When confined to petitions on socioeconomic issues, individual actions were generally regarded as authorized performances, although transgressive tactics were sometimes taken to enhance their effectiveness. Petitioning to upper authorities or even to the Emperor was a long-standing tradition, particularly among elites. Ordinary people in imperial China might occasionally stage collective petition movements on national or local public affairs, but such activities were highly risky and therefore difficult to sustain. In sum, although China has a rich history of popular contention – rebellions, revolutions, social movements, state-sponsored political campaigns, and collective petitioning movements – it is very hard to find a period when collective petitioning movements were frequent and routinized for a reasonably long period of time. In this sense, the surge represents a remarkable change in government-citizen relations in China.

As the examination of participants and demands of contemporary social protests suggests, the rather distinctive trend since the 1990s should be understood in the context of the epochal social change in the Reform Era. The upsurge started about a decade after the beginning of the Reform and Opening in the late 1970s, and the early 1990s was a particularly critical period of deepening structural reform in the Chinese economy.[43] By then a number of population sectors had begun to experience the painful downside of the reforms – they had been deprived of many rights and benefits such as pensions and employment that they had taken for granted for decades. Prevalent corruption among government and grassroots cadres, as well the sense that ordinary people lacked a voice regarding the direction of economic changes, further exacerbated

---

[43] Many scholars have noted the importance of the 1990s for social transformation in China. For examples, see Martin King Whyte, *Myth of the Social Volcano: Perceptions of Inequality and Distributive Injustice in Contemporary China* (Stanford, CA: Stanford University Press, 2010); Sun Lipingj *Shiheng: Duanlie Shehui de Yunzuo Luoji* (Imbalance: The Logic of a Fractured Society) (Beijing: Shehui Wenxian Chubanshe, 2004).

their sense of deprivation. Such grievances clearly motivated an increasingly large number of petitioners to mount collective action.

Of course, these grievances could also motivate ordinary people to make claims in other forms. However, during this period there was no substantial rise in other forms of claim making or conflict resolution, such as individual petitions, litigations, and mediation, even though most of the grievances and conflicts addressed by collective petitioning could conceivably be addressed through these forms. Therefore one of our central tasks is to explain why Chinese people have begun to strongly prefer collective petitions, which were usually reinforced with a variety of "troublemaking" tactics, and how they could get the opportunity to frequently stage this form of collective action. An examination of the political structure in next two chapters will shed light on these questions.

PART II

POLITICAL OPPORTUNITY STRUCTURE

3

Market Reforms and State Strategies

How do we account for the upsurge of collective protest in China since the early 1990s? It is impossible to understand this trend without analyzing the changing political structure surrounding claim making, especially the way in which state agents cope with claim-making activities. Patterns of state strategies – for example, the state's propensity and capacity for repression – have long been regarded as a key aspect of the political opportunity structure that influences popular contention.[1] In the Reform Era, the Chinese state has developed a particular repertoire of strategies for coping with popular contention: generally restrained repression with a goal of containment rather than deterrence, expedient concessions, practical persuasion, and prevalent procrastination. Such a pattern of state strategies make collective petitioning with "troublemaking" tactics a rational and even attractive choice: Such forms of social protests are not overly risky, often somewhat effective, and usually indispensable for their success.

Of course, this pattern of state strategies is itself a product of economic reforms and the sociopolitical transformations they have triggered. Thus this chapter will examine how two important processes in the Reform Era – the changes in state-society linkages and those in the state structure – have transformed the strategic repertoire that state agents use when responding to social protest.

---

[1] Doug McAdam, "Conceptual Origins, Current Problems, Future Directions," in Doug McAdam, John D. McCarthy, and Mayer N. Zald (eds.), *Comparative Perspectives on Social Movements: Political Opportunities, Mobilizing Structures, and Cultural Framings* (New York: Cambridge University Press, 1996), p. 27.

In fact, the study of the participants of protest events and their demands in the previous chapter also suggests a remarkable change in state-society linkages in China: For their essential needs, a number of social groups, such as pensioners, peasants, homeowners, demobilized army officials, and disabled tricycle drivers, began to negotiate with the government directly, rather than with grassroots state agents such as work unit or production unit leaders. This change has deeply affected state agents' propensity and capacity for employing strategies such as repression, concession, and persuasion. In the meantime, market reforms have also considerably transformed the state structure: Divisions among different levels of governments and differentiations among functional state agencies have increased substantially. These transformations in state structure, together with the changes in state-society linkages, have profoundly changed the political opportunity structure for popular contention.

CHANGES IN STATE-SOCIETY LINKAGES

For purposes of simplicity and clarity, we can distinguish two models of state-society structure: the unit system model and the government-citizen model. Features of the unit system model have been well studied by many China experts, particularly Andrew Walder, Andrew Nathan, and Jean Oi.[2] Essentially, the unit system model has three dimensions of the linkages between ordinary people and the authority: (1) organized dependency, (2) particularistic relationships, and (3) dense transaction between the authorities and ordinary people in a relatively closed local community over a long period of time. This kind of authority relationship is typical for the Party-state apparatus and state-owned enterprises, yet it can also be found in collective enterprises and to some extent in people's communes in rural areas.[3] By contrast, the government-citizens model features: (1) lack of dependency, (2) universalistic relationships,

---

[2] See Andrew Walder, *Communist Neo-Traditionalism: Work and Authority in Chinese Industry* (Berkeley and Los Angeles: University of California Press, 1986); Andrew Nathan, *China's Transition* (New York: Columbia University Press, 1997); Jean Oi, *State and Peasant in Contemporary China: The Political Economy of Village Government* (Berkeley and Los Angeles: University of California Press, 1989) and "Communism and Clientelism: Rural Politics in China," *World Politics* 37/2 (January 1985), pp. 238–266.

[3] As Womack points out, there is significant similarity between Walder's neotraditionalism in urban areas and Oi's clientelism in rural areas. See Brantly Womack, "Transfigured Community: Neo-Traditionalism and Work unit Socialism in China," *China Quarterly* 126 (June 1991), pp. 313–332.

and (3) thin transaction between the authorities and ordinary people, usually located in a public space over a short period of time.

As to the first dimension, in the unit system model, ordinary people are highly dependent on the leaders of their unit for most conceivable needs and benefits, such as jobs and housing, and cannot organize themselves autonomously. In contrast, in the government-citizens model, ordinary people obtain most needs and benefits from the market and from society. They rely on the state only for a limited range of issues, such as public security, criminal justice, social security, and so on. As to the second dimension, in the unit system model, the leadership exercises power mainly through a patron-client network, therefore the relationship is highly personal. In contrast, in the government-citizen model, state agents wield power over people generally, and rewards or sanctions are based only on categorized identity. For example, when a policy stipulates that all retired workers in SOEs should get a subsidy of 50 RMB every month, the recipients are not supposed to be distinguished according to their relationship with the officials in charge. Thus, the relationship between the state and the beneficiary is an impersonal one. The third dimension is related to the first one. In the unit system model, state power is very close physically and socially to ordinary people. The agents of the state, with an identity as factory managers or production team leaders, interact with ordinary people face to face every day. In contrast, state power in the government-citizen model is relatively remote, and state agents, as bureaucrats, only temporarily come into contact with people, usually in a public place rather than a closed community.

When viewed in broad terms, state-society interactions in China in the Reform Era have undergone a transition from a unit system model to a government-citizen model. At the same time, the transition should not be understood as a thorough replacement of one model by the other. I am not suggesting that before the transition there did not exist some government-citizen interaction. Although the Party-state and ordinary people usually interacted through grassroots institutions such as work units in the urban areas and production teams or brigades in the rural areas, occasionally people did interact directly with the government. For instance, the xinfang system was supposed to work as a channel for ordinary people to contact government officials directly. In some periods, this sort of contact was relatively frequent and at quite a high volume. For example, in the late 1970s and early 1980s, when the CCP decided to conduct massive reforms and amend many of its previous policies, numerous people lodged their complaints to the government about their suffering in previous political campaigns and particularly during the Cultural Revolution. The first three or four decades of the PRC also witnessed occasional waves of petitions targeting the government directly.[4] Overall, however, the frequency of government-citizen interactions throughout the Mao era was fairly low, with the majority of them taking place in the form of individual contact.[5] Therefore, it is fair to say that direct interactions between the government and citizens were only marginal before the transition began in the 1990s.

By the same token, we cannot say the unit system model of interactions has completely disappeared. Work units as a basic level of social organizations still exist in some sectors, especially within public and semipublic institutions including the remaining SOEs. These work units still assume some political functions on their members such as monitoring, sanctioning, and interest representation. Yet even for these remaining work units, much of their previous power relationships have substantially changed. At the same time, numerous different social and economic organizations, which do not act as state agents in any sense, have developed. Consequently, the majority of political interactions no longer take place within basic social and economic institutions. Instead, ordinary people have begun to directly encounter government officials quite often.

Thus, the changes in state-society linkages should be understood as a shift from the unit system model to the government-citizen model as the dominant pattern of relations. Even though these two models have not fully taken into account regional and sectoral differences, the stark contrast between them captures the change in China overall. This transformation of state-society structures, unsurprisingly, has had a tremendous impact on interactions between state agents and ordinary people. In fact, this transformation has not worked alone. Another important process that has influenced state strategies is the increasing divisions and differentiations within the state structure.

DIVISIONS AND DIFFERENTIATIONS WITHIN THE STATE STRUCTURE

Like state-society linkages, the structure of the Chinese state has also experienced a "quiet revolution from within" in the Reform Era: The divisions among state agencies have increased substantially in both vertical and

---

[4] Elizabeth Perry, *Challenging the Mandate of Heaven* (Armonk, NY: M.E. Sharpe, 2002).
[5] See Laura Luehrmann, Officials Face the Masses: Citizen Contacting in Modern China, unpublished dissertation at Ohio State University, 2000.

horizontal dimensions. Vertically, diverging interests among state agencies in different levels, especially between the central and local governments, has become significantly more salient. Although the principal-agent problem has always existed in the hierarchical system of the Chinese state in the PRC, economic reforms have introduced new divisions of interest between the different levels of government. In particular, fiscal decentralization, as well as the development of local corporatism, has led to the rise of local interests, which often stand opposed to those of the central state. Walder summarizes this process:

> As party-state officials are less dependent upon higher levels of government for these things [sources of revenue, income, and career advancement], and more dependent upon new economic activities emerging locally, officials gradually become oriented more "downward" and less "upward" than at any time in the past. Success for local officials – whether measured in job performance, budgetary revenues, and local economic prosperity, or personal income, is determined increasingly by local activities and opportunities outside the traditional structures and practices of central planning. The greater the departures and alternatives, the greater the change in official orientation, and the weaker the claims of higher levels of government.[6]

C. K. Lee has rightly argued that the division is essentially one between development-pursuing local agents and the center that is more concerned with legitimation. The vertical divisions have been amplified by the decline of the center's capacity for monitoring and sanctioning local agencies. As Shaoguang Wang pointed out in 1995, "In a space of fifteen years or so, the Chinese political structure has been transformed from one that was once reputed for its high degree of centralization and effectiveness into one in which the center has difficulty coordinating its own agents' behavior."[7] The central government's attempts to coordinate and discipline local agents, as well as local agents' efforts to outmaneuver such coordination and discipline, have had a powerful influence on the interactions between the government and petitioners.

Whereas the increasing vertical divisions have been well studied, horizontal differentiations have received little attention. Before the reform

---

[6] Andrew Walder, "The Decline of Communist Power: Elements of a Theory of Institutional Change," *Theory and Society* 23 (1994), p. 311.

[7] Shaoguang Wang, "The Rise of the Regions: Fiscal Reform and the Decline of Central State Capacity in China," in Andrew Walder (ed.), *The Waning of the Communist State: Economic Origins of Political Decline in China and Hungry* (Berkeley: University of California Press, 1995), p. 109.

period, the identities and interests of various public agencies with different functions within the Party-state apparatus were minimally differentiated. The boundaries between the Party and state-owned enterprises, between the Party and the government, and between different departments of the state were often blurred.

As soon as the economic reforms started in the late 1970s, it was clear to Chinese leaders that functional differentiations were necessary for effectively governing a market-oriented economy and an increasingly complex society. The 1980s therefore witnessed impressive momentum of political/administrative reforms that initially focused on the differentiation between the government and state-owned enterprises and between the Party and the government. In the meantime, no longer content with their previous roles as mere instruments of the Party, a variety of state agencies such as the legislature, the judiciary, the media, and mass organizations also started to seek somewhat distinctive identities. For example, some leaders and deputies of the National and local People's Congresses tried to change their image as a "rubber stamp" and to find more or less independent voices as lawmakers, government supervisors, and representatives of their designated constituencies.[8] A massive legal reform has also tremendously transformed the role of the court. Judges have been substantially professionalized, and a variety of legal norms and procedures have made courts evidently distinct from the two other branches of the political and legal system – the police and procuracy. Even the uniform of judges has been changed from a quasi-military style to a Western style to signify their special identity. Similarly, the media has also substantially departed from its previous role as a mere propaganda tool. With the development of a large number of nonofficial media outlets, the media landscape has become much more diversified. Even among official media, commercial and institutional interests have often competed with, or even prevailed over, political considerations in their operation. Mass organizations, such as the official labor union, ACFTU, also sometimes actively take on state interests in their role as an advocate of their constituency. A notable example is the China Disabled Persons Federation.[9] When the chairman of the Federation, Deng Pufang, exhorted his subordinates to defend disabled people's interests, he claimed emphatically,

[8] Murray Scot Tanner, "The National People's Congress," in Merle Goldman and Roderick MacFarquhar (eds.), *The Paradox of China's Post-Mao Reforms* (Cambridge, MA: Harvard University Press, 1999).

[9] Xi Chen and Ping Xu, "From Resistance to Advocacy: Political Representation for Disabled People in China," *China Quarterly* 207 (September 2011), pp. 649–667.

"We need to represent their interest, unite them and educate them, so that the Federation can be a bridge between disabled people and the government. This is the political function of the Federation."[10]

To be sure, the differentiations between various state agencies are still limited, and the progress has not been linear. Although Chinese leaders have allowed or even encouraged functional differentiation to a certain degree, they often re-tighten the leash when they feel that some agencies have strayed too far. For example, in the period shortly after the student movement in 1989, the CCP reasserted its direct control over many state agencies on whom it had previously relaxed its grip.[11] Similarly, after respecting a certain level of judiciary distinctiveness for a few years, Chinese political leaders since the 2000s again have begun to stress the political importance rather than the functional distinctiveness of the court system. Of course, despite their limited scope and back-and-forth style, horizontal differentiations have been both extensive and very consequential for interactions between the government and ordinary people.

THE REPERTOIRE OF STATE STRATEGIES

Before discussing how the changes in state-society linkages and state structures have shaped state strategies for coping with popular claim-making activities, we need to give an overview of major strategies used by the Chinese government in dealing with citizen complaints and protest: repression, concession, persuasion, and procrastination. This is not an exhaustive list of state strategies toward every protest in China, but it covers the most important ones.[12]

As Figure 3.1 illustrates, when ordinary people have made claims to the government via individual or collective action, the state can decide to deal with them instantly or defer action to a later date. If it is the latter,

---

[10] Deng Pufang's internal speech to the Federation in 1999, obtained in Hunan Province in 2002.

[11] For example, see Zhonggong Zhongyang, *Zhonggong Zhongyang guanyu jiaqiang he gaishan dang dui gonghui, gongqingtuan, hulian gongzuo lingdao de tongzhi* (The Central Committee of the CCP on How to Improve the Party leadership on the ACFTU, CYL, and ACWF). This is a circular distributed shortly after the student movement in 1989.

[12] Some scholars on Chinese contentious politics have put forth some interesting formulas of state strategies. Ying Xing proposes a list of state strategies including repression (pulling out nails), punishing officials (removing the cover), and concessions (opening the box). See Ying Xing, *Dahe Yimin Shangfang de Gushi* (the story of the petitioning of the migrants in Dahe town) (Beijing: Sanlian Press, 2002).

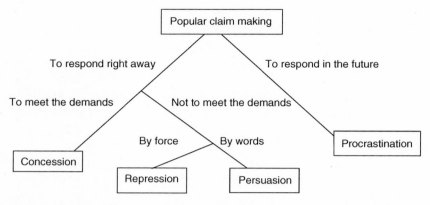

FIGURE 3.1. State strategies when responding to popular claim making.

it is called procrastination. When the state wants to respond right away, it can decide either to meet their demands or to reject them. If the former, it is called concession. If the state decides not to meet them, it can either demobilize people's action by force or by words. If by force, it is called repression; if by words, persuasion.

Repression, concession, and persuasion work best when combined together. Supplementing repression with persuasion can help prevent an escalation of conflicts, and supplementing it with concessions can often divide the challenging groups or demonstrate the state's goodwill. Similarly, supplementing concessions with repression helps prevent people from raising overly high demands and prevents other people from following their example. When persuasion is used alongside state concessions, this can help ensure that the concessions provided by the state do not exceed its means, and make various state strategies of persuasion more effective.

Procrastination has often been overlooked as a strategy. Rather than a strategy, it is often simply regarded as a bureaucratic problem; however, procrastination has an effect not only in demobilizing collective action, but also in helping the bureaucracy distinguish urgent, valid, and determined petitions from less urgent, less valid, and less determined petitions.[13] State officials have actually often consciously used procrastination to

[13] See Ying Xing, *Dahe Yimin Shangfang de Gushi*, and Ying Xing and Jin Jun, "Jiti Shangfang Zhong De Wentihua Guocheng: Xinan Yige Shuidianzhan De Yimin De Guishi" (The Process of Problemization in Collective Visits: A Story of Migration Caused by a Hydroelectric Plant in Southwest China), *Qinghua Sociological Journal*, Special issue (2000), pp. 80–109.

attain such goals. Procrastination usually only works as a supplementary strategy; however, under some special circumstances, as in today's China, when other state strategies have become less effective, procrastination can become a major state strategy. In the following sections, I discuss these strategies individually, with a focus on how the changes in state-society linkages and state structure have transformed them.

REPRESSION

Those who view the PRC as a harsh authoritarian regime are likely to be surprised by protesters' defiance and government officials' restraint in dealing with protesters in today's China. Petitioners not only disrupt social order; they sometimes even directly attack government officials verbally or physically, yet most of these activities have been de facto tolerated and no punishment applied to organizers or participants. In his study of policing strategies in Reform Era China, Tanner also notes this new trend:

> The new goal of security forces today is to minimize popular anger through more moderate, professional policing of protests and to limit police use of violent coercive tactics to incidents of imminent mob violence, arson, looting, or attacks on key government buildings. This approach, of course, implicitly means police will allow many low-key illegal protests to continue while they try to maintain order at the scene.[14]

Government control of protest activities is often not just restrained, but also costly and ineffective. Unable to employ decisive coercive force to deter defiant protesters, local governments have often relied on "resource intensive" means, such as sending out hundreds of cadres from various government agencies to dissolve a protest. The common practice of intercepting skip-level petitioners who are on their way to upper authority or retrieving them from upper authorities (*jiefang*) is also a case in point. An official from the People's Congress in Sichuan Province has estimated that the government needs to spend about 10,000 RMB to take back a petitioner from Beijing.[15] This is a remarkable sum considering the GDP

[14] Tanner, p. 148.
[15] *Jiangnan Times*, "Xinfang Zhidu Gaige Jiannan Qihang, 'Jiefang'Beihou Shi Zhengji Yali" (The Xinfang System Reform Has Started with Difficulty, 'Interception of Petitioners' Is Due to the Pressure of Government Official's Performance), Nov. 16, 2004. For another article discussing the monetary costs of "stabilizing" petitioners, see "Dalu Jiefang Liantiao Diaocha" (Investigation of the Chain of Retrieving Petitioners in Mainland

per capita in Sichuan Province in 2001 was only 5,250 RMB. In City Y in Hunan, a local official told me in 2002 that the government had spent more than 100,000 RMB on controlling a single especially "stubborn" petitioner over many years, who was eventually sent to labor reeducation camp for one year as punishment.[16] Such costly measures contributed to an impressive increase in government spending on stability maintenance in recent years. In 2010, for instance, Liaoning Province in northeastern China devoted 15 percent of its revenues to this task.[17]

Why do local governments not employ coercive force more promptly and decisively? Some observers attribute government restraint to officials' sympathy for petitioners.[18] Such sympathy is indeed quite common among government officials and may have played a role in inhibiting harsh repression. At the same time, it should be noted that such sympathy also existed in many, if not most, protest events in other periods of the PRC's history, but the government had nevertheless cracked down on many of them. Labor unrest in 1956–1957 and student movements in 1989 are two examples.

More important are structural changes in the Reform Era, especially the shift of state-society linkages from the unit system model to the government-citizen model, which have had an enormous impact on the incentive and capacity for state officials to employ repressive means. In the unit system model, organized dependency and dense transaction between state officials and ordinary people in a relatively closed local community over a long period of time facilitate both surveillance and sanctions. As Foucault emphasizes, subject visibility is essential to any disciplinary system.[19] In the unit system model, authorities usually can more effectively monitor ordinary people's actions for two reasons: (1) people's everyday activities are usually confined to a very stable and closed community, and (2) many ordinary people, especially those most loyal to the regime (or "backbones"), would be likely to report others' activities to the authorities. In other words, ordinary people are highly visible in the unit system model.

China), in *Fenghuang Zhoukan (Phoenix Weekly)*, July 17, 2008 (no. 297). It reported a case in which the local government spent over 100,000 RMB in one year on a single persistent petitioner.
[16] Interview at City Y, July 2002.
[17] Andrew Jacobs and Jonathan Ansfield, "Well-Oiled Security Apparatus in China Stifles Calls for Change," *New York Times*, February 28, 2011.
[18] Tanner, p. 144.
[19] See Michel Foucault, *Discipline and Punishment* (New York: Vintage Books, 1977).

By comparison, ordinary people can more easily hide their activities from state surveillance under a government-citizen model. A government official in City Y told me how they tried to control a "long-term" woman petitioner before the annual meetings of National People's Congress and People's Political Consultative Conference in 1999:

> Shortly before the period of the "two annual meetings" (*lianghui*), three government cadres began to closely monitor that woman to prevent her from going to Beijing. One day when they found that that woman had left for the provincial capital, Changsha, they immediately followed her, and caught her at her daughter's home. She assured the cadres that she just came to visit her daughter, and would not go to Beijing. Although the cadres did not quite believe her, they could not stay at Changsha for a long time since they had other work to do. It was also impossible to forbid her from visiting her daughter. So they returned. The next day, she went to Beijing.[20]

When petitioners become more skillful in using the law to defend their rights, surveillance becomes even more difficult. One organizer of a petitioning group in City Y talked about his experience around Army Day in 2002:

> Many officials, including leaders from the organizational department of the city party committee and the district, called me by telephone or visited me around Army Day for I am also a veteran cadre. While they seemingly just wanted to convey greetings, they were actually afraid I would go to visit the provincial government or the central government. I said to them, I appreciate your kindness, but I know your real purpose. You'd better not violate my personal liberties. If you want to come to do thought work on me, please don't come since I know the party policies better than you. If you want to come because I have violated laws, please do it according to legal procedures. To interrogate me, you need to obtain a warrant first. Thereafter they no longer came to disturb me during that period.[21]

The transition to the government-citizen model has not only created monitoring difficulties, but also made sanctioning more costly and ineffective. Here we need to distinguish between two sanction methods: sanctions with hard means and those with soft means. The former refers to legal or administrative coercive sanctions such as arrest or imprisonment, and the latter to social and economic sanctions, such as dismissal

---

[20] Interview, July 2002.
[21] Interview, September 2002.

from a job, salary reduction, deprivation of titles, and so on. Compared to hard means, soft means incur lower costs and lower risk. In the unit system, unit leaders can easily apply soft means on any defiant unit member because ordinary people are dependent on them for most essential needs such as securing a job, promotion, housing, medical and child care, and so forth. Because one cannot easily move to a new unit for a very long period of time, the consequences of repression tactics can be very devastating for "troublemakers."

By contrast, it is difficult for the authorities in the government-citizen model to employ soft means. There are far fewer issues for which ordinary people depend on the government. More importantly, the provision of benefits on such issues is usually categorical rather than particularistic. The government can seldom single out a particular group or individual for withholding such benefits. Governmental officials are therefore often left with only hard means of sanction. The loss of soft means has apparently generated misgivings among many local officials. Some of them even attempted to continue soft-means sanctions in an indirect way. For instance, when a local construction project was met with popular resistance in the Jiahe County, Hunan Province, in 2004, county leaders forced public employees who are relatives of the protesters to persuade protesters to give up resistance. Those public employees who could not fulfill this duty would be penalized with a reduction of salary or even dismissal from their job. In this case, because the government could not sanction protesters with soft means directly, it punished public employees who were the relatives of protesters. Ultimately, because such a practice was widely regarded as illegitimate, the State Council intervened, and this measure was aborted.[22]

In addition to their high costs and low effectiveness, hard means risk angering the population and escalating the contestation between protesters and authorities. This trend is especially problematic as the divisions between central and local governments have increased in the Reform Era, whereby central leaders are particularly concerned about legitimation and have good reason to suspect that some local leaders may want to silence protesters simply with force. Chinese leaders have therefore repeatedly admonished against imprudent use of force.

Premier Zhu Rongji, for instance, in his annual central government work report at the NPC in 1999, emphasized that government officials

---

[22] See Xinhuanet, "The State Council Meeting Agreed with the Decisions for the Jiahe Incident," www.xinhuanet.com, June 4, 2004.

"must appropriately deal with contradictions among the people in new situations" and "must solve contradictions at the initial stage, must not use simple and rude methods to escalate conflicts, and must not use 'means of dictatorship' to deal with people and the masses."[23] Here the "means of dictatorship" refers to harsh coercive measures. This mindset has manifested itself in both central and local policies. For example, as Tanner observes, in the Chinese public safety system, "the predominant concern of police strategists has recently shifted from how to best deter all protests to how to avoid misusing force and accidentally exacerbating popular ire."[24] As a local official told me, as of 2002, Hunan Province's policy was that municipal governments were not allowed to use more than one hundred police in one action without the approval of the provincial government.[25]

The decision to sanction "troublemakers" with hard means has often become risky for local officials. Such risks are often not worth taking, particularly because many local officials in China only serve a short term, after which they will be transferred to other positions, and often to other localities. For example, in 2001, on average, a mayor in China only served 2.5 years in that position.[26] If coercive measures go awry, especially if they have escalated the conflict, the decision makers will have to take responsibility. After a large-scale bridge blockade with more than 1,000 participants in City Y, Hunan, in 1999, the Party secretary and mayor decided to punish the two organizers, who were pensioners in their seventies, to deter similar activities in the future. However, the leaders apparently felt enormous pressure for imposing the sanction. When declaring their decision, they claimed that they were prepared to lose their black gauze cap (their official post). This statement might have been a special way to express their determination, but it would not make sense had there been no such risk. Even with such extraordinary determination on the part of the Party secretary and the mayor, the final penalty was not particularly harsh – the two organizers were sentenced to three years in prison with two years' probation. It should also be noted that as of 2002, this was the only criminal penalty (labor reeducation excluded) imposed on protest activities in City Y, even though there were more than a hundred very

---

[23] *People's Daily*, March 6, 1999.
[24] Tanner, p. 148.
[25] Interview, July 2002.
[26] Pierre Landry, *Decentralized Authoritarianism in China: The Communist Party's Control of Local Elites in the Post-Mao Era* (New York: Cambridge University Press, 2009), p. 90.

disruptive and often illegal protests during the previous ten years. Such a lack of criminal charges indicates that local leaders were obviously very cautious about using coercive force.

Vertical divisions have certainly constrained repression, but bureaucratic differentiations in the horizontal dimension have sometimes offered protection to protesters as well. The media, mass organizations, and courts sometimes have taken on a role as advocates or protectors of protesters. The China Disabled Person's Federation (CDPF) is a case in point. Since the early 1990s, led by its charismatic leader, Deng Pufang, the Federation has fought an uphill battle to resist many local governments' ban on three-wheelers used by disabled people for commercial purpose. During almost two decades of struggle, the Federation and its local chapters have routinely protected disabled drivers from local punishment.[27] For instance, when the police confiscated nine three-wheelers owned by disabled people in City Y in 2002, the owners petitioned to the headquarters of CDPF in Beijing, which eventually pressured local government to release the vehicles.

The presence of various agencies and individuals within the state structure that serve as advocates for protesters has obviously empowered petitioners and constrained government repression. Thomas Bernstein's study of peasants' resistance highlighted the role of a variety of advocates including the rural deputies to the National People's Congress, the members of the agrarian research community of governmental and academic institutions, officials in ministries such as Agriculture, and editors and journalists in the specialized and general media.[28] Such advocates made it considerably more difficult for local officials to deter resistance with harsh repression.

An unintended consequence of the increasing difficulty in penalizing petitioners with hard means is the development of informal or even illegal sanctions implemented by some local governments. Under high pressure from above to maintain stability, but provided by the central government with very limited tools to deter "troublemakers," some local officials have been tempted to use some informal and extralegal means to intimidate petitioners. For example, although local government efforts to retrieve skip-level protesters from Beijing or the provincial capital are not

---

[27] For the advocacy work by the CDPF, see Chen and Xu, "From Resistance to Advocacy: Political Representation for Disabled People in China."

[28] Thomas P. Bernstein, "Farmer Discontent and Regime Responses," in Merle Goldman and Roderick Macfarquhar (eds.), *The Paradox of China's Post-Mao Reforms* (Cambridge, MA: Harvard University Press, 1999), p. 198.

supposed to serve as a punishment for petitioners, it is not unusual for local officials to treat petitioners harshly through imprisonment and torture. Some local governments have maintained detention facilities called "black prisons" (*hei jianyu*), which subject prisoners to miserable conditions and have even used mental hospitals to contain petitioners without mental problems.[29] Moreover, there are even a few rare cases in which brazen local cadres hired hatchet men to attack protesters violently.[30]

The adoption of such informal or even illegal sanctions by local officials underscores the inadequacy of legitimate coercive force. It has also further exacerbated the divergence of interests between central and local governments and makes it even more imperative for the central government to discipline local officials. Because of its lack of legitimacy, however, coercive means such as harsh imprisonment and violent attacks are unlikely to be adopted widely.

Petitioners have quickly perceived the decline of local governments' capacity and propensity for cracking down on social protests. Their fear of and deference to state officials in the unit system model have to a large extent been replaced by bold defiance toward state officials in the government-citizen model. One afternoon in the summer of 2002, when I went to the provincial xinfang bureau in Hunan Province to look up government archives, I witnessed a poor woman petitioner who wrangled with the bureau chief for almost half an hour. Petitioners were supposed to address their grievances at the designated reception area and were not allowed to enter the office area, but somehow the woman snuck in and got a chance to confront the chief face to face. This unfortunate chief took great efforts to explain to her why her problems could not be solved easily and tried to persuade her to go to the designated reception area, but the woman responded by crying and cursing. The chief was obviously annoyed yet refrained from asking security guards to expel her. I was stunned by the woman's defiance, because from an ordinary person's point of view, a provincial bureau chief is a very high-ranking official.

---

[29] Human Rights Watch published a report, entitled "We Could Disappear at Any Time," to describe such human rights violations in 2005. See Human Rights Watch, "Officials and 'Retrievers' Block Citizens' Complaints," http://www.hrw.org/en/news/2005/12/07/china-rampant-violence-and-intimidation-against-petitioners, last visited on June 15, 2010. Also see *Liaowang Weekly* (November 26, 2009).

[30] There are a number of such cases reported by the media. For example, in a clash between petitioners and enforcers in October, 2009, a teenage petitioner accidentally killed one of the hired thugs. See "Zhongguo 16 Sui Shangfang Shaonian Shasi Jiefangzhe, 900 Cunmin Lianming Qiuqing" (A Sixteen Year Old Chinese Petitioners Killed a Retriever, 900 Villagers Pleaded Pardon for Him), *Jinghua Shibao*, June 17, 2010.

Although this is only an isolated incident, it reveals a kind of defiance that had been foreign to Chinese society under the unit system model. Like in imperial eras, Chinese society in Mao's era used to pay great respect to state officials except during some periods of the Cultural Revolution. Freed from grassroots units by the reforms since the late 1970s, however, ordinary people no longer found officials to be as formidable as before.

In sum, the shift in state-society linkages, combined with the increase in divisions within the state structure, has dramatically altered the propensity and capacity of state officials to use coercive force. From the local officials' point of view, harsh sanctions on petitioners are often not only costly but also risky. They therefore have become more hesitant about using them. This is especially true when some other options – concession, persuasion, or procrastination – are available.

CONCESSION

With the explosion of popular collective action since the 1990s, the Chinese state has had to confront the dilemma of concession more frequently. If it does not make concessions, it has few to no means of dissolving collective action; if it gives in to pressure, however, petitioners may come back some time later with greater demands, or other petitioners will follow the model of those successful "troublemakers."

The state in the unit system model seldom encounters such a problem. A comparison between the unit system model and the government-citizen model reveals sharp differences in the state strategy of granting special benefits to ordinary people. In the unit system model, state agents acting on their own initiative routinely grant special benefits to some people. As Walder observes, by providing such positive incentives, work unit leaders can encourage loyalty.[31] In contrast, government officials in the government-citizen model grant benefits only when they are forced to do so. When complaints and protests are rampant, government officials often have to make concessions to those who have exerted the strongest pressure. Therefore, we can see a stark contrast here: in the unit system model, the more loyal the unit members, the more likely they are to get rewarded; in the government-citizen model, the more troublesome the petitioners, the more likely they are to get concessions.

Such a difference can ultimately be attributed to the different nature of the authority relationships under the two state-society structures.

[31] Walder, *Communist Neo-Traditionalism.*

The unit system model features particularistic relationships between the authority and ordinary people, and selective rewards are inherent in this type of relationship. In contrast, the government-citizen model features a universalistic relationship. The state in this model provides services and benefits to its population members based on only categorical affiliation. Consequently, when the state rewards a group, other groups similarly situated are likely to claim the same benefits.

Such a problem is exacerbated by the decline of the authorities' capacity for coercion. The authority in the unit system model has strong coercive capacity, whereas in the government-citizen model it may lack both the capacity and motivation for coercion. When concessions are supplemented with coercion, the side effects of encouraging troublemaking are largely controllable. Concessions to troublemakers without coercive capacity, however, have often caused chain reactions. The case of the Bureau of Industrial and Commercial Administration (BICA) reform in City Y in the early 2000s illustrates this point well.

In response to the reform in the BICA in City Y, the first group, composed of demobilized volunteer army officers (*zhiyuanbing*), staged violent and sustained protests. The government gave in without punishing the protesters. Following this incident, a second and much larger group, composed of demobilized drafted army officers (*yiwubing*), followed their model, and their protests were even more violent than the first group. When the government found it necessary to punish these violent protesters, punishment was too late and too light. The authorities detained a protester thirteen days for damaging public property in the county BICA, yet once he was released, he went right back to the struggle. Finally, the government gave in to the second group. Ultimately, the success of the first two groups then inspired a nonveteran group to begin their own protest, creating further problems for authorities.

Because of the aforementioned dilemma surrounding concessions, governmental officials need to be very cautious in making them. In the meantime, most complaints and protests emerged in response to structural problems, and thus their demands cannot be met in a substantial way within a short time frame. Such issues as pension arrears, peasant burdens, and land disputes all have structural origins. Even if local government had strong incentives to meet petitioners' demands promptly, it is often beyond their capacity to do so. Therefore, they can often only make small and expedient concessions to pacify petitioners.

Such concessions often occur under three situations. First, when protests have started or are about to escalate into serious disruption, the state will meet protesters' most immediate demands as an emergency measure. Second, before important events or holidays, such as the Spring Festival, the government often gives protesters a small cash sum to pacify them. In City Y, this happens many times to pension protesters and savings crisis protesters.

Third, shortly after the government has implemented new policies that affect particular social groups and are likely to provoke protests, the government often gives some compensation to the affected to absorb the shock. For example, when the municipal government in City Y first decided to ban disabled people's motorcycles for use as passenger transport, the resistance was fierce. In response, the city government spent 400,000 RMB to pay about 200 disabled people for one year. One year later, when the government stopped paying the compensation, those disabled people went out to protest again. However, those protests had lost much of their momentum.

The goal of government officials in granting such expedient concessions is usually to avoid the hardest hit and to obtain some time. They often count on the possibility that the contention will be demobilized after a period of time either because the policy will be accepted by the population or other structural causes of the contention will disappear or because the protesters cannot sustain current levels of mobilization. They sometimes make decisions based on individual career calculations as well. As mentioned before, local officials in China tend to serve only a short term. Even if concessions create a chain reaction, such an effect will not be evident in a short period of time. In other words, pacification of protesters with concessions is a safer strategy than repression because concessions often only have long-term side effects, which are unlikely affect an official's career, whereas harsh repression tends to have short-term consequences.

PERSUASION

> *Not the gun but the word is the symbol of authority.*
> Charles Lindblom[32]

There are some scholars who have rightly seen persuasion as a key feature of the Chinese communist system in Mao's era. Charles Lindblom is one of the few theorists who have taken persuasion seriously as a major

---

[32] Charles Lindblom, *Politics and Markets* (New York: Basic Books, 1977), p. 52.

instrument of social control. He points out that persuasion is central and fundamental in all social systems in the world, including totalitarian systems such as German and Italian fascism. According to Lindblom's analysis, however, China serves as the best example of a system of persuasion. He calls the system in Mao's China a preceptoral system (tutelary system) and argues that "a preceptoral system is the most distinctive and ideologically central element of Chinese communism under Mao."[33] Walder also observes that state agents in Mao's China used persuasion extensively, which is quite different from the Soviet system. As he notes, "One searches in vain in the memoirs of people who worked in Russia during those years for accounts of regular group study or group criticism – even within the party itself. By contrast, these themes pervade similar accounts of Chinese organizational life in the 1950s and 1960s."[34]

Such observations are consistent with the official guidelines of the CCP in dealing with popular claim making. As analyzed above, Mao established the principle of persuasion in his famous essay, "On the Correct Handling of Contradictions among the People," in 1957. Denouncing any "means of dictatorship" against people, he proposed using persuasion and education in dealing with "contradictions among the people." The specific methods of persuasion Mao proposes are "criticisms and self-criticisms." In general, he proposed a plan under the slogan "unite-criticize-unite," which he hoped would serve as a formula to govern the proper process of government persuasion tactics in cases of conflict. This formula emphasizes that criticism should be used to promote inclusion and solidarity rather than exclusion and the exacerbation of adversarial relations.

Although the CCP has redefined the boundary between the people and the enemy in the post-Mao era, its emphasis on persuasion as the main strategy in dealing with conflicts among the people remains unchanged. For example, Zhu Rongji argues that the basic method of dealing with conflicts among the people is a combination of "legal, economic, and administrative means, as well as deep and delicate thought education work."[35] Petitions and most social protests belong to the category of

---

[33] Lindblom defines the preceptoral system as "massive highly unilateral persuasion in which a small enlightened governmental elite instructs the masses in much the same way that Rousseau advised teachers to educate a child and imagined a 'superior intelligence' transforming each individual." Lindblom, pp. 54–55.

[34] Walder, *Communist Neo-Traditionalism.*

[35] Zhu Rongji, "zhengfu Gongzuo Baogao" (Central Government's Work Report), *People's Daily*, March 6, 1999.

conflicts among the people, and therefore persuasion is supposed to be the main method to use on them.

From Ideological Persuasion to Practical Persuasion

With the transition from the unit system model to the government-citizen model, the methods and effects of persuasion have changed substantially. As Lindblom notes, efforts to persuade the people can be subdivided into a variety of methods, such as information, indoctrination, instruction, propaganda, counseling, advice, exhortation, education, and thought control.[36] Here I want to differentiate these persuasive methods according to their respective goals and contents. Roughly speaking, persuasion can be distinguished as either practical persuasion or ideological persuasion. In practical persuasion, authorities induce the desired responses by providing information on basic facts and information for cost-benefit analysis. In ideological persuasion, authorities "educate" people to accept a grand ideological aspiration. An extreme form of ideological persuasion is the making of "the new man" or "a new society," which, according to Lindblom, can be found in the USSR, Cuba, China, George Orwell's *1984*, and Victorian England.[37]

We can find a series of themes along a continuum from ideological to practical persuasion: people's acceptance of utopian ideology of making "new men" or "a new society," people's acceptance of other official ideological goals, people's general understanding of public policy, people's understanding of government's considerations and difficulties regarding specific issues, people's understanding of the importance of social stability and legal order, and people's understanding that resistance is useless or counterproductive. As to the effects, ideological persuasion, if feasible, is of course more useful for political control. The making of "the new man" encourages people not only to willingly conform to norms, but also to actively support and defend state authority. An understanding of the state's ideological goals and overall policy can also substantially reduce resistance. When Deng Xiaoping reflected on the lessons learned from the 1989 student movement, he pointed out that the CCP's greatest failure in the Reform Era was education. He is right in attributing the social movement to the CCP's failure in fostering ideological education. However, whether or not such failure was avoidable is itself a matter of debate.

---

[36] Lindblom, *Politics and Markets*, p. 56.
[37] Ibid., p. 56.

With the transition from the unit system model to the government-citizen model, the methods of persuasion have shifted largely from ideological to practical persuasion. Not surprisingly, the effectiveness of persuasion has also substantially decreased. How have changes in state-society structures caused this change? To answer this question, we first need to examine the conditions necessary for ideological persuasion to be effective. Ideological persuasion is most strong when: (1) persuasion is intensive and pervasive, and (2) the ideology is internally coherent and consistent with practice.

As Lindblom points out, "only intense and all-pervasive education can accomplish social transformation."[38] The extreme form of ideological persuasion – the making of "the new man" – is very time-consuming. Persuading people to accept official ideological aspirations and general policy also requires a considerable length of time. In addition to persistent efforts by the state to accomplish social transformation through education, the intensity of persuasion tactics can also be increased by (1) the continued lack of alternative communications; (2) mobilization of collective pressure; and (3) the combination of persuasion with coercion. Small group discussions, educational camps, and public denunciation meetings, pertinent to pre-Reform China, are among the most intense methods of persuasion.

Needless to say, social organizations such as work units are very suitable for carrying out intense ideological persuasion. A work unit features a relatively closed environment in which contact between authorities and ordinary people is long, continuing, and pervasive. Work unit leaders can also easily invoke spiritual coercion by mobilizing mass criticism, as well as economic and social coercion by denying social and economic benefits. In contrast, it is much more difficult for government officials to carry out such intense forms of persuasion because their contact with petitioners is short and superficial. Dialogues or ad hoc meetings typically only last for several hours or, at most, several days. To increase the intensity of persuasion, the present-day Chinese government occasionally sent out work teams to live with petitioners for a short period. Even then, the local community often considered such work teams to be outsiders. Their interaction with petitioners is too superficial to touch the hearts of ordinary people. State-society interactions in the government-citizen model also lack other conditions for intensive coercion: (1) petitioners enjoy other channels of information and communication; (2) petitioners' demands

---

[38] Ibid.

are often collective and, unlike individual resistance, they are not subject to collective pressure; and (3) it is hard for the government to carry out persuasion in a coercive way.

The state-society linkages in the unit system model not only facilitated intense ideological persuasion; in the pre-Reform era, they were also associated with a powerful ideology. The power of ideology relies on its internal coherence and its consistency with practice. Clearly the transition to a market economy has substantially undermined the strength of socialist ideology both in terms of its internal coherence and its consistency with practice. The privatization, exploitation, inequality, and corruption that have emerged in the wake of continued economic reform have shaken people's faith in socialist ideology.

Practical Persuasion and Its Effects

As previously noted, ideological persuasion is more effective for political order than practical persuasion. However, when ideological persuasion is not feasible, the state resorts to practical persuasion. In fact practical persuasion is not always ineffective. To best assess the degree to which practical persuasion is effective in different contexts, we need to first examine its effects according to the different types of practical persuasion used.

The first type of persuasion consists of explanation of facts. When complaints and protests are based on unfounded information, the state has an opportunity to successfully demobilize petitioners by transparently explaining the facts. As a common practice, when the government has investigated individual cases, it will convene a mass meeting to announce its findings. If the investigation procedure looks fair or the evidence it presents is strong, people tend to accept government explanations. Still, it is not rare for people to challenge the credibility of such investigations.

Explanation of policies is the second type of persuasion. There are two main situations under which government officials persuade people by explaining policies. The first situation occurs when petitioners misunderstand particular public policies. For example, quite a few protests against peasant burdens are based on a misunderstanding of confusing state policy. The central government stipulated that the fee exerted by the villages and townships on peasants should not exceed 5 percent of average peasant annual income. In this provision, the fee does not include taxes; however, many peasants understood that the combination of fees and tax should not exceed the 5 percent standard. When government officials clarified such misunderstandings, peasants usually gave up their complaints or protests because most of them were not ready to challenge this central policy.

The second situation occurs when some policies, especially local policies, are challenged by members of the community. For example, when the city government in City Y decided to ban disabled people's motorcycles from use as passenger transport to improve the city's image in 2000, many people with disabilities challenged the policy. They believed the local leaders' concern about the city's appearance was not justified considering the underdevelopment of the local economy. "When so many people do not have a job," an interviewee said, "the local leaders only consider their own promotion." The city government took great efforts to persuade the affected groups to cooperate, but only when the government promised to compensate each disabled person by 200 RMB per month did they temporarily stop their protests. In recent years, petitioners have more often begun to challenge policies themselves rather than limit their claims to the implementations of policies. As a demobilized army officer said in an interview, "if the government does not have good policies, we demand them. After all, policies are made by the government."[39] In such a situation, explanation of policies alone can hardly be effective.

The third type of persuasion, explanation of the government's difficulties, has also been commonly used by government officials. As a local official pointed out, this type of persuasion is quite common, especially because many petitioners complain about the failure of implementing central policies and laws. Government officials in such circumstances usually can only plead with petitioners for their understanding of the government's difficulties in enacting policies. Typically, such persuasion can work only temporarily at best. For example, in a joint letter to the provincial and central government signed by retiree representatives from forty-seven local SOEs in City Y in 2002, petitioners complained:

> The provincial government emphasized that the city government should pay us pensions that the government owed several years ago. Yet our city government always emphasized the financial difficulties. The mayor even complained, "President Jiang and Premier Zhu have only made policies, and not provided us with money. This is why it is difficult for us to carry them out."… We have heard Premier Zhu's speech that our country has the ability to solve such problems [of pension arrears] now.

[39] Interview, September 2002.

As to local government officials' emphasis on financial difficulties, that might be true. But does it mean there is no way to solve our problems? We don't think so.[40]

Emphasis on financial difficulties is often not convincing, especially when the government has spent a great deal of money on wasteful projects such as "image projects" (*mianzi gongcheng*) and "achievement projects" (*zhengji gongcheng*), and when corruption among government officials is rampant.

As a fourth type of persuasion, governmental officials sometimes emphasize the importance of stability and economic development. Social stability and economic development are among the common themes in instances of government persuasion throughout the entire Reform Era. It is worth noting that during both the student movement in 1989 and Falungong movement in 1999, officials also resorted to this theme when dealing with protesters. For example, officials from the National Xinfang Bureau, in their dialogue with representatives of Falungong petitioners on April 25, 1999, asked them to "cherish the stable political situation," because "national pride and economic prosperity are all based on political stability."[41] Persuasion along this line can hardly be effective when important interests are at stake. Petitioners often responded by arguing that "stability is of course important, but subsistence is more important."

In most interactions with petitioners, government officials would like to conclude by reminding petitioners that their collective action has violated some aspect of administrative regulations and laws. This last type of persuasion is called "legal education." However, unless the officials make more explicit threats of punishment, this form of "education" can hardly make any difference because such violations are commonplace and the government has seldom punished them.

It is important to point out that even though most of the aforementioned persuasion methods are not especially convincing, they are still meaningful temporarily and procedurally. The dialogue between government officials and petitioners ultimately consists of claims made by both sides. To effectively engage the protesters, the government representatives must present some kind of argument, regardless of whether these arguments are convincing or not. A government report described petitioners'

---

[40] Interview, September 2002.
[41] People's Daily, "Main Points of the leaders from the Xinfang Bureau in the Central Committee office and State Council Office in the dialogue with Falungong Petitioners," June, 14, 1999.

attitudes at the end of a dialogue: "[T]hey were not satisfied with the reply [by the officials]. Yet they felt they had nothing new to say. Feeling unsatisfied, they still reluctantly left the reception hall."[42]

To enhance their effectiveness, government officials are not reluctant to expend large amounts of resources. They often mobilize dozens or even hundreds of cadres to carry out methods of persuasion, or send work teams to rural areas. They also often take advantage of personal connections when attempting to persuade protestors, as when they send officials who are friends or relatives of petitioners. This strategy is remarkable considering that the authority relationship in the government-citizen model is largely an impersonal one. Sometimes, government officials go too far in using personal relationships, however. In the previously mentioned case in Jiahe County in Hunan Province in 2004, the county leaders forced petitioners' relatives who worked in public or semipublic work units to do the "thought work." If persuasion was not successful, those relatives would be penalized by the government.[43] This case highlights the difficulty encountered by the government in enforcing compliance through persuasion in the government-citizen model. As a result, government officials still feel tempted to take advantage of any connections to the work unit system to solve such problems in an informal way.

PROCRASTINATION

For a political system that relies on petitions and protests as the main form of interest articulation, procrastination is particularly useful. This is due to two factors. The first is the unequal distribution of costs in transactions between the government and ordinary people. Procrastination is a natural remedy for this problem. If we compare the xinfang system with a court system, we can clearly understand the function of procrastination. In a court system, parties in a dispute would assume most costs as well as the obligation of providing evidence. In contrast, the xinfang system does not require ordinary people to pay any fee or fulfill any formal obligation of providing evidence. Therefore, ordinary people may address their complaints in this system at very low costs, for example, by writing a letter to government officials. Because petitioners could initiate the procedure of xinfang at very low costs, they may be tempted to raise

---

[42] Documents collected from City Y, 2002.
[43] See Xinhuanet, "The State Council Meeting Agreed with the Decisions for the Jiahe Incident."

unreasonable demands. To deal with these demands, on the other hand, the bureaucracy needs to assume very high costs. Investigation of even a minor case could be endless and is usually very costly. In the 1980s, there was a saying within the xinfang system, "a stamp costs only eight cents, but it can keep upper and lower authorities busy for half a year."

Procrastination can remedy this problem to some extent. By forcing petitioners to repeat their petitions or to petition other state agencies, procrastination can increase the costs to petitioners and reduce the costs for the government. Because of bureaucratic procrastination, some petitioners have ended up paying very high costs. Some "long-term" petitioners (*laohu*) have spent dozens of years petitioning and sacrificed their normal life completely. The xinfang system thus relies on procrastination to differentiate significant, valid, and determined claims from others, because usually only those petitioners who have significant, valid, and determined claims are likely endure the costs of repeating petitions again and again. Therefore, procrastination can typically reduce the government's total costs of investigation.

The second factor increasing the government's reliance on procrastination is that the government needs time to respond to popular claims.[44] Direct actions, unlike institutionalized political participation, tend to be taken suddenly. Usually the state is not good at dealing with such sudden actions. This is not only because sudden collective actions tend to be more emotional, radical, and therefore less controllable, but also because all major state strategies, including repression, concession, and persuasion, require time. Particularly because most popular claims bear on some structural problems, as shown in many cases of peasant burdens, pension arrears, and land disputes in China, it is usually beyond the capacity of the local government to respond to such demands in a short period.

Whereas the government finds procrastination useful, petitioners have often tried to overcome it by creating a sense of urgency. In their petitions, some retirees stressed, "if you [the government] don't pay the arrears as quickly as possible, we may never have a chance to get them since we are at an old age!"[45] In other cases, petitioners have created a sense of urgency not just by statements, but also by action. Often, they will escalate or

---

[44] Similarly, Murray Scot Tanner, in summarizing Huntington's implicit insights, points out that a key task of state strategies in a developing country is to "buy time for the regime by containing protests and keeping popular demands from overwhelming the state governing capacity before it can undertake needed political reforms." See Murray Scot Tanner, "China Rethinks Unrest," *Washington Quarterly* 27/3, pp.137–56.

[45] Interview in City Y, 2002.

threaten to escalate their mobilization if they are not met with a prompt response. In the struggles between the government and petitioners, time is often a focus. Despite petitioners' efforts to overcome government delays, however, procrastination has still been utilized regularly.

In a sense, procrastination can diminish the difference between direct action and institutionalized participation when originally impulsive protesters are trapped in prolonged bargaining process. In other words, with procrastination, state officials can de facto routinize government-citizen contentious interactions. Consequently, waves of protests can, ironically, function somewhat like institutionalized political participation.

When the state has time, it may make efforts to solve structural problems, especially the "burning issues" that have caused the most frequent and disruptive petitions. As a consequence, petitions on some issues have gradually decreased. For example, collective petitions on peasant burdens and villagers' self-governance issues have gradually declined since 1999 due to policy adjustments in the central government. Similarly, it took about seven years for the government in Hunan to finally solve the problem of the savings crisis.

Of course, local officials need to learn the art of procrastination. In spite of the important function of procrastination, tardy response to petitions and protests or outright inaction is still regarded as official misbehavior, and will therefore be punished by superiors.[46] The really skillful procrastinators therefore usually appear to be prompt and responsive, but in actuality will not solve the problems at hand in a timely manner.

Procrastination has gained a central role only after the transition to the government-citizen model. In this model, preventive repression, expedient concession, and practical persuasion all essentially work for procrastination because all of them can temporarily contain or pacify protesters, and yet no thorough solution is offered by the government. In contrast, the state agents in the unit system model usually only employ procrastination as a supplementary tool. This is mainly because in this model, conflicts are much more likely to be solved promptly through more effective repression, concession, and persuasion.

---

[46] Many local officials have been sanctioned for their irresponsiveness or tardiness. A recent high-profile case took place in Zhuanghe City, Liaoning Province, on April 13, 2010. More than 1,000 petitioners knelt down in front of the municipal government building, but the mayor did not come out to meet them. The mayor was later dismissed from his position. See Xinhuanet, "Liaoning Zhuanghe shizhang bei zeling cizhi" (Mayor of Zhuanghe, Liaoning, was forced to resign), http://www.xinhuanet.com, last visited on April 24, 2010.

CONCLUSION

This chapter has provided part of the explanation for the upsurge of collective petitioning events. It starts with an examination of a remarkable change in state-society linkages, which, combined with increasing vertical and horizontal divisions within the state structure, has dramatically altered state agents' incentives and capacity for coping with popular contention. The new pattern of state strategies – restrained repression, expedient concessions, practical persuasion, and prevalent procrastination – has significantly contributed to the rise of collective petitioning. Restrained repression has reduced petitioners' fear, and oft-used expedient concessions have made "troublemaking" attractive. Because restrained repression, expedient concessions, and practical persuasion have essentially worked to aid government efforts at procrastination, it is often imperative for petitioners to create urgency for their demands. Compared to their usually emphatic statements, collective action with "troublemaking" tactics can convey an even stronger sense of urgency to the authorities.

4

The Xinfang System and Political Opportunity

To explain the dynamics and strategic orientation of popular protests since the 1990s, we naturally look for factors of social and political change in the Reform Era. What have often been overlooked are some enduring elements of the regime that have also profoundly shaped popular collective action. This chapter will show how inherent contradictions of the PRC have played such an important role.

Such contradictions have been most clearly manifest in the xinfang system, one of the primary institutions for the CCP to handle popular claim-making activities. The design of this system is based on the mass line, which simultaneously emphasizes the concentration of political power to Party leaders and nonbinding consultation with the masses. As a consultative apparatus it has been designed to facilitate "managed participation," which means that both the forms and effects of participation are under tight control by the Party-state.[1] Ordinary people can signal their preferences to the state but are not supposed to exert pressure on it. It is up to state officials to decide how such preferences will influence policy making and implementation.

This system largely worked as designed before the mid-1990s. Although some petitioners tried to use some "troublemaking" tactics to push state agents to meet their demands, overall popular participation had been well "managed." However, after the mid-1990s, this system began to work extensively in another way. The state not only often tolerates collective

---

[1] Yongshun Cai, "Managed Participation in China," *Political Science Quarterly* 119/3 (Fall 2004), pp. 425–451.

action, but also uses the xinfang system to facilitate popular collective action by providing them with quasi-legitimacy and pressuring the local government to negotiate with petitioners. Chinese petitioners have thus routinely taken advantages of some mechanisms in this system to challenge local authorities. This is what Kathleen Thelen calls "institutional conversion": institutions with one set of goals in mind are redirected to other ends.[2] How has the xinfang system largely been converted into an instrument for contentious bargaining? This chapter first illustrates how the inherent tensions in mass line politics have made the xinfang system "amphibious," which means an institution can be used for purposes contrary to those it is supposed to fill.

Of course, the "amphibiousness" of this institution may not always facilitate mass mobilization. Another important condition for the xinfang system's conversion is the change in institutional configurations in the Reform Era. In fact, since the 1990s, the xinfang system has worked within a substantially different institutional configuration. Chapter 3 discussed two particularly important changes – the decline of the unit system and the increase in divisions and differentiations within the state structure. The new configuration makes the xinfang system especially favorable to collective petitioning.

To fully take advantage of this political opportunity structure, petitioners still need to choose the right strategies and tactics. When contradictions and divisions of state institutions function as political opportunities, it is especially important for petitioners to play a proactive role in appropriating the institutional space. Such strategies and tactics will be fully discussed in Chapters 5 and 6.

In addition to secondary materials, this chapter mainly relies on data from County H in Hunan, particularly an event catalog of 125 cases. This is mainly because higher-level bureaus tend to transfer most cases to the county level and do not handle the cases themselves. For most cases, county-level bureaus are in charge of coordinating investigation and solutions. County-level archives usually include rich materials of case files and the communication documents among government agencies. They are therefore especially useful for examining the whole bureaucratic process of handling petitions and protests.

---

[2] Kathleen Thelen, "How Institutions Evolve: Insights from Comparative Historical Analysis," in James Mahoney and Dietrich Rueschemeyer (eds.), *Comparative Historical Analysis in the Social Science* (Cambridge: Cambridge University Press, 2003), p. 228.

THE MASS LINE AND THE XINFANG SYSTEM

To understand the evolution of the xinfang system, one must first understand the mass line. Among authoritarian regimes that survived the third wave of democratization, China is distinct from most others in that the CCP consciously and systematically rejects liberal democracy as a political model and instead advocates a rival ideology, namely the mass line, to handle government-citizen interactions. The mass line is defined here as a set of principles for political practice and institutional design, which seeks to integrate extensive mass mobilization and participation with the Chinese Communist Party's monopoly of political power.[3]

Within the Marxist-Leninist tradition, the CCP regime still claims that political institutions of the mass line are superior, or at least not inferior, to those of liberal democracy. After the demise of communist regimes in the Soviet Union and Eastern Europe, scholars in the West have seldom taken such claims seriously. The mass line, together with other aspects of communist ideology, has clearly lost much of its international appeal.[4] Despite whether the claim of the CCP regime is valid or not, the mass line still works as a key guideline for the Party to handle state-society relations.

Scholars who study Chinese politics in the Reform Era have seldom paid attention to the mass line mainly because of two common misunderstandings: (1) identifying the mass line with the Mao era, and (2) identifying the mass line with mass campaigns. Mao is of course one of the most important advocates of mass line politics. However, if we read various speeches by Deng Xiaoping, Jiang Zemin, and Hu Jintao, and other Chinese leaders in the Reform Era, we can easily find that mass line politics is a legacy of the CCP that goes far beyond Mao's time.[5]

The mass line, moreover, is not equivalent to mass campaigns. Liu Shaoqi emphatically rejected such conflation in the early 1960s in the

[3] The mass line is sometimes referred to as a kind of attitude or work method in China. As an attitude, it refers to the Party-state agents' concern with the interests and opinions of the masses. As a method, it refers to extensive consultation and study of popular preferences and interests, and the conduct of extensive persuasion in the process of policy implementation.

[4] The mass line was more popular internationally in the 1960s. See Mark Selden, *The Yenan Way in Revolutionary China* (Cambridge, MA: Harvard University Press, 1971).

[5] For example, see Jiang Zeming, "Jiang Zeming Guanyu Jianchi De Qunzhong Guandian He Qunzhong Luxian De Lunshu Xuanzhai" (Excerpts of Jiang Zemin's Remarks on the Party's Mass Opinion and Mass Line), *Dangde Wenxian* (Documents of the Party), vol. 1996, pp. 1–8.

wake of the disastrous Great Leap Forward (GLF) campaign. Aside from a mass campaign approach to mass line politics, there also exists an institutionalist approach. Many major CCP leaders have in fact sought to establish a set of institutions to carry out the mass line.

The Mass Line

What is the mass line? Mao provided the best description:

> In all the practical work of our Party, all correct leadership is necessarily from the masses, to the masses. This means: take the ideas of the masses (scattered and unsystematic ideas) and concentrate them (through study form them into concentrated and systematic ideas), then go to the masses and propagate and explain these ideas until the masses embrace them as their own, hold fast to them and translate them into action. Then once again concentrate ideas from the masses and once again take them to the masses so that the ideas are persevered in and carried through. And so on, over and over again in an endless spiral, with the ideas becoming more correct, more vital and richer each time.[6]

In practice, as Phyllis M. Frakt has noted, mass line politics is a system "combining a vanguard system with meaningful participation of the masses."[7] Richard Pfeffer makes a similar observation, pointing out that such a system institutes "in a vanguard system the appropriate degree of accountability and responsiveness to the masses of people."[8]

Therefore, it is generally believed that mass line politics consists of two closely related principles: 1) communication between leaders and the masses, and 2) centralization of political power. In mass line politics, political communication in fact includes both participation and persuasion. Participation is especially important in the policy-making stage and persuasion in the policy-implementation stage.

At the same time, however, political power is highly concentrated in a vanguard ruling group. However active the masses are, they do not have decision-making power. Instead the ruling group wields political power in a highly centralized fashion. In de Tocqueville's terms, the Chinese system is a combination of administrative and government centralization.

---

[6] Mao Zedong, "On the Mass Line," in Stuart R. Schram (ed.), *The Political Thought of Mao Tse-tung* (New York: Praeger Publishers, 1969), pp. 316–317.

[7] Phyllis M. Frakt, "Mao's Concept of Representation," *American Journal of Political Science* 23/4 (Nov. 1979), p. 690.

[8] Richard M. Pheffer, "Serving the People and Continuing the Revolution," *The China Quarterly* 52 (Oct.–Dec. 1972), p. 621.

First of all, political power in the polity is concentrated in a colossal Party-state. The CCP regime penetrated deeply into society before the Reform Era and still maintains a high level of control over many social and economic issues. This is essentially what Tocqueville calls government centralization. Within the Party-state system, power is concentrated in the Party. Moreover, within the Party, power concentrates in the central committee, which in turn is ultimately centralized in a few or even in a single Party Politburo leader.[9]

As previously mentioned, there are two basic approaches to mass line politics. Mao's mass line, which emphasizes mass campaigns, is clearly different from Liu Shaoqi and Deng Xiaoping's mass line, which stresses the importance of institutions. Liu Shaoqi and Deng Xiaoping were highly skeptical of mass campaigns, especially since the late 1950s. The differences between their understanding and Mao's became more pronounced when the GLF proved to be a huge disaster. For them, along with some other top leaders, the GLF demonstrated once and for all that the country should no longer utilize massive political campaigns to accomplish national goals.[10]

Liu criticized the excessive use of mass campaigns in 1962, stating "some comrades regard mass campaigns as the only form of the mass line, as if the mass line cannot exist without mass campaigns. Such a notion is obviously wrong. Those so-called 'mass campaigns' that violated the mass line, not only have failed to reflect the masses' opinions and demands, but have also damaged their enthusiasm and the Party's authority and credibility."[11]

Mao's approach dominated mass line practice, however, before he died in 1976. Not only were Liu and Deng unable to carry out their approach except for a short period, but both of them had also personally suffered from mass campaigns initiated by Mao. Liu, as is well-known, even lost his life in the Cultural Revolution, which was one of most radical mass campaigns.

Yet the institutional approach to the mass line largely won out when Mao died and Deng assumed power. Deng emphasized the importance

[9] Liu Zhifeng, "Lun Qunzhong Luxian yu Qunzhong Canyu" (On the Mass Line and Mass Participation), *Kaifang Shidai* 2 (1998), p. 17.

[10] Kenneth Lieberthal, *Governing China: From Revolution through Reform* (New York: W.W. Norton, 1995), pp. 109–110.

[11] The Central Committee of the CCP, *Guanyu Jianguo Yilai Ruogan Lishi Wenti de Jueyi Zhushiben* (Decisions on Some Historical Issues), (Beijing: Renmin Publication House, 1983), p. 546–550.

of institutions. He commented explicitly on Mao's mistakes, "He has not carried through some good working methods, such as the democratic centralism and the mass line, and has not designed or formed good institutions for them."[12]

Of course, although Mao preferred the mass campaign approach, he still found it necessary to establish some institutions. He thus founded the xinfang system among others. However, due to his approach, institution building with the xinfang system was quite limited and was sometimes disrupted during the Mao Era.

DESIGNING THE XINFANG SYSTEM

The xinfang system is in fact an important part of the mass line politics of China. It represents a major effort by the CCP regime to institute political representation. This system is designed to facilitate communication between the Party-state agents, especially the leaders, and the masses. It is one of the few effective channels for ordinary people to make claims to the state. Through this system, information about popular preferences and grievances can be conveyed to Party-state leaders. This is a precondition for the state to be responsive to such claims. In particular, this system stresses the *direct* contact between leaders and the masses. Leaders need to get firsthand knowledge of what ordinary people are feeling and thinking. In a sense, the CCP inherited the Chinese emperors' suspicion of the bureaucracy. As Ocko's study of the Qing dynasty reveals, the system would allow a few cases to reach the throne even at the expense of an excessive overflow of petitions to Beijing.[13]

The xinfang system, moreover, not only facilitates political communication, but also works to strengthen the centralization of political power in two key ways. First, the information inflow through the system also helps the Party-state hold its agents accountable. In fact, most information of cadre malpractice comes from this channel. For example, various statistics indicate that this channel has provided clues for at least 70 percent of corruption cases taken up by legal enforcement agencies in any period of the PRC.[14] Second, the system assists leaders to mobilize all

---

[12] Deng Xiaoping, *Dengxiaoping Wenxuan* (Selected Works of Deng Xiaoping), (Beijing: Renmin Chubanshe, 1994), vol. 2, p. 345.

[13] Jonathan Ocko, "I Will Take It All the Way to Beijing: Capital Appeals in the Qing," *Journal of Asian Studies* 47/2 (May 1988), pp. 291–315.

[14] For example, see Diao Jiecheng, *Renmin Xinfang Shilue* (A Brief History of People's Letters and Visits) (Beijing: Beijing Xueyuan chubanshe, 1996).

relevant public agencies to respond to popular claims. One of the basic duties of xinfang agencies is to work on behalf of leaders to designate cases to relevant agencies and oversee the process of case investigation and handling.

Setting Up Xinfang Agencies

The CCP leaders decided to set up special xinfang agencies in 1951. It is worth noting that the CCP regime did this much sooner than the Soviet Union, which did not set up its own Department of Letters until 1978, about sixty years after the founding of the regime.[15] By contrast, the CCP regime did it no more than two years after it was founded.

The CCP's official history treats May 16, 1951, as the starting date of the xinfang system.[16] It is the date when Mao issued his famous written instruction to Party and government authorities above the county level to establish "special organs or personnel" for handling petitions. In these instructions, he first stressed that this work was one of the Party-state's main methods to strengthen its ties with the people.

Mao continued, "When there are too many letters from the people for [the leaders] to handle by themselves, some special organs with an appropriate number of staff members should be set up, or special personnel should be appointed. If letters are not too many for leaders and their secretaries to handle, such organs and personnel are not needed."[17] From such instructions, it is clear that special agencies or personnel are established only to assist leaders and their secretaries to handle letters. It seems that at that time, Mao and other CCP leaders were not sure how far such institution building should go.

In June 1951, shortly after Mao's instructions were issued, the General Administration Council (GAC), which was the administrative branch of the Central Government, issued Decisions on Handling People's Letters and Meeting Petitioners. This document first reiterates some principles of the mass line that the "People's government at each level should maintain a close contact with the masses, whole-heartedly serve the people, and

---

[15] Nicholas Lampert, *Whistle Blowing in the Soviet Union: Complaints and Abuses under State Socialism* (London: MacMillan, 1985).

[16] For examples, see Diao Jiecheng, *Renmin Xinfang Shilue*; Ying Xing, "Zuowei Teshu Xingzheng Jiuji De Xinfang Jiuji" (The Xinfang Remedy: A Special Form of Administrative Relief), *Faxue Yanjiu* 3 (2004), pp. 58–71; and Laura Luehrmann, "Facing Citizen Complaints in China, 1951–1996," *Asian Survey* 43/5 (2003), pp. 845–86.

[17] Diao, *Renming Xinfang Shilue*, p. 32.

also encourage the masses to monitor their own government and government cadres." Then it required the government at each level to set up special personnel to handle letters and a special consulting or reception office to receive visitors.

However, like Mao's instructions, this document did not specify to what extent the work of handling petitions should be specialized. From the perspective of the Party-state, establishing special agencies would not necessarily improve its relationship with the masses. The first concern was whether or not a few xinfang cadres would be capable of handling petitions that covered all areas of government function.[18] This problem could be solved by limiting xinfang agencies' duties to preliminary handling and coordinating other agencies to do further work. Yet there was another fundamental paradox: Specialized agencies can facilitate communication between Party-state leaders and ordinary people, but they can also impede it because this means that most ordinary people will no longer have direct contact with the leaders. If bureaucratization went too far, the mass line would be compromised.

In response to Mao's instruction and the GAC's Decisions, the Party and the government at the county level and above began to set up special personnel or departments to handle petitions.[19] However, in the first several years, they still struggled with the dilemma of the specialization of xinfang work. At that time, there was a debate about whether full-time personnel or part-time personnel were better for handling petitions. After several years of experimentation, specialized agencies or personnel proved to do the work better for two main reasons. First, part-time officials tended to give priority to their own work rather than that of handling petitions. Second, when petitions were concentrated in specialized agencies or personnel, information about popular demands and grievances was easier to collect and process. It was not until 1956 that this had become a general consensus.

The ambiguous attitude toward specialization of xinfang work constrained the process of building up xinfang agencies for at least several years. For example, the development of specialized agencies or personnel remained quite limited in local governments in the 1950s. According to a study of twenty-two provincial governments by the Secretariat of the State Council in 1957, there was large variation among the provinces. Shanghai appointed fifteen cadres for xinfang work, whereas Hunan

[18] Ibid., p. 27.
[19] Ibid., p. 53.

only had one cadre. The xinfang agencies in local governments below the provincial level were even more underdeveloped.

To promote such specialized agencies, the CCP held its First National Conference on Xinfang Work in 1957. This conference helped clarify the confusion about the dilemma of specialization in xinfang work and pointed out that specialized xinfang agencies were indispensable for leader-mass relations in a polity as large as China. It claimed that:

> Leaders' involvement must be combined with the role of specialized xinfang agencies. Since there are many letters and visits, 'leaders should pay attention' would be an empty slogan without the work of specialized xinfang agencies and personnel. At the same time, without leaders' support, xinfang officials could hardly fulfill their duty by themselves. The vast number of ordinary petitions needed to be handled by xinfang agencies.[20]

Institution building overall had improved to some extent in the 1960s before the Cultural Revolution. In 1966, most provincial governments had even established bureau department-level (*chuji*) xinfang agencies. Except during the period of the Cultural Revolution, there had been a self-reinforcing mechanism that worked in this process of institution building. As xinfang agencies become built up, more petitions will be addressed to them; when there are more petitions, the xinfang agencies will be further strengthened. Furthermore, several dramatic waves of petitions also accelerated this process. The tide of petitions in the period between 1978 and 1982 and those since the mid-1990s have prompted the regime to continue building up xinfang agencies. Yet the basic structure, as analyzed later, remains unchanged since it was laid out in the 1950s.

Structures of the Xinfang System

When discussing the structure of the xinfang system, a distinction between xinfang agencies and the xinfang system must be made. Xinfang agencies are usually called xinfang bureaus or xinfang offices. They are set up at the Party committee and the government at the county level and above.[21] They answer to both upper-level xinfang agencies and to

---

[20] Ibid., p. 101.

[21] There has been an enduring debate within the CCP regime whether the xinfang bureau/offices in the government should be separate from or combined with the xinfang bureau/office of the Party. Since the late 1990s, the prevalent practice is that the two bureaus should be combined into one, which is mainly run by the government.

the leadership at the same level. Beside this main hierarchy of xinfang agencies, many smaller xinfang agencies are set up in a variety of public and semipublic agencies, such as in the People's Congress, the People's Political Consultation Conference, the courts, the procuratorate, SOEs, and colleges. This chapter discusses primarily the main hierarchy of xinfang agencies.

The xinfang system is a set of state agencies including, but not limited to, xinfang bureaus involved in handling petitions. Compared to xinfang agencies, the xinfang system is a broader concept that includes three components: (1) xinfang bureaus, (2) Party-state leaders, and (3) other state agencies routinely involved in handling petitions. In Chinese official jargon, there is a distinction between the "small xinfang" and the "big xinfang." Generally speaking, the "small xinfang" refers to xinfang bureaus and the "big xinfang" refers to the xinfang system. For the CCP regime, this distinction holds one very important policy implication. The Party-state has advocated the concept of the "big xinfang" to clarify and strengthen the responsibility of local leaders and other agencies in handling petitions. Therefore, the "big xinfang" is not just an empirical concept, but also a normative one.

To further explore the structure of the xinfang system, two key sets of relationships should be examined: (1) the relationship between xinfang agencies and Party-state leaders; and (2) the relationship between xinfang agencies and other state agencies. Two features stand out: (1) xinfang agencies are highly dependent on Party-state leaders; and (2) a wide range of public or semipublic agencies are involved in responding to petitions.

First, let us look at xinfang agencies' dependence on Party-state leaders. Indeed, they were never meant to fulfill any function other than assisting the leaders. They screen petitions and select important ones for leaders to review; they also synthesize information to help leaders evaluate political situations; they carry out leaders' instructions; and they coordinate and supervise other agencies to handle petitions on behalf of the leaders. This is why their role has been traditionally defined as that of secretarial staff.

To fulfill their function, xinfang agencies are heavily dependent on the leaders for authority. Although xinfang agencies need to coordinate and supervise other agencies to handle petitions, they lack sufficient authority to do so. For a long time, the rank of xinfang agencies was at least half a level lower than other departments of the Party and the government. This situation changed to some extent in the 1980s when county- and city-level xinfang bureaus were elevated to the same rank as the other departments. But the rank of the provincial level and national level still remains lower than other equivalent department-level agencies. For example, currently, the Hunan Provincial Xinfang Bureau is still half a level lower than other departments of the provincial Party and government.

Because xinfang work is "leaders' work," the regime has continuously urged leaders to take an active attitude toward handling petitions. In November 1957, for instance, the State Council stated, "Experiences have indicated that, in order to handle people's letters and receiving people's visits well, the key is for [Party-state's] organ leaders to pay attention to and personally get involved in this work."[22] In 1964, it reaffirmed this statement, "The key to the work of handling letters and visits is leaders' serious involvement."[23]

Yet, there is little institutional arrangement to support leaders' incentives for handling petitions. It is hard to evaluate their performance and reward their efforts for such work. The effect of reading letters, dialoguing with petitioners, or holding meetings is less evident. In contrast, the achievements in economic development or in implementing required tasks, such as tax or grain collection and enforcement of the one-child policy, are more manifest. Usually local leaders' performance in handling petitioning can be evaluated in a negative way: They can hardly get rewards for handling petitions well, but they may get sanctioned for failures or mistakes. However, of course, there are many ways for local leaders to circumvent such negative evaluations. It is still one of the major problems for xinfang institutions that draw out an essential role for the leaders but still provide little incentive for them to actively handle petitions.

Second, we can examine the relations between xinfang agencies and other Party-state agencies. Except for their work on information flow, to fulfill their functions, xinfang agencies usually need to coordinate with other public agencies. A wide range of agencies are routinely involved in the process of responding to petitions. The all-encompassing structure of the CCP regime has been regarded as one of the biggest advantages of this political system, because the Party-state can easily mobilize various agencies to attain some goals, such as handling petitions.

Of course, such a structure also has its problems. For example, many public agencies have overlapping functions. When peasants want to complain about overtaxation, they can resort to the Party, the government,

---

[22] Diao, *Renmin Xinfang Shilue*, p. 358.
[23] Ibid., p. 364.

TABLE 4.1. *Government Agencies Investigating Xinfang Cases in County H, 1991–2001*

	Xinfang Alone	Xinfang with Another County Department	Xinfang with a Town or Township Government	Xinfang with Two or More Other Agencies	N/A	Total
Cases	8	24	18	69	6	125
Percentage	6.4	19.2	14.4	55.2	4.8	100

Source: CHXB.

the People's Congress, the People's Political Consultative Conference, the official media, and others. This situation can cause inconvenience to petitioners because they are often confused about where to complain. But knowledgeable petitioners may also take advantage of this situation and use one agency's response to bargain with another. This has also become a concern of the regime.[24]

To avoid problems caused by the all-encompassing structure of the Party-state, the xinfang agencies are supposed to coordinate public agencies. The xinfang agencies can play two kinds of roles when coordinating with other agencies: (1) supervision (*duban*): after they transfer cases to relevant agencies, they supervise the process of handling cases and, as discussed earlier, usually need to borrow authority from leaders for this work; and 2) cooperation (*heban*): xinfang agencies form joint investigation or work teams with other agencies to handle cases. Such joint teams can be very big, consisting of several agencies. They can also be small, consisting of the xinfang agency with one other agency.

Joint investigation or working teams are very common in China. As Table 4.1 shows, among the 125 cases that the xinfang system put on file for investigation in County H, only 8 were handled by the county xinfang bureau alone. In contrast, forty-two cases were handled by the xinfang bureau with another government agency, either one of the county departments or one of town or township governments, and sixty-nine cases by the xinfang bureau with two or more other agencies in the form of joint teams.

The relationship between xinfang agencies and the leaders and other public agencies will be further illustrated in the discussion on various working mechanisms in the xinfang channel. Yet even this brief analysis

[24] Ibid., p. 65.

of its basic structure indicates that the xinfang system has been designed as an instrument for assisting Party-state's leaders to mobilize all resources within the political system to respond to popular claim making.

Dilemma of Mass Line Institutions

Designing and redesigning the xinfang system presents many difficult tasks. What can sustain Party and government leaders' motivation to handle petitions? What can ensure that bureaucratic procedures do not obstruct the communication between petitioners and the leaders? What can maintain social control when claim-making activities tend to concentrate in power centers? Many such concerns are deeply rooted in this centralized system of political consultation, and are therefore difficult to solve.

Two dilemmas have the most significant impact on popular claim-making activities. First, because Party and government leaders can only handle a tiny portion of cases, a large majority of cases will be processed by government agencies that lack power or incentive. The system also relies on the way in which petitions are delivered to determine the significance of the petitions, and "troublemaking" tactics are often believed to signify the petitions' credibility and importance. This system therefore tends to frustrate moderate petitioners and encourage "troublemakers" who can exert pressure on the government and distinguish themselves from other petitioners. In other words, a strong incentive of petitioners to appropriate the system is expected, although this is certainly contrary to the intention of the designers. This dilemma may be partly remedied if the regime can impose high costs on troublemaking activities, but it cannot always do so effectively. Second, the system needs to be flexible enough so that a few important petitions and appeals can reach the leaders, but also rigid enough so that an overflow of claim-making activities will not overwhelm or disrupt the power center. The system is therefore tempted to formalize and standardize procedures and norms, but ultimately remains vague and ambiguous about them.

WHY DO MODERATE PETITIONS NOT WORK?

According to the standard procedures of the xinfang system, petitioners need to overcome several barriers for their demands to be effectively addressed. They first need to be selected as important cases for Party-state leaders to review. If Party-state leaders believe it necessary to handle them seriously, they will give written, or in some cases oral, instruction to relevant agencies. Most cases need to be investigated to verify the information in the petitions. If petitions are believed to be valid and important, some measures of rectification and remedy will be implemented. We examine these four regular procedures: sorting out petitions, giving instructions (*pishi*), investigation, and solution. For most ordinary petitions, each step amounts to a formidable barrier.

Sorting Out Individual Cases

In this large and centralized political system, the amount of information about individual cases far exceeds Party-state leaders' capacity to process. Reviewing a few letters by leaders has been regarded as quite important. The CCP always emphasizes that however busy the leaders are, they should spend some time reading petition letters themselves. At the First National Conference on Xinfang Work, Yang Shangkun emphatically pointed out that being busy cannot be used as an excuse for not reading letters. He said, the central leaders were even busier than provincial leaders, yet they still often reviewed letters.[25] This policy has not changed in the Reform Era. Most leaders on each level still review some letters themselves. However, even the most compassionate and hardworking leaders can only read a very limited number of petitions. Premier Zhu Rongji was one of the top leaders who took this work very seriously. On average, he received 800 to 1,000 petition letters addressed to him personally each month. He reviewed the original copy of a few most important letters, excerpts of relatively important letters, and a summary report on all other less important letters. He expressed his expectation for xinfang officials who were in charge of sorting out his letters, "Don't worry about my busy schedule. Try to transfer letters to me as many as possible."[26] But xinfang officials should certainly know the limits.

Likewise, although local leaders' direct involvement of handling a few truly important "visits" (petitions delivered personally) is preferred, their time and energy are scarce. Therefore, valuable information should be differentiated from less valuable information. As discussed earlier, ever since the establishment of specialized xinfang agencies, one of the basic principles has been "to treat petitions differently."[27] Sorting out petitioning is

[25] Ibid., p. 104.
[26] Zhu Rongji, "Opening Speech in the Fourth National Conference on the Xinfang Work, 1996," a document obtained from CHXB.
[27] Diao, *Renmin Xinfang Shilue*, p. 59.

thus the first work a xinfang agency needs to do after receiving petitions. Xinfang agencies have sometimes been ridiculed as mailrooms because of this function. Of course, their work is actually more sophisticated; it needs to evaluate the significance of each case, which requires political knowledge and skill.

What are the key criteria to judge significance? Significance is usually evaluated according to (1) the content of petitions and (2) the form of delivery. According to a training manual used by the Hunan provincial bureau in 1991, petitions are supposed to be put into files for investigation if they report the following issues: (1) important problems or situations regarding main public policies, especially relevant to the Reform and Opening policy; (2) serious violations of law, government rules, and party discipline; (3) social problems that are prevalent or are likely to become a trend; or (4) emergency problems that threaten social stability.[28] The last criterion is concerned with not just the content of petitions, but also the method of delivering petitions. With the rise of collective petitioning in the 1990s, the last criterion has become more important. When there are too many petitions that bear on important issues, petitioners often distinguish themselves by using special tactics to signal to the authorities that they have "emergency problems that threaten social stability."

After evaluating the significance of the cases, the xinfang agency will transfer them to different destinations. This procedure varies to some extent at different levels of government. In principle, higher-level agencies will transfer most petitions to lower-level agencies, and only the county-level agencies are supposed to handle most cases by themselves.[29] However, agencies at every level are very selective. Even at the county level, only a small number of cases will be reviewed by leaders.

Having selected a few important cases for the leaders to review, xinfang agencies will transfer most cases to relevant functional departments or to lower-level government. There are two different ways of transferring cases: (1) assignment (*jiaoban*) and (2) passing on (*zhuanban*). In the first situation, the higher-level xinfang agencies will put the cases into file and request the relevant departments or lower-level bureaus to deal with such cases within a limited time period. In the second situation,

---

[28] Tang Junjie, "On the Work of Handling Letters and Visits Cases." This is an unpublished training manual for the xinfang cadres in Hunan Province, 1991, which was obtained during fieldwork.

[29] This principle was first stipulated in the State Council, "Renmin Laixin Laifang Gongzuo de Jiben Jingyan (Caogao)" (Basic Experiences in Handling People's Letters and Visits-A Draft), 1964. See Diao, pp. 364–369.

they will not register the cases but transfer them wholesale. Such cases will be treated as ordinary ones without any preferential status. For example, if the provincial bureau transfers a case to a city bureau as an assignment, the city bureau usually will also put it into a file for investigation, and will report the results to the provincial bureau after handling it. In contrast, if the provincial bureau transfers a case in the "passing on" style, the city bureau will treat it as a normal case that it received directly.

The provincial bureau in Hunan Province received 17,975 letters from January to June in 1996.[30] Among them, 13,520 letters were written to the bureau directly and 4,455 to the central government and then transferred to the provincial bureau. Among these 17,975 letters, only 50 were sent to provincial leaders for review and 70 letters were directly sent to leaders of relevant departments or lower-level bureaus; 255 other letters were put into file and then sent to relevant departments or lower-level bureaus. These 375 letters were sorted out as important enough for serious treatment. A vast majority of letters had been sent to lower-level bureaus wholesale without special registration. Other levels of xinfang agencies work similarly. At the bottom level, when the xinfang bureaus have nowhere else to transfer the cases, they shelve them in their own quarters.

Written Instructions

Among Chinese petitioners, there exists a widespread "myth of written instructions." They are willing to pay a tremendous price for a written instruction from a leader, preferably from a high-ranking leader. However, many petitioners who managed to get written instructions were disappointed and disillusioned. Written instructions are certainly important, but they are not a sufficient condition for a thorough government response.

Typically, however, written instructions are a necessary condition to initiate a serious investigation and handling. As previously discussed, xinfang agencies do not have sufficient authority to order relevant agencies to handle a case. So they borrow it from Party-state leaders. If the leader approves xinfang agencies' proposals, he or she will usually write an instruction or, in some cases, at least give a relevant oral instruction.

---

[30] Calculated from the monthly summaries of petition letters (*laixin jiankuang*) produced by Hunan Provincial Xinfang Bureau, which the author obtained in 2002.

TABLE 4.2. *The Highest Levels of Leaders Issuing Written Instructions in County H, 1990–2001*

	Cases	Percentage
Provincial and central	17	13.6
City	14	11.2
County	56	44.8
N/A	38	30.4
Total	125	100

Note: For cases in which leaders at several levels issued written instruction, this table only counts the highest level.

As Table 4.2 shows, among the 125 cases in County H files, written instructions from leaders at various levels can be found in 87 cases. For the other 38 cases, it is reasonable to assume that oral instructions were given for at least some of them.

When a central or provincial leader has given an instruction, leaders at lower levels will add their own instructions as follow-up. Therefore, when a case with instructions from central leaders has been transferred to the county level, provincial, city, and county leaders' instructions can usually also be found in the file.

Instructions can be written on petition letters or special reports. In some cases, leaders give instructions in comprehensive reports. For example, the National Xinfang Bureau periodically sends comprehensive reports to the Hunan Xinfang Bureau about all petitions addressed to the National Bureau by Hunan petitioners in a set period. Beside a description of the overall situation and some statistical data, some specific cases will be given as examples. Typically, a provincial leader will circle such cases and write instructions in the margins.

Why does a leader's instruction not guarantee sufficient investigation and handling? The primary reason is that most instructions are quite general and formal, seldom expressing unreserved support for petitions. They only take such petitions as signals of possible problems and usually refrain from making a judgment before receiving further investigation reports. Therefore, in a majority of cases, leaders only request their subordinates to investigate, and nothing beyond that. Of course, they can express different levels of concern in some delicate way. For example, a central leader may refer cases to the Provincial Party Secretary or governor personally, or he or she may add some words such as "pay attention to it" or "treat it seriously." If they want to express a stronger concern, they may write longer instructions. In such longer instructions, they often reiterate some principles or remind lower level officials of the importance of dealing with such problems seriously.

Premier Zhu Rongji acknowledged that even his written instructions did not always work. At the Fourth National Conference on Xinfang Work in 1996, he admitted that many letters with his personal instructions got no substantial response, like "a stone dropped into the sea." He added, "To be honest, I do not have many ways to change this. But I still want to express my concern for those cases [by writing instructions]. After all, when I have given instructions, lower level authorities will pay relatively more attention to those cases."[31]

Although lower-level officials will pay more attention to cases with higher-level leaders' instructions, as discussed later, there also exist strong incentives and good opportunity for them to cover up for themselves and their subordinates. Furthermore, upper-level leaders' attention is often short-lived. Usually, a formal report is enough to satisfy them.

Investigation

For most cases, investigation is the core procedure. In the Chinese political system, it is not just a process of fact-finding. It is politics itself. First of all, investigation of lower-level officials by itself is often a sign of mistrust and can possibly exert much pressure on them.[32] Secondly, it is a multiparty game, and therefore involves very complicated calculations. For example, when investigators want to protect their subordinates, they face many choices. They may pacify petitioners by: (1) admitting to less serious problems while hiding more serious ones; (2) attributing problems to village-level agents while clearing township-level agents of any responsibility; or (3) concentrating on finding the petitioners' own problems. This section will examine the extent to which investigations are likely to yield truth.

As discussed earlier, higher authorities are usually far away from the facts. When they review petitions, they can only make some preliminary judgment on their credibility. The available information is usually far

---

[31] Zhu Rongji, "Opening Speech in the Fourth National Conference on the Xinfang Work, 1996." This is a document collected from CHXB, 2002.
[32] Ying Xing and Jin Jun, "Jiti Shangfang Zhong De Wentihua Guocheng: Xinan Yige Shuidianzhan De Yimin De Guishi" (The Process of Problemization in Collective Visits: A Story of Migration Caused by a Hydroelectric Plant in Southwest China), *Qinghua Shehuixue Pinglun (Qinghua Sociological Journal)*, Special issue (2000), pp. 80–109.

from sufficient to either support or deny demands. One central agency once adopted three standards for preliminary judgment on the credibility of claims in the early 1950s – petitions are likely to be false if: (1) there is inconsistency in the content, (2) the handwriting does not match the identity of petitioners, and (3) the petitions have suspicious origin.[33] From these standards we can see how weak their judgments often were.

While upper authorities need to get more information, they usually avoid investigating by themselves. Instead, they delegate this job to their local subordinates. However, because of the symbiosis among local officials, one can assume that lower-level authorities will often have a strong incentive to cover up for their agents. This problem has existed in almost all big, hierarchical bureaucratic systems, from imperial China to the Soviet Union.[34] William Alford's case study of late Qing clearly indicated how strong such tendencies could be. An ordinary criminal case in Zhejiang Province gradually implicated dozens of high-ranking officials because (1) officials wanted to protect their subordinates, and/or (2) when higher-level officials got involved in the investigation process, they needed to defend their positions for their own sake. This case shows a snowball effect: In the process of investigation, more and increasingly higher-level officials will be drawn into the conflicts, therefore increasing the motivation for a cover-up.[35]

Given this symbiotic relationship, why do upper authorities not regularly dispatch their own teams to conduct investigations? The first reason is limited resources. Upper authorities cannot afford to dispatch investigation teams to the grassroots on a regular basis. The second reason is practical difficulties. Unfamiliar with the complicated local situations, officials from upper authorities will have great difficulty in finding the truth by themselves. The third and most important reason is that such direct investigations may undermine the relationship between upper and lower authorities. Depriving local authorities of the opportunity to investigate cases within their jurisdiction indicates a very strong sense of mistrust. Consequently, such investigations, if too frequent, are

---

[33] Diao, *Renmin Xinfang Shilue*, p. 46.
[34] For research on Imperial China, see Zhou, "Illusion and Reality in the Law of the Late Qing," Ocko, "I Will Take It All the Way to Beijing," and William Alford, "Of Arsenic and Old Laws: Looking Anew at Criminal Justice in Late Imperial China," *California Law Review* 72 (1984), pp. 1180–1255. For research on the Soviet Union, see Nicholas Lampert, *Whistle Blowing in the Soviet Union: Complaints and Abuses under State Socialism* (London: MacMillan, 1985).
[35] William Alford, "Of Arsenic and Old Laws: Looking Anew at Criminal Justice in Late Imperial China," *California Law Review* 72 (1984), 1180–1255.

TABLE 4.3. *Levels of Government Agencies Investigating Xinfang Cases in County H, 1990–2001*

	Case Number	Percentage
City and above	4	3.2
County leaders	14	11.2
Joint team at the county level	55	44.0
Grassroots*	48	38.4
NA	4	3.2
Total	125	100

* Grassroots organizations refer to county bureaus, township or village authorities, or work units.

likely to be resisted by local authorities and will severely hurt intra-bureaucratic relations.

Among the 125 cases in County H files, 86 cases were first addressed to city, provincial, or central authorities, and then transferred to the county government. Among these eighty-six cases, thirty-one received written instructions from leaders at the city level and above. However, as Table 4.3 shows, the city authority and above only conducted investigations in four cases. In all others, the county government was delegated with the final power of investigation and upper authorities only requested a final report.

To increase the effectiveness and credibility of investigations, the county government usually (1) designates one or more county leaders to lead the investigation, (2) organizes joint teams of investigations, or (3) requires the county xinfang bureau to supervise such investigations if they are done by grassroots authorities. As Table 4.3 shows, the majority of cases have been handled in one of these three ways. County leaders led investigations in fourteen cases; joint teams consisting of county agencies (township-level officials participated in some of them) conducted investigations in fifty-five cases; and grassroots agencies conducted investigations under xinfang bureaus' oversight in forty-eight cases. Clearly investigations are usually done by lower-level agencies.

Different levels of investigators yield different results. Investigations conducted by upper authorities (the city and above) or by county leaders are more likely to acknowledge that factual statements in petitions are true or partly true. As Table 4.4 shows, among fifteen such cases, 93 percent of them were regarded as true or partly true. In comparison, among ninety-seven cases that were investigated by county-level departments or lower authorities either jointly or individually, this percentage is

TABLE 4.4. *Relations between Levels of Investigators and Investigation Results in County H, 1990–2001*

	Grassroots or Departments	County Leaders or Upper Level	Total
Not true	31 (32.0)	1 (6.7)	32 (28.6)
Partly or basically true	66 (68.0)	14 (93.3)	80 (71.4)
Total	97 (100.0)	15 (100.0)	112 (100)

Note: Thirteen cases have been filtered because there is no information about the outcome of the investigations either because the data is missing or because the there was no investigation conducted in such cases.

only 68 percent. This difference demonstrates that the higher the level of the investigators, the less likelihood of a cover-up. Of course, we need to exclude an alternative explanation, namely that this correlation is caused by the fact that upper authorities or county leaders are more likely to conduct investigations when petitions are more credible. In fact, all 125 cases were considered quite credible upon preliminary judgment. Otherwise, they would not have been put into the file for investigation at all, as they all passed a highly selective screening procedure by xinfang agencies.

By comparison, the different levels of leaders who gave written instructions do not have significant impact on investigation outcomes. As Table 4.5 shows, among twenty-nine cases in which city leaders or above gave instructions, factual statements in 76 percent of petitions were regarded as true or partly true. In contrast, among fifty-two cases in which county leaders gave instructions, the percentage was 73 percent, and among thirty-one cases in which no written instructions can be found, the percentage is 65 percent. Although positive correlations still exist between levels of written instructions and investigation outcomes, they are weak. The comparison between the effect of levels of investigations and that of written instructions indicates that upper authorities' intervention in local conflicts is more forceful when conducting investigations rather than merely issuing instructions.

It should be noted that, even though the process of investigation is typically not open to petitioners, local officials, if accused by petitioners, do have a chance to defend themselves. In this aspect, the xinfang system is different from judicial procedures where both parties have an equal opportunity to argue and cross-examine the evidence. In the xinfang system, petitioners are typically notified of the findings only when the investigations are over. If they dissent, they have to deliver another petition.

TABLE 4.5. *Relations between Levels of Instructions and Investigation Results in County H, 1990–2001*

	No Instruction	County	City and the Above	Total
Not true	11 (35.4)	14 (27.0)	7 (24.1)	32 (28.6)
Partly or basically true	20 (64.6)	38 (73.0)	22 (75.9)	80 (71.4)
Total	31	52	29	112 (100)

Because of the unequal opportunities available to petitioners and their adversaries, cover-ups are relatively easy. Beside hiding or distorting facts, one common strategy is to defame petitioners by challenging petitioners' behavior, personalities, and their intentions in petitioning. Yet petitioners usually do not have a chance of defending themselves. In some cases they are not even aware of such accusations. In the County H data, investigation reports in thirteen cases challenged the petitioners', especially the organizers', credibility or intentions. Petitioners are often described as unwilling to comply with laws and policy, jealous of grassroots cadres, or having other personal grudges. In one case, organizers of a collective petition were accused of being involved in underground religious activities. This is a very serious accusation in China, because such activities are believed to have a negative political nature, although the outcome of that case indicates that upper authorities did not take the accusation seriously.

Upper authorities usually understand investigation biases. Yet they still tend to approve investigative reports unless petitioners strongly challenge them by petitioning again. Of course, in some rare cases, the inconsistencies, bias, and superficiality of such reports were so evident that they were rejected right away. However, upper authorities are generally less concerned about truth than about whether such reports will help stabilize conflicts. Given that in many cases petitioners do not wholeheartedly agree with the conclusions of investigations, local authorities are typically required to conduct "thought education work" on petitioners after investigations.

Solutions

Many petitions involve rectification of state actions (and inactions) or policies that affect the interests of petitioners. Even if local officials did not have a role in the original issues, their failure to solve them often becomes a liability for those officials who handle them. How often will upper authorities sanction local officials for malpractice? The 125 cases in the County H data indicate a tendency to avoid severe sanctions on local cadres. Among 125 cases, local cadres' responsibility is not an issue in 32 cases. Among the other ninety-three cases, local cadres were found to have no responsibility in forty-six cases. Among the other forty-seven cases in which local cadres were found to have some sort of responsibility, in thirty-one cases the sanctions were confined to criticism, much lighter than what petitioners expected. In only sixteen cases did local cadres get more severe sanctions such as admonishments or dismissal from their posts. The underlying reasons for upper authorities' reluctance to sanction their subordinates severely are somewhat similar to their reluctance to investigate cases directly. The intra-bureaucratic relations are often more important than meeting petitioners' demands or having justice realized. This phenomenon might be common for all large hierarchical systems. Therefore, Zhou Guangyuan's observation of the Qing Dynasty can be applied to today's China quite well: "[A] provincial governor had to be realistic: official corruption was ubiquitous, and yet he had to rely on local officials to fulfill tax quotas for the central government. In doing so, his first goal was to keep the people quiet."[36]

How Does "Troublemaking" Make a Difference?

The above analysis of procedures of the xinfang system illustrates why the vast majority of moderate petitioners will be frustrated. Popular collective action with "troublemaking" tactics is staged precisely to overcome the stated procedural barriers. In many collective petitioning events, protesters demand a direct dialogue with local leaders and refuse to address ordinary officials. Their "troublemaking" tactics can sometimes elicit different government responses. Local leaders, or at least department leaders, actually often talk to protesters directly. Rather than comfortably reading reports and then giving instructions in their office, local leaders are pressed to conduct face-to-face dialogues. This is a significant shift. The leaders will confront quite a different mindset, and are faced with quite different choices of strategies. Ironically, it is contention that brings leaders closer to the masses. Even when petitioners fail to force local leaders to meet them, their "troublemaking" tactics make it more likely for xinfang officials to report them to local leaders as important cases.

[36] Zhou, "Illusion and Reality in the Law of the Late Qing," p. 451.

In addition, investigations are often unnecessary for such cases. Indeed for many petitions, especially for many collective petitions on "burning issues," governmental officials are usually quite familiar with the problems raised in the petitions. For example, when a group of pensioners mount some collective action to pressure the government to pay their pensions, they are not informing the government about some unknown facts. In such cases, the issue is not whether petitioners' claims are true or false, but whether the petitioners can create enough pressure for the government to meet their demands. When investigation is needed for some cases, the pressure exerted by collective action makes it less likely for local officials to cover up.

Moreover, even though a thorough solution is rare, as discussed in the previous chapter, some expedient concessions are likely to be made by the government quickly in such cases. In the face of pressure from collective actions, the government usually needs to find some way to pacify petitioners. Of course, this does not mean that special procedures triggered by collective action are always effective. Indeed, many collective actions have been dissolved and no substantial promises have been made. Yet the pressure created by many collective actions still leads to serious deliberation by local leaders and makes it more difficult to cover up for the accused officials. In addition to expedient concessions, some substantial policy change may result from sustained popular contention.

AMBIGUOUS NORMS

Another consequence of contradictions within the xinfang system is ambiguous norms on claim-making activities. As Tilly points out, "at any given time, governments themselves react differently to the various claim-making performances currently available to claimants."[37] He distinguishes such performances into three categories: prescribed, tolerated, and forbidden. The different scopes of these categories have significant impacts on the interactions between the state and ordinary people.

In China's case, a more refined differentiation is necessary. Specifically it is useful to differentiate two types of performance within the category of tolerated activities: (1) desirable and (2) undesirable but tolerable. This distinction highlights a gray area of which ordinary people can take advantage. Local officials do not feel comfortable about the pressure

---

[37] Charles Tilly, *The Politics of Collective Violence* (Cambridge: Cambridge University Press, 2003), p. 47.

exerted by "troublemaking" tactics, but they are often unable to prevent them by harsh repression because many such tactics are not entirely outlawed. The norms of the xinfang system have two features: (1) a large number of activities fall into the category of the undesirable but tolerated; and (2) the boundary between this category and the forbidden is very vague.

Desirable Performances

What forms of petitioning are desirable? Petitioning via mail is obviously preferred. The xinfang system was originally designed to handle letters, and visits only came up as a substitute for letters. When Mao and other CCP leaders first conceived the xinfang system, they mainly had letters in mind. This is indicated by Mao's instruction on May 16, 1951. Indeed, if petitions are meant only to inform the Party leaders of people's demands and opinions, letters are enough. At the same time, letters can save both the government and petitioners much cost and trouble because mail is both cheap and peaceful. Therefore, the regime consistently advocates letter writing as the main form of petitioning. In the Regulations in 2005, Article 17 still stipulates that ordinarily petitioners usually should address their grievances via mail, e-mail, or fax. Aside from petitioning via mail, moderate and individual "visits" are also acceptable to the authorities. In practice, if there is no attempt to exert pressure on government officials, such "visits" would be treated similarly to petitioning via mail.

Two caveats need to be made here. First, even the desirable forms of petitions are not necessarily welcome by state agents, especially local agents. Indeed, no matter how moderate the complaints are, they are often annoying to local authorities. Nicholas Lampert describes the situation in the Soviet system, "[B]y raising a fuss, and above all by trying to take the complaint outside the organization, they will quickly be seen as troublemakers, as 'scribblers' (*pisaki*) and 'nit-picking critics.'"[38] This is often the case in the Chinese system. Therefore, the desirability of petitioning via mail can only be understood in a relative sense.

Second, petitioning via mail does not necessarily exclude collective action, because some letters are jointly signed. Therefore, some letters, particularly joint letters, may still exact considerable pressure on the authorities. However, to the regime this form of collective action is still much more preferable to delivering petitions in person. Article 12 of the

[38] Nicholas Lampert, *Whistle Blowing in the Soviet Union*, p. 117.

Regulations in 1995 therefore stipulates that when many people want to express their common opinions, suggestions, and demands, they should usually take the form of letters or phone calls.

Even though this system prefers some performances to others, it has a big problem: It does not reward the preferred performances. On the contrary, it rewards undesirable ones. So it is no surprise that petitioners are often tempted to engage in some undesirable performances. There are four common types of such performances: skip-level petitioning, repetitive petitioning, collective petitioning, and disruptive petitioning.

Skip-Level Petitioning

The state is in a difficult position to regulate the skip-level petition. On the one hand, the skip-level petition should not be outlawed, because one of the main merits of the xinfang system is that ordinary people can approach upper authorities to redress their grievances. Grassroots authorities are often accused in petitions, and their immediate superiors tend to share common interests with them. Therefore, it is unreasonable to always require petitioners to go to low-level authorities first. Also from the standpoint of the regime, it is necessary for the upper authorities to get information directly from ordinary people to hold local agents accountable.

On the other hand, skip-level petition tends to cause trouble for the regime. The primary concern of the regime is that skip-level petitions will concentrate conflicts, as well as disruptive activities, at political centers. In a centralized system such as China, many important political activities take place in the political centers. One might also suppose that political rituals are of greater significance for the legitimacy of the regime. Therefore, the regime wants to make sure there is no disruption of such ritual political activities. Moreover, political centers also tend to be economic centers, and therefore economic interests are at stake when preventing disruption in big cities. Unfortunately, big cities are especially vulnerable to petitioning activities. As a provincial leader in Hunan pointed out in a conference in 1988, "Cities are different from the countryside. In the cities, the population is concentrated, and information can be conveyed quickly. If one person who takes a piece of cloth with characters on it stands at the gate of the Provincial Government, or if a person wrangles with the guard, immediately dozens of people will gather there to watch."[39]

---

[39] Documents collected from HNPXB.

For these reasons, although the regime can tolerate, or sometimes even welcome, petitioning directly to upper authorities via mail, it has tried very hard to prevent petition activities, especially collective ones, from physically taking place in political centers. Of course, Article 16 of the Regulations attempts to restrict only skip-level petitions delivered in person, not those via mail. This dilemma is nothing new. It has bothered rulers of dozens of dynasties in ancient China. An opening to the capital has to be maintained, but ordinary petitioners must be discouraged from taking their cases to the capital. There has never been a satisfactory solution to this dilemma. [40]

In the 1990s, Hunan Province, among others, experimented with a system of "petitioning level by level." In such measures, the government tries to specify the level to which a petitioner should first resort. Only when the first level fails to redress the problem should the petitioners go to the next level. This type of procedure has also been written into the Regulations in 1995 and 2005. However, such measures could never be strictly carried out. Not only have petitioners refused to observe them, but the state itself has also left much room for exceptions.

In other words, the regime has never decisively outlawed skip-level petitioning. It tries to reduce skip-level petitions mainly by pushing local governments to exert social control. However, the ambiguous attitude of the regime has sometimes caused confusion for local governments. In some areas, local governments even painted slogans along the highways, saying, "Crack down on skip-level petitions!"

Repetitive Petitioning

From the early years after its founding, the xinfang system began to differentiate repeated petitions from first-time petitions. Repetition of petitions has been regarded as a negative sign of ineffectiveness of handling petitions. Of course, this is a problem for the bureaucracy, and not necessarily the petitioners' fault. Therefore, repeating petitions usually has not been treated as illegitimate.

However, the regime is concerned with excessively repetitive petitions, especially those to political centers. In China, many petitioners spent years delivering their petitions. Such petitioners are often designated as long-term petitioners (*laohu*). Even though the regime is wary of *laohu*s, it cannot outlaw them. It has always been acknowledged by the xinfang

[40] Ocko, "I Will Take It All the Way to Beijing."

system that a significant portion of *laohu*s have legitimate claims to make. Indeed, endless repetition of petitions can signal to the authorities the petitioners' credibility and determination. In many cases this is the only way to catch the attention of Party-state leaders. There are many cases in which justice could not be realized until the petitioners struggled for ten years or even longer.

However, the regime has found it necessary to put *laohu*s under control. A speech by the chief of the National Xinfang Bureau in 1987 justified the control of *laohu*s:

> While a majority of petitioning masses really want to report the situations and problems, and observe rules and laws, there are indeed a few petitioners, esp. some *laohu*s, who insist on unreasonable demands, make trouble and cause the government to lose face (*chuchou*), and threaten social order. Some *laohu*s instigated other petitioners to make trouble, compiled and sold lists of central leaders' addresses and car plate numbers, counterfeited central documents, caused shame in front of foreigners, and interfered with the work order of handling petitions.[41]

From the standpoint of the regime, the most disturbing aspect of *laohu*s is not their own claim-making activities, but their impact on other petitioners. Some government documents call *laohu*s "yeast." Others call them "specialized petitioners" (*shangfang zhuanyehu*). Because they have accumulated much information and experience in petitioning, they like to pass on to other petitioners the knowledge concerning how to "make trouble" for the government. Also, because they stay in the cities all the time, they have the potential to organize collective actions among petitioners from different regions.

There is also an additional reason for local governments to be wary of *laohu*s: Repeated petitioning to higher authorities affects evaluation of local government performance. *Laohu*s have been the main source of some strictly controlled forms of petitioning, such as visits to the central authority. For example, a Hunan provincial government document in 1998 indicates that among petitioners who went to Beijing for petitioning that year, 47.3 percent were *laohu*s.

Being listed as *laohu*s is not necessarily a bad thing for the petitioners because this often implies unusual concessions by the government. Local governments are required to take a much more flexible stance to meet *laohu*s' demands. In 1987, the Hunan provincial government specified its policy toward handling *laohu*s' petitions: (1) their cases should be

---

[41] Documents collected from HNPXB, 2002.

reviewed again no matter how many times they have been officially settled before; (2) regarding demands that the government had the capacity
to meet, local government should treat them leniently and thoroughly; (3)
for issues where no clear policy can be resorted to, they should be treated
with flexibility with the spirit of general policies.[42] Of course, along with
lenient treatment, most *laohu*s will be put under more stringent control,
and occasionally severely punished.

Collective Petitioning

Likewise, the regime finds it difficult to take a clear and consistent stance
on collective petitioning. Among these undesirable performances, collective petitioning is the biggest concern for the CCP regime. However, as
indicated in the Regulations in 1995, among other official documents, the
regime acknowledges the possibility that many people may legitimately
want to express their opinions and demands together. It does not deny the
legality of collective petitioning unqualifiedly.

In a conference on handling collective petitioning in 1986, a document from the central authorities tried to define the nature of collective petitioning. It clarified the point that collective petitioning could not
be entirely prevented under the "socialist democratic system" in China.
However, it claimed that reporting problems with collective action could
have "very limited positive social effects, but often had very strong negative effects." Specifically, the main problem of collective petitioning is that
it is very easy to be taken advantage of by "vicious people." Obviously,
this stance is quite different from prohibiting collective petitioning outright, although the regime certainly does not encourage or support it.

Although collective action cannot be generally forbidden, the regime
tries to define the boundaries specifically in the form of law. The
Regulations of 1995 stipulated that collective petitions should not be
delivered by more than five representatives. Yet this stipulation has seldom been enforced. Indeed, each year, tens of thousands of petitioning
groups – if not more – violated this norm.

Local officials do not have a good way to deal with those "illegal" petitions. Punishment of every violation is infeasible because they are so common. Refusing to meet the petitioners is inappropriate because it is the
officials' duty to respond to popular demands, especially those that may
affect social stability. The officials' common strategies in dealing with this

---

[42] Documents collected from HNPXB, 2002.

are (1) pretending that there is no violation of the rules or (2) requesting the petitioners to elect no more than five representatives on the spot. The second strategy is smart because it allows petitioners to demonstrate their power by collective action, but at the same time can fulfill the requirement according to the law. Of course, despite the fact that they tolerate such violations of the rule, local officials usually will criticize the petitioners for the violation. In other words, this norm has often been confirmed in words but seldom enforced in action.

Disruptive Petitioning

The CCP regime does not have a problem outlawing disruptive petitioning activities in theory. However, in practice, numerous disruptive petitioning activities have been de facto tolerated. How has the regime defined the boundary between prohibited and tolerated? It sometimes depends on whether the government wants to send a signal to the larger society that such actions will no longer be tolerated. The Chinese government frequently employs selective and exemplary punishments to send such signals. From the viewpoint of ordinary people, however, it is still far from clear what activities will definitely be punished. Indeed, such selective and exemplary punishments are inherently arbitrary for three reasons. First, while some disruptive or illegal activities will be punished, many other similar activities are tolerated. For example, in the same city, blocking bridges has been punished but blocking highways is tolerated. Both tactics violate the law and are disruptive, so why is the government response different? Second, it is more confusing when different areas take different standards. Blocking government entrances or highways was generally tolerated in City Y, but several organizers of the same type of activities were imprisoned or detained in other cities in Hunan in the early 2000s. Third, such punishments are often based on a cumulative effect. For example, a long-term petitioner made various troubles for the government for almost twenty years without being punished, but in 2000, local leaders somehow decided that she was no longer tolerable. Such cases of selective and exemplary punishments actually send confusing signals to the population, and thus look arbitrary. As a rule, arbitrary punishment has not led to conformity to the law, but instead to opportunism in violating the law.

In sum, two points should be underscored here. First, the state has *not* outlawed most of those unwelcome performances. Therefore, such performances still enjoy legitimacy to some extent. Second, the state's attempts to define norms do not always succeed. When petitioners collectively ignore some of its formal norms, the state often concedes. The limit of five participants for collective petitioning is a good example.

WHY IS THE XINFANG SYSTEM INCORRIGIBLE?

With the rise of social protests, the xinfang system has increasingly come under official scrutiny. The Chinese leadership seems to be well aware of the defects in the system, and has therefore made great efforts to reform it in order to promote orderly participation. For instance, it has attempted to enhance the efficiency by improving and standardizing the organizations and procedures so that the system will be less likely to frustrate moderate petitioners; it has formalized the procedures and rules to solve the problems of vague norms; it has also strengthened the mechanisms for local responsibility to make sure that local officials can handle petitions promptly and properly. However, the system seems to be incorrigible. Most of the similar government's efforts have been either futile or counterproductive.

The problems such reforms have sought to solve are deeply rooted in the grand institutional framework of mass line politics. Without changing the framework, such specific adjustments are bound to fail. The preceding discussion of vague norms has illuminated this point. Similarly, the efforts to improve the organization of the xinfang system have hardly attained their goal. As the xinfang agencies started to assume heavier and more important duties since the rise of collective action in the 1990s, the CCP tried to promote their status and authority to some extent. A common assumption in the xinfang system is that if xinfang agencies have enough authority, they can efficiently handle many less important cases independently, and can thus relieve the leaders of much of their burden.

The Hunan provincial government in fact decided to elevate the rank of officials in the xinfang bureau by half a level. Consequently, the bureau chief enjoys the same rank as the directors of other provincial departments. However, even such equal status is still not high enough to coordinate and supervise other agencies. So they still have to rely heavily on the leadership, and the leaders still have to play an important role in responding to protests.

Another improvement is that, since the late 1990s, xinfang bureau chiefs have been concurrently appointed as the deputy secretary generals of the government at the county, city, and provincial levels.[43] It should be noted, however, that these measures only enhance the status of xinfang cadres rather than of xinfang bureaus. Why not substantially empower the xinfang bureaus, as some Chinese scholars have suggested? The reason is simple: The dependence of xinfang agencies on the leaders is deliberately designed. Xinfang agencies are not created to substitute for leaders, but to assist them.

The Chinese government has also experimented with some new channels and procedures, such as the "leader's hotline" and "leader reception days," to enhance efficiency. Such experiments promised to provide an opportunity for ordinary people to directly contact their leaders. Not surprisingly, they have made little difference. Those "hotlines" are operated by low-rank officials who can only relay information to leaders, because it is impossible for major leaders to answer phone calls all day. Therefore, this channel faces the same procedural barriers as the ordinary xinfang channel. Only a tiny portion of the cases can catch local leaders' personal attention; most others will be handled by powerless officials.[44] Likewise, leader reception days will also be faced with the problem of overwhelming demands if local leaders take the procedure seriously. Then the question arises again how cases can be differentiated in a way that does not encourage "troublemaking" activities.

Another, more promising reform is to reduce the role of the xinfang system and shift most dispute-related petitions to the legal system. Since the legal reform began in the early 1980s, there has been very impressive progress in the institution building of the judicial system. Not only have the judicial apparatus and procedures been improved and strengthened, but the notion of "the rule by law" or "the rule of law" has also become more prevalent. Thus C. K. Lee claims that law has become a new official ideology in China.[45] Given that the xinfang system is widely regarded as a symbol of "the rule by men," it is believed it will be replaced by a formal

---

[43] It seems that this is a measure that was adopted nationwide. In Zhejiang Province, for example, all xinfang bureau chiefs at the city and county level had been concurrently appointed as deputy secretary general or deputy director of the general office before the end of 2001. See *Zhejiang Nianjian* (Zhejiang Yearbook) (Hangzhou: Zhejiang Nianjian Bianweihui, 2002), p. 72.

[44] There are many articles in Chinese media to cover the failure of "hotlines." For example, see *Gongren Ribao*, "Rexian De Lengyu: Bufen Chengshi 'Shizhang Dianhua' Anfangji" (The Cold Experience of Hotlines: A Covert Investigation of 'Mayor Hotlines' in Some Cities), *Gongren Ribao* (Workers' Daily), June 13, 2005.

[45] C. K. Lee, *Against the Law: Labor Protests in China's Rustbelt and Sunbelt* (Berkeley and Los Angeles: University of California Press, 2007), p. 27.

legal system sooner or later. In fact, however, the position of the xinfang system has not been weakened, but rather substantially strengthened. An analysis of the incentive structure herein for both the regime and ordinary people sheds light on this puzzle.

Let us first take a look at the pros and cons of the judicial system as compared with the xinfang system from the standpoint of Party leaders. Almost all undesirable activities that have been involved in the xinfang system are less likely to take place in the ideal-type judicial process. First, because judicial procedures are supposed to be more formal and independent, collective and disruptive activities would not have much impact on such decisions. Consequently, ordinary people are less tempted to engage in them. Secondly, the strict procedures in the judicial system can largely eliminate the problem of skip-level and repetitive appeals. When a final decision has been made, the disputing parties normally cannot challenge them. Therefore, the judicial system can help relieve the administrative powers of much of the burden of conflict resolution. Even though the judiciary in China is not very independent, it still enjoys these two advantages over the xinfang system, to a degree.

However, from Party leaders' point of view, the judicial system also has some clear disadvantages. First, its capacity is limited. This is not just because its institutions are still underdeveloped. More importantly, a relatively autonomous judiciary cannot mobilize many resources to tackle social problems. The CCP has been particularly good at mobilizing necessary resources throughout the political system to attack difficult tasks. This campaign style has survived the Maoist era even though political campaigns have been formally renounced as a main governing tool, and a specialized judiciary seems to be at odds with this approach. The weakness of the judiciary is especially evident when dealing with highly contentious issues. The CCP often requires a variety of public agencies to get involved to effectively solve such problems. Thus, courts have often been discouraged to accept cases involving confrontational social protests.

Its second perceived disadvantage is that judicial considerations are not always consistent with political considerations. Consequently, whereas Party leaders have no interest in getting involved in many ordinary cases, they are tempted to intervene in a few cases that have political significance. For example, if local authorities believe enforcement of a judicial decision will cause social unrest, they may request a halt in enforcement.

Such an incentive structure has influenced CCP leaders' strategy: on the one hand, they encourage the judicial system to play a bigger role in conflict resolution; on the other hand, administrative powers reserve the right to intervene in cases where significant political interests are at stake. From the early stages of the Reform Era, the CCP leaders in fact began to support the expansion of the judicial system's role for conflict resolution. In the early 1980s, Hu Yaobang, General Secretary of the CCP, pointed out that the regime should try to let judicial organs handle more cases. In 1989, Wen Jiabao, Director of the General Office of the CCP, requested that xinfang agencies not handle cases that should be handled by judicial and law enforcement organs. Premier Zhu Rongji expressed a similar view about ten years later, "for the problems that are supposed to be handled by the judicial organs, [the xinfang bureaus] should instruct the petitioners to report to the judicial organs so that such problems can be resolved by means of law. The more institutionalized and legalized channels have more direct and quicker effect than the xinfang channel."[46]

At the same time, Party-state leaders insist that in the present situation the xinfang system can only be strengthened, not weakened. For example, Vice Premier Tian Jiyun said in 1987 that xinfang work is an important and long-term task. At present, it can only be strengthened, not weakened.[47] Such a statement can be heard many times in leaders' speeches throughout the Reform Era.

When significant political interests are at stake, administrative powers do not hesitate to intervene with the judicial process. Indeed, there is hardly any limit to its intervention. It can influence the acceptance, decision, and enforcement of a decision of a case. As Ying Xing has nicely argued, while in the United States even political issues can be taken to court, in China every judicial issue can be decided by administrative power.[48] Party and government intervention has unfortunately become even more common since the mid-2000s.

Of course, the choice between courts and the xinfang system is not entirely up to the state to decide. If ordinary people persistently choose the xinfang system over the courts, the xinfang system has to handle such conflicts. Therefore, ordinary people's incentives for choosing these two channels also need to be examined here.

From the standpoint of ordinary people, the xinfang system has several advantages: (1) it is cheap, and possibly quick; 2) it can be more effective

---

[46] Deng Shuisong and Fang Tengsheng, "Shixing Youxu Fenliu, Zuohao Xinfang Gongzuo" (Differentiating cases orderly and doing xinfang work well), *Mishu Zhiyou* (Friends of Secretaries), 7 (2000), p. 465.

[47] A document collected from CYXB, 2002.

[48] Ying, Xing, *Dahe Yimin Shangfang De Gushi* (The Story of the Petitioning of the Migrants in Dahe Town) (Beijing: Sanlian Press, 2002).

in enforcement than the judiciary; (3) it does not have strict requirements on evidence; (4) it does not have limits on jurisdiction, that is, any issues can possibly be taken up; and (5) it is possible to influence results with demonstrations of power. All of these advantages are significant for some people, especially some disadvantaged groups.

Of course the judicial system also has some advantages. Every case that meets legal requirements will be accepted and be heard in a formal procedure. By contrast, a majority of cases addressed to the xinfang system cannot get a substantial response at all. Moreover, engaging in litigation will usually have no personal risk, whereas collective petitioning may be subject to possible repression. Finally, if their cases win, the remedy by the courts is usually more sufficient, even though the decisions sometimes are not enforced. The xinfang system, in contrast, can seldom fully meet petitioners' demands even if their claims are valid. Usually both the state and petitioners have to make some compromise therein.

Each institution has its advantages, so ordinary people need to decide which method to use according to their specific situations. Of course, they do not have to choose only one. In many cases, people choose both at the same time or one after another. It is thus very likely that the xinfang system will continue to be used as a primary institution for conflict resolution for a long time. Many Chinese people who cannot or are unwilling to afford legal fees, who cannot bear long judicial procedures, who have not collected enough evidence in their transactions, who believe in the supreme capacity of administrative power, whose cases cannot be taken up by the courts for various reasons, and, most importantly, who have a capacity for collective action will therefore regard the xinfang system as the more advantageous choice.

In sum, within the centralized system of mass line politics, the Chinese state and protesters are still strongly attached to the xinfang system. Absent a radical overhaul of the political system, it is hard to imagine that a large number of social conflicts will shift from the xinfang system to the judiciary. Incremental reforms of the xinfang system tend to be futile because it is deeply entrenched in mass line politics, which remains a pillar of the political system.

WHY ARE SOME INSTITUTIONAL ADJUSTMENTS COUNTERPRODUCTIVE?

A number of efforts of procedural adjustments have focused on strengthening the responsibility of local governments for demobilizing collective petitioners. In such a highly centralized system for political consultation, as discussed earlier, there is a strong tendency for popular claim-making activities to move to the power center. Political centers, such as Beijing and each provincial capital, are faced with the formidable task of social control. Therefore, a basic principle of the regime is to "rather have disorders in localities than in the center." The most important measure is to clarify and strengthen local officials' responsibilities, because it is top-down pressure that ultimately provides local officials with incentives to work hard and properly handle social protest. However, such reforms have largely been counterproductive; they have provided petitioners an even stronger incentive to stage collective action with troublemaking tactics.

Speedy Information Flow

The xinfang system has set up procedures for reporting urgent information since the mid-1990s. Such requirements serve two purposes. First, the upper-level authorities will be better prepared if such events escalated into more violent or skip-level petitioning. Second, this can exert pressure on local officials to take petitions seriously.

The government stipulated a series of issues that local governments must report to the leaders at the same and upper levels.[49] In Hunan Province, "must report" issues include: (1) collective petitioning with participants of more than 50 people that have been addressed to the county government or above; (2) potential collective petitioning activities with more than 100 people; (3) information about collective petitioning events to the provincial government or Beijing; and (4) events that evolved from ordinary petitioning to "erupting mass incidents" (*tufaxing qunti shijian*) that have disrupted normal work, production, business, and daily order. The first three should be reported within the same day, and the fourth should be reported instantly. The report should include the time, location, number of participants, forms of action, the claims, government responses, and the trend (*dongtai*). When necessary, the local xinfang bureau should send follow-up reports.

Screening "Elements of Instability"

With the surge of social protest, the xinfang system has tried to enforce more effective surveillance of protest organizers. There are two types

[49] State Council, Regulations on Letters and Visits, 2005.

of primary targets: long-term petitioners (*laohu*) and collective petition organizers. Before the rise of collective petitions, long-term petitioners were the primary targets.

Every xinfang bureau above the county level periodically designates some persistent petitioners as "long-term" petitioners, and makes a list for each of the lower levels of government. When the lower-level agencies receive the list, they must implement some "stabilizing" measures and report the result after a certain period. These lists are refreshed, and some *laohu*s have been stabilized while some new persistent petitioners have emerged. To illustrate how this procedure works, we can take a look at a report by the Hunan Provincial Bureau to the National Xinfang Bureau in response to a list distributed in July 1997. This report describes how the Hunan Provincial Bureau had handled certain *laohu*s:

> Up to the end of September, among the 129 *laohu*s who petitioned to Beijing, fifty-two have been stabilized by relieving their difficulties further and with more flexible [favorable] measures. For another forty-one who insisted on unreasonable demands even though their issues had been dealt with, we have done thought stabilizing work again and also strengthened control and education measures. For the other thirty-six *laohu*s, we are still working on them.[50]

Since the mid-1990s, the primary target has shifted to collective petitioners. Although the xinfang system still compiles lists of *laohu*s, nowadays it has started to pay more attention to collective petitioners. Xinfang agencies have begun to periodically compile lists of "instability factors" shortly before important occasions: the New Year Day and the Spring Festival, the "Two Conferences," the National Day, and so on. This is because it is generally believed that collective petitions are more likely to take place on such occasions and will also have a relatively greater impact on society during such periods. Therefore, local governments have often designated such moments as "specially protected periods" (*tebuqi*). In some years, xinfang agencies were especially busy when there were many important occasions. In 1999, for example, besides regular "important periods," there were some other special events when collective petitioning activities should be strictly prevented: the crackdown of Falungong, the tenth anniversary of the crackdown on the Student Movement, the turnover of Macau to China, and the fiftieth anniversary of the founding of the PRC. In that year, the city bureau and seven

[50] Documents collected from HNPXB.

county-level bureaus in City Y compiled 43 lists, in which they identified 739 "instability factors."

Screening "instability factors" is not temporary work. The xinfang system tried to institutionalize it as a standard procedure. It was thus written into the Regulations on Letters and Visits in 2005. Such a practice is remarkable in that those petitioning groups who have demonstrated a high capacity and/or tendency to stage collective action can maintain pressure on local governments even without actually carrying out collective action.

Responsibility for Demobilization

The Chinese government has also tried to clarify local government responsibility for demobilization. Local officials will be sanctioned if they fail to effectively monitor or confine protest organizers, or intercept and bring back petitioners to higher authorities.

After having identified "elements of instability," xinfang agencies will coordinate relevant agencies to implement surveillance, and, if necessary, impose confinement on activists. As analyzed in the previous chapter, with the decline of the work unit system, this work has become much more difficult to carry out than before. A common practice is the so-called "five-to-one" or "four-to-one" procedure, which requires four or five state agents to be responsible for controlling one designated target. These agents usually are a combination of a local leader (for example, deputy town or district head), a local police officer, a residential cadre, and a work unit leader. Besides surveillance, local governments sometimes implement some form of confinement, such as house arrest. They usually try to implement such measures in a legal way, although this is not always feasible. In some cases, local cadres in City Y not only watched the activists during the daytime, but also even slept in their homes at night.[51] Officials in other areas tried a variety of unusual methods to control activists. For example, in Hunan Province, local officials reportedly tried to get activists drunk by enticing them with delicacies.[52]

When collective or some individual petitioning activities take place in the location of higher authorities, or on their way to upper authorities, local governments are required to promptly intercept them or bring the

---

[51] Interview, September 2002. Similar measures were taken by Beijing authorities in 2005 when they tried to prevent continuing anti-Japanese demonstrations.
[52] Wang Amin, "Yiwei Xiafang Ganbu De Kunhuo" (The Puzzlement of a Cadre Who Visited the Grassroots), *Liaowang*, no. 14 (2005).

petitioners back. A case in District HS of City Y illustrates this responsibility very well. In 2000, thirty-nine workers who contracted shop floors at a major local department store came to the city government at 9:40 in the morning to protest against a reform policy affecting the department store. After listening to their petitions, as is standard practice, the xinfang cadres notified the district general office and the xinfang bureau, requesting them to send a district leader and other officials from relevant departments. However, no one was dispatched by the district government for six hours. The city xinfang bureau contacted the district government five times. It was not until the City bureau chief called the deputy magistrate of the district at 4 PM that the district finally dispatched two vice directors of the District Supply and Marketing Cooperative and a vice manager of the department store. Because these three officials did not have enough authority to give petitioners an authoritative promise, petitioners, feeling unsatisfied, stayed in the city government office until 9:40 PM.

Afterward, the xinfang bureau, under the name of the City Leading Group of the Xinfang Work, issued a public denunciation of the district government for its failure to respond promptly and sufficiently. The denunciation specifically mentioned that the ranks of the officials dispatched by the district government were too low for effective bargaining. This case illustrates the responsibility of the local government for preventing collective petitioning to upper authorities or bringing back protesters. To effectively fulfill this duty, local officials with decision-making power should be promptly dispatched, because protests can seldom be demobilized without a negotiation. In recent years, this norm has been clarified and entrenched in routine practice in many local governments. For petitioners who have almost no hope of catching the attention of power holders through moderate activities, collective action with "troublemaking" tactics is certainly tempting.

In sum, some institutional and procedural adjustments purported to reduce popular collective action have nevertheless provided more favorable conditions and stronger incentives for collective action. When "troublemaking" petitioners are further differentiated from moderate petitioners, and obtain a more privileged status, local governments are under strong pressure to buy them off. At the same time, enhanced scrutiny by upper authorities further constrains local officials' use of coercive force. Upper authorities are generally less approving of high-handed measures and more supportive of comprehensive solutions. Local officials are therefore under greater pressure to solve the problems rather than just temporarily crack down on protests.

INSTITUTIONAL CONVERSION AND POLITICAL OPPORTUNITY

After a long analysis of the xinfang system, we are now ready to explain why and how it can be converted to a facilitative institution for popular contention. This conversion is based on two preconditions – institutional amphibiousness and changes in institutional configurations – and it has been achieved through the mechanism of social appropriation and government response.

Amphibiousness

One favorable condition for institutional conversion is institutional amphibiousness, a term coined by X. L. Ding.[53] By institutional amphibiousness, Ding means that the nature of individual institutions is indeterminate. As he describes it, "An institution can be used for purposes contrary to those it is supposed to fulfill, and the same institution can simultaneously serve conflicting purposes."[54] The examples he gives include such organizations as trade unions, youth associations, and women's organizations. According to Ding, these organizations "bore a strong resemblance to voluntary associations in liberal democracies but were actually pre-emptive organizations." They were set up both to serve "the regime's mobilization goals and ... [in particular, to inhibit] the formation of private loyalties."[55]

Whereas Ding applies this concept mainly to "mass organizations," institutional amphibiousness can be found in a wide range of government agencies, too. The official media, for instance, is notably amphibious. Although it is designed to be a mouthpiece of the Party-state, it also reports ordinary people's opinions and reveals misconduct by state agents. It is not surprising, therefore, that the mass media briefly adopted an openly oppositional and exhortative role during the 1989 student movement.[56]

Amphibiousness is best treated like a variable. Not every state institution is amphibious, and some institutions bear this trait more than others.

[53] X. L. Ding, "Institutional Amphibiousness and the Transition from Communism: The Case of China," *British Journal of Political Science* 24 (1994), 293–318.
[54] Ibid., p. 298.
[55] Ibid., p. 298.
[56] Andrew Walder, "Collective Protest and the Waning of the Communist State in China," in Michael Hanagan et al. (eds.), *Challenging Authority: The Historical Study of Contentious Politics* (Minneapolis: University of Minnesota Press, 1998), p. 71.

Institutions of interest articulation in state socialist regimes tend to be more amphibious; in contrast, the function of the army, police, and Party propaganda apparatus is more clearly defined and therefore they have lower levels of or no amphibiousness.

Amphibiousness is an enduring or even permanent feature of some state institutions. The official trade union in socialist countries is a case in point. Under state socialism, an official trade union sometimes shifts between the role of a "transmission belt" and that of a corporatist organization. Jonathan Unger and Anita Chan observe that, even in Stalin and Mao's era, when the peak trade union was charged only with disseminating central directives, it still allowed for articulation of grassroots rights and interests, especially during periods of liberalization. This is an important reason why Mao finally decided to dissolve the labor union during the Cultural Revolution.[57] During the student movement of 1989, the All-China Federation of Trade Unions once again played a significant part in facilitating contention.[58]

In the case of the xinfang system, Chinese petitioners tend to appropriate the xinfang system to stage collective action with "troublemaking" tactics mainly because of: (1) the low efficacy of normal petitioning and preferential treatment of "troublemaking" tactics; (2) the government's ambiguous attitude toward the legitimacy of "troublemaking" tactics; and (3) officials' pressure on subordinates to maintain social stability. These three factors are built-in features of the xinfang system. In this sense, this system is amphibious by its design. Most reforms aimed at changing the structure have failed.

However, contradictions and ambiguities are not necessarily favorable to the subordinate classes. In history, most dictatorial regimes featured arbitrary rules, which were full of contradictions and ambiguities, and this only made the rulers even more tyrannical. By themselves, contradictions and ambiguities can work to the advantage of either the rulers or the ruled. Only under certain conditions can such contradictions and ambiguities provide political opportunity for popular resistance.

In the case of the xinfang system, changes in institutional configuration and the appropriation-reaction mechanism are also indispensable for realizing the potential of institutional conversion. An institution

---

[57] Jonathan Unger and Anita Chan, "China, Corporatism, and the East Asian Model," *Australian Journal of Chinese Affairs* 33 (January 1995), p. 37.

[58] Elizabeth J. Perry, "Casting a 'Democracy' Movement: The Roles of Students, Workers, and Entrepreneurs," in Jeffery N. Wasserstrom and Elizabeth J. Perry (eds.), *Popular Protest and Political Culture in Modern China* (Boulder, CO: Westview, 1992), p. 159.

functions differently when it is located in a different institutional configuration. This has also been emphasized as an important condition in McAdam's study of the conversion of Black churches. In his case, changes in social, economic, and political institutions, such as the rapid urbanization of Blacks from the 1930s to the 1950s, came together to make social appropriation possible.[59]

Changes in Institutional Configurations

The xinfang system has operated in a dramatically different institutional setting since the 1990s. Chapter 3 discussed two of the most important institutional changes that substantially impacted how the xinfang system functions: the decline of unit systems and the increase of divisions within the state structure.

Under the unit system model, state agents at the grassroots level fulfilled the function of surveillance, sanction, and containment. Because such a system features long and dense interactions between ordinary people and state agents within a very limited space, surveillance is usually prevalent and effective. Also, the "organized dependence" of ordinary people on their work units makes sanctions formidable. As analyzed in Chapter 3, with the unit system, the Party-state effectively prevented most defiant activities. Contradictions and ambiguities of mass line politics have only reinforced the arbitrary power of grassroots state agents.

The unit system did not work in isolation. There were a variety of other institutions that worked with it to maintain social control: the food rationing system in urban areas, the system of custody and repatriation, and the railway system. All these apparatuses served to limit social mobility, especially population flow from rural to urban areas. None of them were specially instituted to constrain petitioning activities, but all of them worked very effectively for this purpose. The food-rationing system was created in the early 1950s and began to be extensively used during the extreme economic difficulty shortly after the GLF to limit consumption of food and other important consumer goods, as well as to restrict population flow from rural to urban areas.[60] Because peasants were unable to support themselves in the city, petitioning in person to political centers became extremely difficult. To maintain a balance between controlling

---

[59] Doug McAdam, *Political Process and the Development of Black Insurgency, 1930–1970* (Chicago: University of Chicago Press, 1982).

[60] Kenneth Lieberthal, *Governing China* (New York: W. W. Norton, 1995), p. 109.

and facilitating petitions, the government provided some remedies for petitioners conditionally so that petitioning to political centers was still possible. For instance, the State Council and the Bureaus of Food in Beijing instituted policies to provide subsidies and rationing coupons to petitioners in 1958 and 1960. Later on, the city of Beijing established a service center where petitioners in extreme economic difficulty could obtain free board and lodging.[61] However, such measures not only facilitated some petitioning activities, but also helped control them because petitioners' reliance on such services made social control much easier.

The system of custody and repatriation was formally instituted in 1982, but a less formal system was in effect as early as the 1950s. Like the rationing system, it also served as a barrier for population flow into the cities. This system was managed by the bureaus (ministry) of civil affairs. Although formally it was designed to expel vagrants and beggars, it has been used to control and expel two other types of individuals: petitioners and peasant laborers.[62] This system worked effectively as a coercive tool until it was abolished in 2003, when an incident of abuse caused the death of Sun Zhigang, a college graduate who worked in Guangzhou, which aroused enormous public opinion pressure to abolish the system.

Even the railway system also worked as a tool for social control before the 1990s, because most Chinese petitioners went to provincial capitals or Beijing by railway. For the first four and half decades or so after 1949, buying train tickets required introduction letters issued by work units or People's Communes. In this way, the railway system worked with work units for the purpose of social control. In the Reform Era, it has still been used to control petitioning activities, but less frequently and less effectively.[63]

Along some important railway lines, the government set up some "dissuasion stations" (*quanzu zhan*). Such stations were even formally included in the xinfang system. In a national conference on controlling collective petitioning to Beijing in 1986, the dissuasion stations in Shenyang City and Tianjin City were invited, along with the Ministries of Public Security and Railways, as well as xinfang bureaus in thirteen provinces and the cities.[64]

[61] Diao, *Renmin Xinfang Shilue*, pp. 150–155.
[62] Xu Zhiyong, Guo Yushan and Li Yingqiang, "Xianzheng Shiye Zhong De Xinfang Zhili" (Regulating Xinfang from the Perspective of Constitutionalism, http://www.yannan.cn/data/detail.php?id=7453, last visited on Sept. 15, 2005.
[63] Yu Jianrong, "Zhongguo Xinfang Zhidu Pipan" (Critique of Chinese letters and visits system), a speech at Beijing University, www.yannan.com, Dec 6, 2004.
[64] Diao, *Renmin Xinfang Shilue*, p. 298.

Work units no longer structure life to the extent they once did, rationing disappeared in the 1980s, and the custody and repatriation system was abolished in 2003. This wave of transformation created considerable challenges for state control of petitioning.

The other institutional change that has benefited petitioners recently derives from increased divisions and differentiations within the state structure. Differing interests between upper and lower authorities have always existed in China. However, as discussed in Chapter 3, bureaucratic differentiations and divisions have substantially increased in recent years.[65] In this situation, the xinfang system's function of holding local officials accountable has often led to coalitions between petitioners and upper authorities, thereby encouraging collective action directed against rogue officials at the grassroots.

In broad terms, the xinfang system operated under two quite different institutional configurations: (1) the xinfang system + the unit system and associated institutions + low bureaucratic differentiations and divisions; and (2) the xinfang system + the decline of the unit system and associated institutions + high bureaucratic differentiations and divisions. Under the second configuration, the potential for the xinfang system to facilitate collective action has been enhanced substantially.

The Appropriation-Response Mechanism

Studies of contentious politics have recently isolated an important mechanism: institutional appropriation. This is a mechanism through which social actors convert or incorporate existing organizations or institutions for their own purposes. Institutions can be appropriated not only from outside, but also from within. X. L. Ding argues that this pattern was at work in the spring of 1989. At this moment, "because of the political orientation or personal connections of those working within, institutional structures were manipulated, becoming means for protest and

[65] See, for example, Wang Shaoguang, "The Rise of the Regions: Fiscal Reform and the Decline of Central State Capacity in China," in Andrew Walder (ed.), *The Waning of the Communist State* (Berkeley: University of California Press, 1995), pp. 87–113; Andrew Walder, "The Decline of Communist Power: Elements of a Theory of Institutional Change," *Theory and Society* 23/2 (1994), pp. 297–323; Dali Yang, "Reform and the Restructuring of Central-Local Relations," in David S. G. Goodman and Gerald Segal (eds.), *China Deconstructs: Politics, Trade, and Regionalism* (London: Routledge, 1994), pp. 59–98; Richard Baum and Alexei Shevchenko, "The 'State of the State,'" in Merle Goldman and Roderick MacFarquhar (eds.), *The Paradox of China's Post-Mao Reforms* (Cambridge, MA: Harvard University Press, 1999), pp. 333–360.

opposition."[66] Although he calls such a mechanism "manipulation," it is essentially a form of institutional appropriation.

Indeed, institutional appropriation is a sensible choice for people who are unable or unwilling to create resources on their own. However, social appropriation by itself is seldom sufficient to account for the dynamics or trajectory of mobilization for at least two reasons. First, it does not explain success at some times and failure at others. Institutional amphibiousness creates favorable conditions for appropriation, but at most times this potential will not be realized. Second, appropriation is usually only one element of state-society interactions. State agents will usually respond to such attempts quite forcefully. In his discussion of protest in rural China, O'Brien describes how local cadres tried to overcome peasants' efforts to use law and state policies to press claims: "Many cadres use these conflicting norms and expectations to make rightful resisters appear unreasonable and to justify not implementing a popular measure or institutional protection ... [therefore] a strong legal case and the use of compelling normative language is merely the ante for rightful resistance."[67]

In the case of the xinfang system, state responses have not overcome social appropriation. On the contrary, they have further encouraged such efforts by exerting higher pressure on local officials to engage in contentious bargaining and avoid escalation of disruption. This in turn will lead to more efforts to appropriate the system. Thus we find that it is the appropriation-response mechanism as a whole that contributes to institutional conversion.

Finally, it should be noted that institutional conversion is not limited to the xinfang system. There are a number of official channels and agencies that have been or will be converted into instruments for popular contention. Notable channels include the court system, the labor mediation and management system, and the official media. Among public or semipublic agencies, the most likely ones include some mass organizations such as official labor unions and the Federation for Disabled people. A conversion of those channels and agencies will further contribute to prevalent contentious bargaining.

---

[66] Ding, "Institutional Amphibiousness," p. 306.
[67] Kevin J. O'Brien, "Rightful Resistance," *World Politics* 49/1 (October 1996), p. 43.

PROTEST STRATEGIES AND TACTICS

5

Between Defiance and Obedience

The two chapters in Part II have identified a particular institutional configuration that have facilitated and shaped popular protests in China. In Part III, my focus will shift from structure to agency. Despite the obvious importance of structures in explaining historical change, they can only constitute part of the story. As William Sewell remarks, "Structure forms the capacities and provides the resources necessary for human agency, enabling humans to reproduce themselves and their social world, but also enabling them to act in innovative ways and therefore occasionally to modify the very structures that shaped them."[1] Similarly, Doug McAdam argues, "Movements may largely be born of environmental opportunities, but their fate is heavily shaped by their own actions."[2] This and the following chapters thus focus on protesters' strategies and tactics. Indeed, given that the political opportunity structure identified in this book puts a special emphasis on contradictions and ambiguities, protesters' strategic decisions deserve a particularly important role in the explanations.

Ordinary people are often faced with a dilemma in their contentious interactions with an authoritarian state. To enhance their bargaining power, they need to employ some sort of "troublemaking" tactics such as engaging in disruptive activities or forming autonomous organizations.

---

[1] William H. Sewell, "Space in Contentious Politics," in Ronald R. Aminzade et al. (eds.), *Silence and Voice in the Study of Contentious Politics* (New York: Cambridge University Press, 2001), p. 55.

[2] Doug McAdam, "Conceptual Origins, current Problems, Future Directions," in Doug McAdam, John D. McCarthy, and Mayer N. Zald (eds.), *Comparative Perspectives on Social Movements: Political Opportunities, Mobilizing Structures, and Cultural Framings* (New York: Cambridge University Press, 1996), p. 15.

However, if they go too far, radical tactics may not only alienate their supporters, but also incur state repression.[3] The choice between efficacy and safety appears as a trade-off, and it is very difficult to attain both at the same time. Yet ordinary people sometimes manage to engage in resistance while somehow remaining submissive. Their most common strategy is what James Scott calls "everyday forms of resistance:" Ordinary people carry out *covert* and *individualized* resistance while feigning obedience. Can ordinary people also mount *public* and *collective* resistance while remaining submissive? Rarely. Yet there are some cases, and China since the 1990s is one of them.

A remarkable aspect of the surge in social protests is the fact that most of these collective actions, even when they involve confrontational tactics, are still generally perceived as essentially submissive rather than rebellious.[4] How have Chinese petitioners achieved the difficult task of maintaining a balance between defiance and obedience?

This chapter describes and explains this paradoxical aspect of protest tactics in today's China, which I refer to as "protest opportunism." It is "opportunism" in that protesters do not take a principled or consistent position toward being either obedient or defiant, and they are ready to employ any tactics they think useful. As this chapter shows, Chinese protesters have a strong tendency to operate close to authorized channels and to take dramatic actions to demonstrate their obedience. At the same time, when they find them useful, they are ready to engage in very troubling activities from the viewpoint of government officials: staging large-scale, public, and disruptive protests, establishing cross-sector ties, or forming semiautonomous or autonomous organizations. They can pursue both strategies at the same time or shift from one to another freely.

Scholars have noted that popular collective action in Reform-Era China has a tendency to operate near the boundary of authorized channels. Kevin O'Brien and Lianjiang Li's concept of "rightful resistance" offers important insights into this point. They highlight three key elements of "rightful resistance:" (1) it operates near the boundary of an authorized channel; (2) it employs the rhetoric and commitments of the powerful

---

[3] For a comparison of advantages of radical and moderate protest strategies, see Ann-Marie Szymanski, *Pathways to Prohibition: Radicals, Moderates and Social Movement Outcomes* (Durham, NC: Duke University Press, 2003).

[4] This can be illustrated by the Chinese term to describe such actions – visits (*shangfang*). Meaning citizens' visits to government, this type of collective action clearly differs from rebellious action.

to curb political or economic power; and (3) it hinges on locating and exploiting divisions among the powerful.[5]

The concept of "rightful resistance" is confined to moderate forms of collective action. As O'Brien and Li note, "rightful resisters stop short of violence" and "in its basic form, rightful resistance is a rather tame form of contention that makes use of existing (if clogged) channels of participation and relies heavily on the patronage of elite backers."[6]

However, social protests in China have sometimes been quite confrontational. It is not rare for angry protesters to assault government officials or damage government property. Even many nonviolent protests have been very disruptive. A blockade of a main bridge can paralyze a big city for half a day or even longer. Indeed, Chinese protesters have usually behaved as "opportunistic troublemakers." They do not have to shy away from confrontational activities, although they often balance such activities with action or statements demonstrating their obedience. In a sense, the concept of protest opportunism more accurately describes an important aspect of the orientation of collective petitioners in China.

The particular orientation of social protests as captured by the term "protest opportunism" did not emerge until the 1990s. To be sure, there has been a long tradition of Chinese petitioners employing opportunistic "troublemaking" tactics to press their claims on the authorities. In the imperial era, for example, petitioners occasionally tried to commit suicide or block officials' sedan chairs when delivering petitions. Although many of these tactics were often quite dramatic, they mostly remained individual activities, and the disruption they caused was rather limited. Therefore, the tension between defiance and submission was not as great as in today's collective petitioning.

This orientation is in fact a product of a unique political opportunity structure that emerged in the 1990s. As analyzed in Chapters 3 and 4, a particular configuration of political and social institutions in this period transformed the behaviors of government officials and ordinary people. The CCP's mass line – and, in particular, its xinfang system – have the potential to inadvertently facilitate and encourage popular collective action. This potential was realized when the unit system model was being replaced by the government-citizen model and when the divisions within the state structure increased concurrently. Consequently, local officials'

---

[5] Kevin J. O'Brien, "Rightful Resistance," *World Politics* 49/1 (October 1996), p. 33.
[6] Ibid. p. 34; Kevin O'Brien and Lianjiang Li, *Rightful Resistance in Rural China* (New York: Cambridge University Press, 2006), p. 68.

ability to repress protesters tends to be severely constrained, and expedient concessions are often their only sensible choice. At the same time, procrastination has become the predominant strategy, with repression, persuasion, and the granting of concessions all serving as specific forms of procrastination.

These changes in state strategies in turn have had a significant impact on protest behavior, contributing to the rise of public, collective, and disruptive popular resistance. The relative decline in repression emboldened protesters, expedient concessions encouraged troublemaking, and procrastination drove people to disruptive troublemaking to counter government foot-dragging.

However, although there is considerable space for troublemaking activities, the threat of state repression still hangs like the sword of Damocles over the heads of protesters. Even though the Chinese state began extensive legal reforms more than two decades ago, it still relies mainly on selective and exemplary punishments, which are inherently arbitrary, to deter disruptive collective action. Consequently, while Chinese petitioners find it necessary to maintain obedience, they also understand that a large number of illegal activities are tolerated de facto. Therefore, such arbitrary punishment has led not to passivity, but to an opportunistic approach to the law.

FOUR CASES

To illustrate how the political opportunity structure has translated into specific popular behavior, and how Chinese petitioners have maintained a balance between defiance and obedience, I will examine the protest strategies of four petitioning groups that engaged in extensive contentious interactions with the government in City Y. For the sake of convenience and confidentiality, I refer to these four groups as A, B, C, and D. Group A is a group of disabled people residing in the urban area. Group B consists of more than a dozen cadres of a branch company of the City Y Supply and Marketing Cooperative. Group C are retired workers at a state-owned factory that employs about 1,000 workers. Group D is composed of dozens of demobilized army officers, including staff and workers in state-owned or collective enterprises, and some peasants.

These four groups are different from each other in many aspects: the group size, their claims, the background of their members, and so forth. Yet they share one important experience: They all struggled with the local government for at least one year. I chose groups with a relatively long experience of struggle mainly because their strategic choices are more readily observable over a long period of time. Two of them, Groups B and C, struggled for seven or eight years; Group A protested for two years, and Group D for about one year. It should be noted that most groups with a shorter experience of struggle share the same strategic orientation with these four groups.

Although these case studies are mainly based on interviews with the groups' organizers, I have attempted to cross-check their statements with government reports, as well as through interviews with government officials. In the interviews with the protest organizers, I pay the most attention to their troublemaking activities, their obedient actions, and their own understanding of their relationship with government officials.

Group A: Disabled Urban Residents

In 2000, most cities in China began to ban motorized tricycles for passenger transport because of traffic, environmental, and urban image problems. This policy created serious difficulties for many disabled people who made a living by transporting passengers in their special vehicles. Because of the high unemployment rates, they had virtually no hope of finding alternative sources of income. Not surprisingly, they fiercely resisted this policy.

Troublemaking. The City Y government officially banned motorized tricycles for passenger transport in November 2000. As soon as they heard this news, Group A, together with other motorized tricycle owners who were not disabled, went to the district government to protest. On November 7, 150 tricycle owners joined the protest and on November 8, 275 more joined. However, soon thereafter, the disabled people decided to act on their own. On December 18, forty-four disabled people paid a collective visit to the city government. Dissatisfied with the official reply from the government, they occupied the reception rooms of the bureau of letters and visits for one night.

Three months later, they blocked the gate of the provincial government. Although they admitted that this was an "excessively radical action" (*guoji xingwei*), they downplayed the disruptiveness of the event:

> There are three entrances to the main gate, and we only blocked one on the side, not at the main entrance. Actually, we did not block the entrance. We only sat-in by the entrance. We distributed handbills, but

we did not display banners. Each of us held a piece of paper, on which
was written "Disabled" and "City Y." We just wanted to tell people passing by that some disabled people from City Y had come here. We also
prepared a placard for a hunger strike, but actually we did not go on a
hunger strike.[7]

Later, the city government made a significant concession, agreeing to
compensate each disabled person 200 RMB per month for one year.
Although the petitioners were not fully satisfied because their ultimate
goal was to continue to use the motorcycles for passenger transport, they
were considerably pacified by this measure. They did not resume petitioning until the government was about to end the compensation at the end
of the year.

On March 15, 2002, which was a national holiday – Help Disabled
People's Day – they manipulated an officially authorized parade. They
slipped in a slogan among those that had been prepared or approved
by the local chapter of China Disabled Persons Federation, which read:
"Support and Thank the Government for Permitting Disabled People to
Use Motorized Tricycles for Passenger Transport." Although this seemed
to be a false statement, given that the government never said it would lift
the ban, the disabled people claimed that this slogan was in accord with
an internal speech given by a vice governor of Hunan Province. Whether
this was true or not, the slogan annoyed the city government because it
publicly challenged its policy and implied that the provincial government
did not agree with the city government's policy. Consequently, the insti-
gators were summoned to the public security bureau on three occasions
to undergo criticism and education. The government also issued a public
disciplinary warning in the local newspapers.

Before the parade, the ban had not been strictly implemented, and
disabled people could still use their vehicles for passenger transport without being penalized if they were cautious. After the parade, however, the
government began to enforce the ban more strictly. In May, the government confiscated five vehicles used for passenger transport. This triggered
another round of troublemaking activity.

When they could not recover their tricycles, twenty-six disabled people, demonstrating indomitable spirit and solidarity, went all the way to
Beijing to submit a petition. In response, the city and district governments
dispatched four officials to Beijing to bring the protesters back to the city.
The local officials partially accepted Group A's bargaining conditions,

---

[7] Interview, City Y, September 2002.

agreeing to release the confiscated vehicles on the condition that the owners sign a written statement that they would not use the vehicles for passenger transport again. The interviewees seemed satisfied with their partial success and expressed a willingness to repeat their strategy if need be. If future demands were not met satisfactorily, the interviewees said, "We will first give them [the local government] a warning, and then go to Beijing again."

Moderation. The first example of moderate behavior can be found in an official report by the bureau of letters and visits:

> On November 14, 9:30 am, 47 disabled people from both ZY and HS districts who were owners of motorcycles lined up to enter the government compound, and attempted to apply for administrative reconsideration of the policy to ban passenger transport with motorized tricycles....[8] They expressed their support for the policy generally, and their willingness to give up their vehicles voluntarily. Yet they claimed that the policy would deprive them of their source of income.... The deputy director explained to them the rationale behind the policy, and told them that the procedure of administrative reconsideration could not legally be applied in this case. The deputy director praised the disabled tricycle owners for their civilized behavior on this visit.... In response, the disabled owners warmly applauded. At 10:30, they lined up again and exited the government compound.[9]

During this event, the protesters' behavior was so obedient that it appeared that they were convinced. They even applauded a speech that rejected their demand and lined up in an orderly fashion when entering and exiting the government compound.

The complainants also refrained from forming alliances with disabled people from other cities, even though such collaboration might have been more forceful. They regarded such action as inappropriate:

> We City Y people should go [to upper-level government] by ourselves, they [people in other cities] should go by themselves. On this issue we should not go together. Going together would violate the party's policies. Establishing ties (*chuanlian*) would give our action a political nature, and our petition would become a political event. Since we disabled people live close to the limit of the law, we should be careful so as not to violate the law.

[8] Administrative reconsideration is an administrative procedure through which citizens request the government to reconsider its decisions.
[9] Government documents obtained in CYXB, July 2002.

However, even though they refrained from petitioning jointly with disabled people in other cities, they maintained relationships with them to share information. From disabled petitioners in other cities they acquired some internal documents, including an internal speech by Deng Pufang, chairman of the China Disabled Persons Federation, which proved to be very useful for justifying their petition.

They also showed restraint with respect to the provincial games held in City Y in that year. An interviewee reported:

> Yesterday an officer from the city police came to my work unit to see me. He warned me that we should not launch a petition during the period of the provincial games. I said we would not petition on two occasions: the first was during times of fighting floods and sending disaster relief, and the second was during important events. I said that I know that you [the government] have your own business to attend to, and we will not disturb you then. Only when you do not have important things to handle will we pay you a visit.

Relationship with the Government. The interviewees believed that their relationship with the government was quite positive. One of them said, "The China Disabled Persons Federation's chapter in the city and the district have praised us highly." This might have been true, judging from some favorable descriptions of this group in government reports. They also mentioned that officials who met them were usually quite nice to them. In return, they demonstrated an understanding of the government and its policies, at least superficially. However, such apparent mutual understanding could not disguise the tension in their relationship. The interviewees claimed, "Overall, the city government has not paid enough attention to the cause of helping disabled people. When we visited the city's chapter of CDPF, they didn't care about us. They treated us like terrorists, like Bin Laden." Obviously, they were aware that the government was concerned about their troublemaking activities. As one of the interviewees said, they lived close to the limits of the law. However, as another interviewee claimed, "The most important point is that we are not against the party or against the society." Not surprisingly, their description of their relationship with the government was not wholly consistent. Neither were their actions, which fluctuated between confrontational and obedient strategies.

In sum, Group A's experience reveals an attitude typical of opportunistic protesters. They found both "troublemaking" and appearing cooperative to be important and therefore tried to maintain a balance between them. They were well aware that their bargaining power came from "troublemaking" tactics, such as their collective petitioning to Beijing. At the same time, however, they recognized the importance of maintaining a positive relation with the local government. For example, after they annoyed the police by manipulating the approved demonstration, they realized that this action led to the local police more strictly enforcing the ban on tricycles. They therefore downplayed the seriousness of their troublemaking action and deliberately showed both an understanding of the local officials' position and a willingness to cooperate. They seemed to be quite conscious of the prescribed bounds of their activities, even though such a boundary was far from well defined. They believed that their defiance was likely to be tolerated by the local government as long as they did not engage in any "political" activity or form cross-sector or cross-regional alliances with other protesters.

Group B: Retired Cadres from a Small State-Owned Company

Group B consisted of about twenty cadres in a small state-owned company. Like many other enterprises in City Y, this company had difficulty paying pensions and health insurance to its retirees. Probably because of its small size, the group of petitioners had a strong incentive to form a coalition with other similar groups. Although Group B is small, its core leader, Mr. L, is well known among retiree pensioners in City Y. I first ran across his name when reading a government report, on which the mayor had written an instruction specifically requiring relevant government agencies to control him and educate him against establishing illegal ties with other groups. He seemed to be the mastermind of a coalition of retirees from forty-seven different enterprises, which was established around 2002.

Pensioners in these forty-seven enterprises had experienced similar contentions with the government. Their goals had also changed over time. Most started their struggle around 1995, when their enterprises were undergoing structural reform. At first, their major goal was for the government to pay their basic salary on time. When this goal was achieved, they demanded that the local government add to their salaries a subsidy of 51 RMB, as stipulated by the central government. When some of them successfully forced the government to comply with this initial request, they followed up with demands for health insurance and back pay. In 2002, they made a remarkably bold demand: As retirees from enterprises, they demanded a status equal to that of retirees from administrative and nonprofit work units.

Troublemaking. Mr. L would not talk about specific protest events, but he was willing to speak generally about the tactics he and his group employed in their petitioning. Their two favorite tactics were writing joint letters to provincial and central government officials and collectively visiting the city government repeatedly. They did not write individual letters or pay collective visits to upper-level government officials because these two tactics were believed to be either useless or unnecessary:

> I have almost never written anything in my own name. Letters from famous people may be able to attract attention, but letters from ordinary individuals seldom get any response. We have written many joint letters [to upper-level government officials]. Whenever we found some policies that had not been implemented thoroughly, we would write letters. I have never visited the upper-level government, not even the provincial government. I have no objection to those who want to do so, but I think the effect would be the same [as writing letters to upper-level government officials]. However, we have frequently visited the city government. It is our "staple diet" (*jiachang bianfan*).[10]

Generally, he was satisfied with the effect of these two troublemaking tactics. "They are useful," he said, continuing on:

> At first the government was extremely intransigent (*tieban yikuai*). For example, as to the subsidy of 51 RMB, the officials in the social security bureau told me in 2000 that it was impossible for them to pay it since the local government did not have any money. I said, 'I don't believe it. The subsidy is stipulated in official policy, and I don't believe you can cover the sky with only one hand.' So we organized many collective visits … now this problem has been solved for those enterprises owned directly by the city government.

He believed that collective action was not only useful, but also legitimate and legal. He said:

> Sometimes, they [government officials] criticized us for having too many people join the petitions. We believe we have not violated the law. In a TV opera, "Black Face" (*heilian*), there is an old comrade who spent two or three years collecting ten-thousand signatures for a joint letter to accuse the party secretary. It was the party secretary, not the old comrade, who was finally punished. If our action were not legal, such an opera would not have been shown on TV. Furthermore, we also rebuked the officials, saying that if our action was illegal, you [the government] violated the law before we did, since you did not fulfill your obligation as stipulated by law.

[10] Interview, City Y, September 2002.

As an old party cadre, he was well aware that although the coalition of retirees from the forty-seven enterprises was a very powerful weapon for the petitioners, it was also very troubling from the viewpoint of the government. So he downplayed the mobilizing efforts in establishing the coalition:

> They [the government] especially oppose ties across industrial sectors. I told them that we did not establish such ties deliberately. We old comrades often got together to chat about things. On occasion we found that the local government had not implemented national policies and laws, and we felt it necessary to report such problems to the upper-level government. We thus all wanted to write letters jointly. Our action has always been voluntary.

According to him, the coalition was formed naturally rather than from explicit organizational efforts. Asked about the future of the coalition, he was optimistic: "Previously we only had fourteen work units, and now we have forty-seven. The number will increase in the future. Other enterprises can join us if they are willing. But they'd better join voluntarily."

Moderation. Group B has never engaged in severely disruptive action. When asked about his opinion toward the disruptive tactics taken by Group C and many other groups, Mr. L replied:

> It is not right to block the gate [of the government]. We have never done such things as blocking gates. Old people may sometimes hurl curses, and easily become emotional. Yet never will we engage in acts of smashing and seizing, or blocking roads or bridges. We do not support radical behavior that violates principles. Such actions are not right, and also provide them [the government] with a chance to "pull our queue." We need to act within the boundary of the law.

He did not regard minor disruptive activities that took place in the course of collective action as a problem. From his perspective, those are normal and justifiable given the cause. According to him, old comrades do not like such things even as a last resort. He noted, "We old people cherish quietness. We cannot stand noise even when we watch TV. Why would we want to make noise in the government?" While minor disruption is normal, Group B would avoid deliberately organizing seriously disruptive activities.

Mr. L was careful to distinguish the coalition from a formal organization. Although enthusiastic about a large coalition for collective action, he refrained from organizing cross-sector or cross-work unit organizations.

In his understanding, the regime permits associations within a work unit, but organizing associations across work units could cause trouble. In each enterprise that made up the coalition, there existed an association of senior people. According to him, the best form of organization is the party team of retirees because it is "perfectly legal." He actually organized such a party team within his own work unit. However, he said he would not form any formal organization across work units. "If you want to form such an organization, you need to get approval from the government, which is almost impossible. If you form it without approval, they [the government] can say you violated the law. So why ask for trouble?"

Relationship with the Government. Despite their often intense struggles with the government, Mr. L believed that he and the other comrades behaved as party cadres. "We will absolutely never do anything antiparty or antisocialist," he said. "Most of us are Communist Party members whose mission is to defend the laws of the nation and the socialist system."

He was also aware of the possibility of repression, but not especially concerned about it. He sought security from the law: "We have never demanded anything without a legal basis." He claimed, "Whenever we do something, including writing letters, I consult things like the Law on Marches and Demonstrations, and the Regulations on Public Security Management." He did not take the threats by the government seriously. One time an official threatened him, saying that the police had been looking for him for several months. He commented with scorn, "The police could not be so stupid. I have been home all the time. This is only a bluff."

In his view, coercive measures taken by the local government were not a deterrent. He talked about his experience after the mayor instructed that he be controlled. In response, he wrote another letter to upper-level governments, accusing the mayor of vindictively attacking the petitioners. He also sent a copy of that letter to the mayor: "The mayor was fine about it, and did not do anything to me, although he must have felt pretty uncomfortable reading my letter."

He also believed that many officials were reluctant to carry out coercive measures. The city government required that the party secretary and the manager of their company monitor and control the pensioners, but the company leaders were reluctant to comply: "They would not do anything without pressure from the government even though they need to protect their official posts." He was confident that their cause was just and that the government officials actually acknowledged it.

Compared to Group A, Group B is smaller in size, and is a less-marginalized group – most of its members were retired CCP members or even cadres. Yet it shared some strategic thinking with Group A. For example, Group B activists also counted on troublemaking activities for bargaining power, although they preferred different types of tactics. They eschewed excessive disruption or skip-level visits, and instead chose skip-level joint letters and collective petitioning to the city government. One of their most alarming activities was to play an important role in a cross-sector/region alliance, although they claimed that the alliance was not an organization. Like Group A members, Group B activists were aware of the importance of adhering to prescribed "rules." Of course, they were even more politically savvy and more skillful at using laws in their struggle. They also seemed to have a somewhat different understanding of the "rules" than Group A activists. For instance, they did not find the cross-sector/region alliance against the official rule because it was formed spontaneously rather than deliberately organized. Finally, Group B activists also described themselves as part of the regime, even more so than Group A members. They were not just local citizens; they were actually "old comrades."

Group C: Retired Workers from a Large State-Owned Enterprise

Group C consisted of several hundred retirees from a large state-owned enterprise (SOE). It was part of the coalition of the aforementioned forty-seven enterprises. Yet joining this coalition to write joint letters was but a minor part of its long struggle. The earliest protest recorded in the government report was a collective visit by 200 people to the city government in 1994. Group C changed its demands over time in a process similar to that of many other enterprises described earlier.

Troublemaking. In its long struggle with the government, Group C experimented with almost every major variety of troublemaking activity: large, disruptive, public, and symbolic actions, as well as skip-level visits. Government reports recorded a series of large-scale collective petitioning by Group C: more than 200 participants (with pensioners from another factory) in June 1994, 150 participants in December 1995, more than 300 participants in February 1996, 85 participants in May 1996, 350 participants in October 1996, 40 participants in September 1999, 240 participants in September 2000, 400 participants (with pensioners from three other enterprises) in June 2001, and more than 200 participants in September 2001.

Mrs. W described their experience as a logical reaction to the government's bureaucratic behavior:

> At first we sent written requests to the government through four or
> five representatives. According to the Regulations for Letters and Visits,
> there should be no more than five people. We knew the policy. However,
> they [the government] won't receive you or pay attention to your request
> if you don't have many people making a commotion. On December 24,
> 2000, before the Spring Festival, I went with another retired representa-
> tive to submit our petition. We waited about one month, but there was
> no response. When we went to the bureau of letters and visits again to
> ask a bespectacled official whether our petition had been submitted to
> the mayor, it turned out that it was still in the drawer. They had not even
> read it. We thus were forced to return en masse.[11]

Strictly speaking, her narrative is misleading because it implies that Group
C did not engage in large-scale collective action until it experienced bureaucratic obstruction in December 2000. As previously stated, the group
actually started its collective action much earlier. However, the narrative
illustrates the typical reasoning behind their "troublemaking" activities.

Members of Group C believed that collective visits were fairly effective. Mrs. W talked about how the government increased their pension
payments, "at first they [the government] just gave us 80 RMB [per
month], and then they added several RMB when we made a real commotion. Later on, our pensions were increased to 130 RMB, and after we
struggled for another several years, we got 200 RMB. They treated us like
kids, and wouldn't give us [our pensions] unless we made a fuss."

To "make a real commotion" (*chaode lihai*), they repeatedly used disruptive and public tactics. In Mrs. W's narrative, such troublemaking was nothing but a natural and necessary extension of normal visits. For example,
she talked about their occupation of a government office for one night:

> We went there to ask for rice [pensions]. We clamored until half past
> twelve o'clock [am]. We could not go home so late. There was no boat,
> and it was very cold. We are all elderly people, and most of us aren't in
> good health. Since the office was warm, we decided to stay overnight.
> The director of the office despised us, and called the police. The police
> came with batons and handcuffs. But they said, "it is right for you to ask
> for rice," and then they left.

She also talked casually about their experience of blocking the gate of
the city government: "At that time, only a few old comrades blocked the

---

[11] Interview, City Y, July 2002.

entrance, while hundreds of other comrades sat down inside the government compound."

Like Mr. L, Mrs. W justified her troublemaking activities as a rightful cause. She often said, "We are old comrades educated by Mao Zedong Thought. We do not like to make trouble. We have been forced to beg for rice. Collective visits are always exhausting, especially for us old comrades. If the government had paid the pensions as it should have, we wouldn't have made collective visits even if you had begged us."

Moderation. According to Mrs. W, the protesters always sent warnings before they actually started disruptive or public actions. Their threats were seldom empty, but they also hoped to resolve the problem without resorting to troublemaking.

When forced to engage in disruption, they nevertheless managed to maintain discipline: "Before we went to petition, we told workers not to shout abuses or damage goods. We always emphasize discipline. As a result, we have never damaged a cup, a window, or a chair. Sometimes we even cleaned the office before we left. We have paid visits in a civilized way."

Like Group A, they also refrained from disrupting the provincial games held in City Y:

> The manager of our factory passed on warnings [from the government] to several of our representatives. He said anybody who plotted or organized activities to disturb the provincial games would be deprived of their salaries or even arrested. He said the government had convened an emergency meeting to make this decision. We replied that we were not afraid of this kind of warning. But we knew enough not to pay collective visits during the provincial games. We are City Y people ourselves, and holding these provincial games is an honor for all of us. Therefore, we did not disturb them. We are old enough to understand this.

Relationship with the Government. Mrs. W often referred to the attitude of the government as "they treated us like kids." From the protesters' perspective, the government preferred to buy them off with small favors whenever they engaged in troublemaking activities. The protesters did not believe that the government really wanted to resort to heavy-handed repression. Like Mr. L, Mrs. W regarded the government's threats of force as a bluff. She expressed defiance:

> Once an official said we had violated the Regulations of Public Security Management. We replied that it was not the time for them to label us with such a hat (*daimaozi*). When the police threatened to arrest five

representatives if we went on with the march the next day, I replied, "If you want to arrest me, I can help you do that. I have nothing to fear. My mom died when I was only 8, and I became a child bride at 12. I have never been involved in adultery, burglary, or embezzlement of public property. We are just asking for rice, and asking for rice does not violate the law. If you arrest one person, we will send several hundred people to ask for him or her back. Where there is repression, there is resistance. You'd better talk rather than threaten us.

As previously mentioned, Mrs. W referred to the petitioners as "old comrades," and she liked to say, "We are all old comrades who have been educated by Mao Zedong Thought. We will not make trouble."

Although Group C is much bigger than Groups A and B, it also demonstrated a similar form of "protest opportunism." It relied heavily on "troublemaking" activities. In fact, because of its more abundant resources for mobilization, it created more disruption. But it also emphasized its moderation and restraint. Members downplayed their "troublemaking" and showed their understanding of local officials. Like Group B, they also stressed that they were "old comrades" and, despite being dissatisfied, were still unquestionably loyal.

Group D: Demobilized Army Officers

Group D consists of demobilized army officers who participated in the Sino-Vietnam War of 1979. Demobilized military officers have been a continuing concern for the regime as a possible threat to political stability for three reasons. First, they have a strong capacity for mobilization. In many areas throughout the country there exist de facto associations of demobilized soldiers. Second, they are better educated than the average population and enjoy a superior understanding of public policies and laws. Third, despite the fact that they have made sacrifices for the nation, many of them are living in poverty. Consequently, many veterans harbor deep grievances against the state.

Group D did not start its contentious activity until the restructuring of SOEs and collective enterprises began in the mid-1990s. Although Group D included some peasants, its core leaders worked in collective or state-owned enterprises. These demobilized army officers faced unemployment as a result of the industrial reforms. With an average age of forty, they found it very difficult to find other jobs. They consulted brochures of central policies and laws and discovered that, as one of them claimed, "many favorable policies and laws affecting demobilized army officers had not been implemented by the local government." Yet their demands were not limited to the implementation of preexisting central policies. They also made proactive claims, demanding new and more favorable policies.

Troublemaking. Like Group C, Group D combined most major varieties of troublemaking: collective, public, symbolic, and disruptive. But its utilization of these various tactics was rather tame compared to that of Group C.

Group D justified its actions in terms similar to those of other groups: "We have to petition collectively. Individual petitions never work, and attract no attention." According to a government report, Group D's largest collective petition movement occurred in January 2002 when twenty-six demobilized army officers paid a highly charged visit to the district government. That July, the officers planned a large event, a march on Army Day, but they failed to carry it out due to forceful measures taken by the government. They also paid several visits to the government, each time with five representatives. During every petition drive, they claimed they represented about 300 Sino-Vietnam War veterans in their district.

According to members of Group D, the planned march was a response to the government having broken its promise. As one of the interviewees explained, "Previously, every time we visited the government it promised to issue a document that would solve our problems. Then in June it said it would not issue the document, and therefore we would get nothing. We comrades-in-arms became indignant since we had been deceived. This is why we submitted an application for the march."

The veterans adopted symbolic tactics that emphasized their military background. In the Points of Attention drafted for their planned march on Army Day, it required that everyone wear old-style military uniforms and carry medals and their certificates of military background or disability. The organizers stipulated that participants should sing revolutionary songs during the march, such as "The Internationale" and the "Three Disciplines and Eight Points of Attention."[12]

Although members of Group D had not yet undertaken skip-level visits when I interviewed them, they clearly intended to do so. They acknowledged they ultimately might need to go to Beijing. One of the interviewees said, "We will not give up until we have visited Beijing."

---

[12] This is the PLA code of discipline, which emphasizes that army officers should not disturb civilians.

Although their petitioning tactics did not seem especially confrontational, their organizational activities caused deep suspicion on the part of the Party-state. The government archives include a speech by a major local leader, requesting that the district government declare the club of comrades-in-arms illegal, and that the police collect information and evidence about the club's activities for future use in a possible crackdown.

Group D's mobilizing rhetoric is highly militant. The following are excerpts from a proposal the group circulated to all Sino-Vietnam War veterans in their district:

> Comrades-in-arms: we will not form an illegal organization, or do anything illegal. But if we cannot attain our goal, we will have to submit petitions level by level. We must use our power of unity to change the leaders' opinion of us, and struggle to obtain the concern of the upper-level leaders.... In order to defend our dignity, we shall always be on call, ready to sacrifice everything we have. Comrades-in-arms: Let's act![13]

Because this group was characterized by an autonomous organization, illegal assemblies, and militant language, the government's suspicion of it is understandable, even though its activities were not as disruptive as those of other groups, such as Group C.

Moderation. Group D refrained from large-scale actions. This was a self-conscious strategy: "We shall try to limit the number of participants. When there are too many participants, we shall divide into groups and petition separately." As mentioned earlier, usually only five representatives delivered their petitions. Apparently they did this to avoid possible repression by the government.

Additionally, they usually refrained from publicizing their actions, as noted in their program: "To reduce the social impact [of our petition], we better not wear army uniforms while petitioning."

They also emphasized discipline and eschewed disruption, as indicated in their program of action, "We should maintain strict discipline while petitioning; petitioners should strictly comply with party discipline, national laws, and the Three Main Disciplines and the Eight Points of Attention. We shall petition in a civilized way, without hurling curses, wrangling bitterly, coming to blows, or damaging public property."

Relationship with the Government. Although among the four groups Group D had the most strained relationship with the government, it did

---

[13] Documents obtained in CYXB, September 2002.

not challenge the legitimacy of the regime. In fact, several times the four leaders emphasized, "We have all been Communist Party members for more than twenty years; none of us will act recklessly." In their program of action, they specified one of their principles to be "to strengthen our confidence, and trust the party":

> Since the establishment of the PRC, the party and the country have taken the greatest care of us. After the War to Resist U.S. Aggression and Aid Korea, the War of Resistance to U.S. Aggression and Aid Vietnam, and the Sino-Vietnam War, the Party Central Committee and the State Council issued timely policy documents that gave us priority in job assignments, provided us with economic security, and confirmed our values. We are deeply confident that the party and the country are greatly concerned about us.[14]

Compared with the other three groups, Group D had even stronger capacity for mobilization. Although it had not yet created much disruption, its organizational efforts already deeply concerned local leaders. Its organizers actually consciously exerted pressure in this way. However, similar to the other three groups, they also showed restraint, moderation, and discipline to avoid government repression. For example, they deliberately renounced disruption and limited the scale and publicity of their petitioning activities. They also emphasized that they were CCP members and avoided any hint of protest against the regime. They actually had an even stronger reason to stress their close relationship to the regime – the regime was indebted to them.

ANALYSIS

We can now provide a systematic comparison of the four groups to further illustrate the key features of protest opportunism.

The struggles of these four groups share remarkable similarities. First, all of the participants portrayed themselves as loyal members of the regime and explicitly rejected any activities directed against the Party-state. Even Group A, the disabled urban residents, who belonged to one of most marginalized segments of the population, appeared to be very understanding of the government on issues such as fighting floods and sending in disaster relief, as well as holding the provincial games. The members identified themselves as City Y citizens who shared interests with their government. Organizers of Group B, who were retired cadres,

---

[14] Interview, City Y, September 2002.

and Group D, who were demobilized army officers, emphasized that they were Communist Party members. Similarly, members of Group C, the retired workers from an SOE, described themselves as "a generation educated by Mao Zedong Thought."

Consistent with the above self-identities, all of the groups demonstrated a strong tendency to operate close to the boundary of authorized channels. For example, Group A challenged public policy by slipping a subversive slogan into an authorized parade. Both Groups A and C occupied government offices as an extension of a legal form of petitioning. Unsurprisingly, they always tried to portray their actions as a natural outgrowth of legal claim making, downplaying any disruptiveness and mobilization effort. Furthermore, they showed certain sympathy toward government officials. For example, they refrained from making trouble when the government was most vulnerable.

At the same time, all of the groups demonstrated some tendency to overstep prescribed bounds: staging large-scale, public, and disruptive protests; forming cross-sector coalitions; and establishing autonomous or semiautonomous organizations. They all insisted that troublemaking tactics were essential. For most of them, troublemaking constituted a necessary, albeit not sufficient, condition for success. Without any troublemaking activities, their demands were almost certain to be ignored. As the popular saying goes, "big troublemaking leads to big solutions, small troublemaking to small solutions, and no troublemaking to no solution." It is worth noting that troublemaking is not confined to these groups that have actually carried it out. Many other groups have not engaged in sustained troublemaking activities, but this is only because they lack the necessary resources and capacity to do so.

In the course of their resistance, the groups all demonstrated an impressive degree of defiance. They often treated the officials' threats as bluffs. This is not to suggest that they were unafraid. Actually, as Solinger indicates, the mindset of protesters in contemporary China is a mixture of daring and fear.[15] They are aware of a sizable space for resistance within which repression is considered unlikely. However, they can never exclude the possibility of punishment. What fuels their defiance is a combination of legal consciousness, understanding of the strategies of government officials, and belief in the righteousness of their cause.

---

[15] Dorothy Solinger, "The New Crowd of the Dispossessed: The Shift of the Urban Proletariat from Master to Mendicant," in Peter Hayes Gries and Stanley Rosen (eds.), *State and Society in 21st-Century China: Crisis, Contention, and Legitimation* (New York: Routledge, 2004), pp. 50–66.

Equally defiant and obedient, the petitioners exhibit a host of contradictions: (1) between words and deeds; for example, although they all verbally denounced disruption, they all engaged in various forms of disruptive activities; 2) among words; for example, Group A portrayed its relationship with the government as both positive and tense; 3) among deeds of the same group; for example, although members of Group C engaged in many disruptive actions, they sometimes cleaned the offices they occupied before they departed; and 4) among the deeds of different groups. However, the petitioners did not seem concerned about such contradictions. Instead, what they worried about most were protest efficacy and personal safety.

Despite the remarkable similarities listed previously, these four groups also demonstrated quite different behavioral patterns. For example, whereas Group A refrained from acting together with disabled petitioners from other areas, Group B did not hesitate to form cross-sector coalitions, although it did refrain from forming a formal organization beyond the work unit. In contrast, Group D was not afraid of forming a lateral organization.

As rational actors, these groups tended to choose strategies that they perceived as legitimate and effective. The previous case studies indicate that these groups sometimes had different understandings of the effectiveness and legitimacy of the various strategies. Whereas Group A found collective visits to Beijing very effective, for instance, leaders of Group B believed that such skip-level collective visits incurred higher costs and would not make much difference.

The groups also differed in terms of their perceptions of the boundary line separating permissible from impermissible actions. Close observation reveals that their perceptions were largely consistent with the strengths and needs of each group. In other words, the various groups tended to regard what they could and needed to do as appropriate behavior and what they could not or needed not do as inappropriate. For example, the leaders of Group B, which had a small constituency but could find many other similar groups, had a strong incentive to form a large coalition for collective action, and therefore regarded such action as legitimate. In contrast, Group A had no intention of forming such a coalition, and therefore believed that establishing such a coalition amounted to political provocation. In another situation, whereas Group B regarded it inappropriate to form a formal organization, Group D thought it was legitimate, largely because its organizational capacity was its most powerful weapon.

The groups demonstrated a certain trade-off in balancing their collective action strategies. For example, whereas Group D favored a strong organization, it tended to refrain from large-scale activities and widespread publicity. Conversely, Group C enjoyed a large number of participants but was not enthusiastic about developing a strong organizational presence.

These similarities and differences in these groups' protest strategies underline their opportunistic approaches. They are ready to employ any useful tactic available, no matter whether it is defiant or obedient. Moreover, for the sake of effective and sustained struggle, they all find it necessary to employ both defiant and obedient tactics.

These features are not confined to the four groups studied here. Among petitioning groups, a tendency to employ troublemaking tactics is prevalent, as indicated by the remarkable rise of confrontational protests throughout the country in the recent two decades. As I have noted, even those groups that have not carried out considerable troublemaking activities have demonstrated the motivation to do so. What they usually lack, however, are the resources and capacity for mobilization. In the meantime, among petitioners, especially among those who have engaged in powerful troublemaking activities, the tendency to indicate obedience is also widespread. One of the most striking slogans in China is "we don't want democracy, we want food" (*buyao minzhu yao chifan*), which appeared during a demonstration by the unemployed in Shenyang city, Liaoning Province.[16] What is important here is not whether those petitioners really rejected democracy, but that they had a strong incentive to show their obedience. Another impressive case is a statement by some Hunan peasants who were trying to organize an autonomous peasant association, "Be loyal to the Communist Party forever."[17] In the post-Mao era, when ordinary people no longer need to demonstrate their loyalty in such an ostentatious way, such postures usually can be found only among those who engage in defiant activities. Paradoxically, the Chinese people are obligated to show their obedience only when they have been defiant.

---

[16] Liu Binyan, "Xueji Qian De Sisuo" (Thoughts in Front of the Bloodstain), http://bjzc.org/bjs/bc/50/06 (accessed on January 8, 2005).

[17] Yu Jianrong, "Dangdai Zhongguo Nongmin Weiquan Zuzhi De Fayu Yu Chengzhang: Jiyu Hengyang Nongmin Xiehui De Shizheng Yanjiu" (Growth and Development of Peasants' Organizations of Rights Defense in Contemporary China: An Empirical Study of the Hengyang Peasant Association), *Zhongguo Nongcun Guancha* (China Rural Survey) 2 (2005), pp. 57–64, 71.

TABLE 5.1. *Relations between the Duration of Petitioning Activities and the Level of Confrontation in City Y, 1992–2002*

	All Petitioning Events	Highly Confrontational Petitioning Events
Temporary	517 (57%)	39 (36%)
Sustained	385 (43%)	69 (64%)
Total	902	108

CONFRONTATION AND DURABILITY

Protest opportunism has an important consequence: It enables petitioning groups to stage protests that are both confrontational and protracted. The data from City Y actually confirms this assumption.

Among the 902 events in the dataset, I classified 108 events as highly confrontational. In these events petitioners employed one or more of the following tactics: staging blockades of roads or bridges, blockading government entrances, attacking government officials, damaging office buildings, self-immolation, marching, staging sit-ins, displaying big banners, kneeling in public, and carrying victims' bodies. At the same time, all 902 events have been divided into two categories: temporary (shorter than six months) and sustained (six months and longer). If an event is coded as sustained, it means that the event is part of a struggle that lasted at least six months.

As Table 5.1 shows, highly confrontational events are more likely to be part of long-lasting struggles. Of the 108 events deemed "confrontational," 64 percent were sustained longer than six months, whereas only 43 percent of all 902 events fell into this sustained category. This is a surprising finding because it is normally expected that confrontational protests are more likely to be put down by the government, and therefore are less likely to be sustained. This surprising fact actually underscores the importance of protest opportunism, in which petitioning can be both confrontational and sustained.

This fact has two important implications. First, it suggests that some social groups can possibly exert considerable influence on policy-making/implementation processes through protests. Because those groups can bargain with local governments forcefully over a relatively long time, they can possibly achieve a status similar to pressure groups. Second, as good news for the regime, many of those supposedly most threatening protests have also been routinized, and are therefore unlikely to do real harm to the regime.

CONCLUSION

These four groups' experiences help us understand how petitioners under the current Chinese political system tend to develop a common orientation, protest opportunism, despite all the differences and contradictions among their actions and statements. The transition from the unit system model to government-citizen model and the increase of divisions within the state structure clearly had a significant impact on their behavior. Their defiance would be hard to imagine had they not all been free from the constraints of the unit system. When they had to defend their interests by making claims directly to the government through the xinfang system, they did not find government officials particularly formidable. Government repression was not impossible, but it was unlikely, especially if the petitioners chose their strategies prudently. They were also well aware of the potential advocacy from upper authorities or from other state or quasi-state agencies such as the China Disabled Persons Federation, and did not hesitate to take advantage of such opportunities.

Protest opportunism is an essential aspect of the surge of popular collective action since the 1990s. Petitioners have gained a certain degree of bargaining power through collective action with "troublemaking" tactics. Although obedient tactics usually cannot directly create pressure on local governments, they can demonstrate that the petitioners are reasonable claim makers and help them sustain collective struggles. Without protest opportunism, it is hard to imagine the dramatic rise and routinization of social protests.

6

"Troublemaking" Tactics and Their Efficacy

September 1 is usually the first day of class for Chinese schools. On September 1, 2010, however, twelve recent elementary school graduates from Yancheng City, Jiangsu Province, did not go to class in a middle school. Instead, they went to the municipal government offices to have their first class. Outside the government compound, they began to study an essay with the title, "Opening Doors for Yourself." In the rain, they read loudly, "there is no door in this world that you cannot open, only if you persist." Those schoolchildren were protesting a local education reform policy, which stipulated that students should be assigned to schools according to their residential address. Originally, they expected to go to the best middle school in the city because of their parents' employers' monetary contribution to the school. Suddenly deprived of this expected privilege, those most persistent twelve families found a very special way to "open the door."[1] Their protest was peaceful and hardly disruptive in any sense. However, it was clear to government officials, as well as to the petitioners themselves, that this was a method of petitioning with "troublemaking" tactics.

The previous chapter shows that Chinese petitioners have developed a strategic pattern, protest opportunism. "Troublemaking," as an essential aspect of protest opportunism, is generally viewed by petitioners as indispensable for the efficacy of their struggle. This chapter will continue to

---

[1] Zhengzhou Wanbao, "Jiangsu 12 Xiaoxue Biyesheng Weijin Minxiao Zai Zhengfu Menqian Shangke" (12 Graduates from Elementary Schools Had Class outside the Government Compound because They Were Not Admitted to an Elite Middle School). See http://news.xinhuanet.com/edu/2010-09/06/c_12521041.htm, last visited on September 6, 2010.

probe into "troublemaking" tactics in a more systematic way, noting in particular the range of such tactics and their actual effectiveness. Because the range and effectiveness of protest tactics can reveal some essential features of the political system, this study of specific "troublemaking" tactics can help us further understand how the particular political structure in China since the 1990s has shaped petitioners' behavior.

The study is also expected to contribute to general theories on protest efficacy. A central task for understanding protest efficacy is to identify mechanisms that mediate the link between protest tactics and their outcomes.[2] Our current understanding of such mechanisms, however, is both biased and incomplete. A dominant view in social movement studies "equates the effectiveness of social movements with their ability to achieve bargaining leverage through disruption."[3] Such an overemphasis on disruption tends to obscure other mechanisms, such as persuasion, publicity, and elite advocacy, which are often equally instrumental in allowing protesters to achieve their goals. This problem is even more serious for studies on authoritarian regimes because such regimes are generally believed to lack an institutional basis for nondisruptive mechanisms.

More importantly, this biased view reflects an oversimplification of the power relationship between ruling elites and subordinate groups. It assumes that wealth and power are concentrated in the hands of a few groups, thus depriving most people of any real influence over the major decisions that affect their lives.[4] An extreme version of this view therefore contends that the ruling group would not care about popular claims unless they were compelled to do so by the disruption tactics of poor people.

In reality, however, many protest tactics employed by ordinary people do not actually seek to create disruption. By the same token, when elites respond – or even concede – to protests, it is not just due to fear of disruption. The interactions between elites and subordinate classes are often more nuanced and reciprocal than what disruption theory assumes. Even though ruling elites usually have no intention of granting power to the subordinate classes, they are often constrained by the divisions among themselves, or by contradictions and ambiguities within their ideology and institutions. Indeed, Chapters 3 and 4 thoroughly explored

---

[2] Doug McAdam and Yang Su, "The War at Home: Antiwar Protests and Congressional Voting, 1965 to 1973," *American Sociological Review* 67 (2002), pp. 696–721.
[3] Ibid., p. 700.
[4] Doug McAdam, *Political Process and the Development of Black Insurgency: 1930–1970* (Chicago: University of Chicago Press, 1999), p. 5.

such features in Reform-Era China. As a result of these divisions and ambiguities, subordinate classes may mount effective protests without resorting to disruption if they can appropriate symbols, statements, and institutions of the ruling class to press their own claims.

This study therefore advocates an expanded view of mediating mechanisms for protest efficacy and proposes a conceptual framework for thinking about these mechanisms. Protesters in China have employed a variety of tactics such as demonstrations, self-inflicted suffering, and traffic blockades. These tactics, which are commonly called "troublemaking" (*nao*), include but are not restricted to activities we might recognize as disruptive. Many "troublemaking" tactics, which can be easily confused with disruptive activities, actually work based on a different logic. A close examination of "troublemaking" tactics can thus help differentiate mediating mechanisms for protest efficacy.

MEDIATING MECHANISMS

Analysts have long recognized the importance of disruption when evaluating protest activity. James Wilson is among the first to regard disruption as a primary, and perhaps the only, mechanism for determining protest efficacy. He conceives of protest as a special type of bargaining, where the relatively powerless groups lack the political resources to negotiate changes in government policies. These groups obtain bargaining leverage through negative inducements – threats.[5] Many activists seemed to share this view; Martin Luther King, Jr. once remarked, "The purpose of direct action is to create a situation so crisis-packed that it will inevitably open the door to negotiation."[6] The effect of disruption has been confirmed by many empirical studies of protest and social movements. For example, in a very influential study, William Gamson showed that social movements that deployed either "violence" or "nonviolent constraints" were more likely to succeed than their more moderate counterparts.[7] In a later study, Piven and Cloward concurred: "It is usually when unrest among the lower classes breaks out of the confines of electoral procedures that

---

[5] James Q. Wilson, "The Strategy of Protest: Problems of Negro Civic Action," *Journal of Conflict Resolution* 3 (1961), p. 292.

[6] Cited from Aldon D. Morris, "Birmingham Confrontation Reconsidered: An Analysis of The Dynamics and Tactics of Mobilization," *American Sociological Review* 58 (October 1993), p. 606.

[7] William Gamson, *The Strategy of Social Protest* (Homewood, IL: The Dorsey Press, 1975), chapter 6.

the poor may have some influence, for the instability and polarization they then threaten to create by their actions in the factories or in the streets may force some response from electoral leaders."[8]

There are, however, some works that cast doubt on the effect of disruption. Not only do some studies find only moderate positive effects,[9] but other studies even suggest a negative impact on the success of particular movements.[10] After reviewing the relationship between disruption and protest efficacy in the "urban disorders" literature, McAdam and Su note that the bulk of the studies find "no effect or mixed results that do not allow for a definite answer to the question."[11] Some analysts attribute such inconsistent findings to an imperfect conceptualization of the dependent or independent variables. As a result, many have tried to refine the measurement of social movement outcomes.[12] Other analysts advocate a more nuanced conceptualization of independent variables. For example, Kurt Schock distinguished violence from disruption.[13] Similarly, McAdam and Su differentiate between violence by demonstrators and violence by police.[14] Even with such improvements, however, there is still no guarantee that disruption will elicit the desired outcome. As some analysts have argued, the effect of disruption is mediated by contextual factors. For instance, Amenta and his colleagues suggest that disruptive tactics may be less important in a strongly sympathetic political context.[15]

The real problem is not that we find situations in which disruption does not work; rather, an overemphasis on disruption has obscured other important mechanisms, such as persuasion and third-party leverage. Such a bias originates from a flawed understanding of the political process of popular contention. Since the 1970s, theorists in contentious politics

[8] Frances Fox Piven and Richard Cloward, *Poor People's Movements: Why They Succeed, How They Fail* (New York: Vintage Books, 1977).

[9] For example, see Peter K. Eisinger, "The Conditions of Protest Behavior in American Cities," *American Political Science Review* 67 (1973), pp. 11–28.

[10] For example, see David Snyder and William R. Kelly, "Industrial Violence in Italy, 1878–1903," *American Journal of Sociology* 82 (1976), pp. 131–162.

[11] McAdam and Su, p. 719.

[12] For example, see Daniel Cress and David Snow, "The Outcomes of Homeless Mobilization: The Influence of Organization, Disruption, Political Mediation and Framing," *American Journal of Sociology* 105 (2000), pp. 1063–1104.

[13] Kurt Schock, *Unarmed Insurrections: People Power Movements in Nondemocracies* (Minneapolis: University of Minnesota Press, 2005).

[14] McAdam and Su, p. 701.

[15] Edwin Amenta et al., "The Strategies and Contexts of Social Protest: Political Mediation and the Impact of the Townsend Movement in California," *Mobilization* 4 (1999), pp. 1–23.

have generally rejected the pluralist model as a description of the political system in liberal democracies.[16] Instead, their central arguments were based on Tilly's polity model, which assumes that polities are organized around a division between members with routine low-cost access and challengers who are excluded.[17] Excluded groups resort to unruliness because of their lack of access. Yet disruption theory has carried this view too far by asserting that powerless people have virtually *no* institutional resources with which to advance their interests. Such an extreme view leads to James Wilson's definition of protest as *exclusively* using negative inducements, as well as Piven and Cloward's argument that disruption is the *only* power source for the poor, and that any resort to institutionalized participation will surely lead to their failure.

Clearly, however, there are some other mechanisms that can mediate protest efficacy. As early as the 1960s, Lipsky criticized Wilson's overly narrow understanding of protest efficacy and pointed out that some nondisruptive mechanisms, such as third-party engagement, might play a more important role. His particular stress on communication and reference publics has also been supported by other studies.[18] Similarly, McAdam and Su's study on the "War at Home" movement finds that persuasive mechanisms can predict increases in relevant roll-call votes in the U.S. Congress.[19]

Disruption theory also involves conceptual confusions, as in cases where some nondisruptive mechanisms have been mistaken for disruption. This problem is especially serious for studies on authoritarian regimes where many nondisruptive activities lack legality. For example, self-inflicted suffering, such as self-immolation, is usually treated as a disruptive means of protest. Yet, as Michael Biggs has analyzed, despite their violent nature, they can better be understood as "costly signaling." McAdam and Su offered a similar observation, noting that "courting violence by one's opponents can be seen as an extreme form of persuasion – an effort to curry favor by mobilizing sympathy on behalf of the movement."[20] Likewise, unfavorable publicity directed at the government, especially in authoritarian regimes, tends to be regarded as disruptive. Yet it works

---

[16] Doug McAdam, *Political Process and the Development of Black Insurgency*.
[17] Charles Tilly, *From Mobilization to Revolution* (Reading, MA: Addison-Wesley, 1978); J. Craig Jenkins and Kurt Schock, "Global Structures and Political Processes in the Study of Domestic Political Conflicts," *Annual Review of Sociology* 18 (1992), p. 170.
[18] For example, see Kurt Schock, *Unarmed Insurrections*, pp. 169–170.
[19] McAdam and Su, p. 717.
[20] Ibid., pp. 716–718.

on a different logic from disruption. Unlike disruption, publicity works through the capacity of engaging sympathetic third parties, particularly the reference public. This is why Biggs argues that it is theoretically counterproductive to confuse these two mechanisms.[21]

Therefore, to understand protest efficacy, an expanded view of mediating mechanisms is needed. Among the mechanisms that have been identified by analysts so far, four appear most important: disruption, persuasion, publicity, and elite advocacy. For the sake of clarity, we can arrange them in a two-dimensional framework that distinguishes between *means* and *routes*. The classical dichotomy between threat and persuasion refers to the means utilized by protest or social movements to induce certain outcomes. In the meantime, we can also draw a distinction between the routes according to whether the impact is direct or indirect. The most common indirect route is often called third-party leverage, which is achieved through either the public or elite groups.

DATA

This study is primarily based on a data set I created from government documents collected from City Y in Hunan Province. The main data source is a government publication – *Information Express (xinxi kuaibao)* – published by the City Xinfang Bureau. I have collected almost all editions of the *Information Express* from January 1992 to July 2002. This internal publication is provided to local leaders with information on petitions, and is not accessible to the general public. It not only reports on petitioners' actions and statements, but also often includes descriptions of how the government has handled them. Compared to the very limited media coverage on collective action in China, government reports can provide more reliable and systematic information, although they have their own bias and incompleteness. In addition to the reports in *Information Express*, I also used other documents including leaders' speeches, meeting records, and internal announcements. The City Y dataset includes 902 petitioning events.

THREE ROUTES OF CLAIM MAKING

Before we discuss specific "troublemaking" tactics, we can briefly examine the routes of claim making. One of the first strategic choices faced

---

[21] Ibid., p. 717.

by Chinese protesters is whether they want to produce direct or indirect leverage. This choice will have a significant impact on the petitioners' choice of tactics. For example, if they choose indirect leverage, they may want to employ publicity tactics to mobilize the sympathy of the elites or public. Government officials and petitioners often regard a shift from direct petitioning to indirect petitioning as a strategy of escalation because this is likely to expose local problems to outsiders and bring external pressure on local officials.[22] As illustrated by Figure 6.1, protest strategies can generally be divided into three models according to the routes they choose: direct petitioning, advocacy and publicity. It is clear how direct petitioning works, so my analysis will be focused on indirect routes.

Petitioners' choice of indirect routes can clearly reveal their perception of the political opportunity structure. If they want to exploit the divisions between upper and lower authorities, they are likely to deliver skip-level petitions. If they trust certain state or quasi-state agencies as their potential advocates, they may petition to official newspapers, TV stations, People's Congress, People's Political Consultative Conference, the official trade union, Disabled Persons Federation, and so forth.

Advocacy differs from other forms of political representation in that advocacy requires little participation by the represented.[23] However, petitioners' efforts to engage elite advocates can be combined with other troublemaking tactics such as disruption. Because Chinese institutions of political representation are very weak, advocacy has been a major way of channeling interest.[24] Among advocates, the most popular have been upper-level government agencies and the media. The importance of other advocates, such as mass organizations and people's representatives, has also increased substantially in recent years.

Petitions delivered to upper-level governments are usually called skip-level petitions (*yueji shangfang*). Among 902 cases in City Y, 143 were delivered directly to provincial or even the central government and 637 to the city government, even though almost all 902 cases were supposed

---

[22] This view differs from O'Brien and Li's argument, which regards the shift from indirect to direct action as escalation. See Kevin O'Brien and Lianjiang Li, *Rightful Resistance in Rural China* (New York: Cambridge University Press, 2006), chapter 4.

[23] Theda Skocpol, "Association without Members," *American Prospect* 45 (July–August 1999), pp. 66–73.

[24] Thomas Bernstein, "Farmer Discontent and Regime Responses," in Merle Goldman and Roderick Macfarquhar (eds.), *The Paradox of China's Post-Mao Reforms* (Cambridge, MA: Harvard University Press, 1999), pp. 197–219.

I. Direct Petitioning Model

II. Advocacy Model of Petitioning

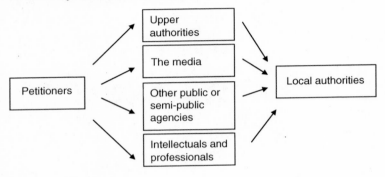

III. Public Model of Petitioning

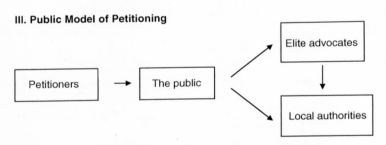

FIGURE 6.1. Three routes of popular claim making in the PRC.

to be handled only by county-level or even lower government agencies. Of course the large percentage of petitions to the city government is partly due to the bias of this data set, which tends to record petitions to the city government more than those to county-level governments and lower. Still, the high frequency of skip-level petitions demonstrates popular trust in higher authorities consistent with empirical studies that show higher authorities enjoy greater political trust than lower authorities.[25]

---

[25] Lianjiang Li, "Political Trust in Rural China," *Modern China* 30/2 (April 2004), pp. 228–258.

This phenomenon is in fact not unique to modern times. For thousands of years, aggrieved Chinese peasants have traveled to the capital to lodge their most serious grievances.[26]

Other elite advocates include the official media and other public or semi-public agencies, as well as some individuals. The official media in China sometimes does not work as the communicative media of the protests or social movements. Instead, it works as if it were part of the government in that the media assumes the responsibility of dealing with petitions.[27] It sets up a special department (the Department of Mass Work) for this purpose. As Liebman points out, "The role of many media outlets in receiving popular complaints and referring them to other government actors further underscores the media's position as a Party-state institution."[28] Even the dramatic commercialization of media outlets in recent years has not entirely changed this role. Clearly the media's commercial interests can often provide them with an additional incentive to cover the protest or the issues raised by protesters. As O'Brien has observed, "Increased editorial freedom and competitive pressures have given rise to a more market-oriented media, and exposés of official wrongdoing can generate a huge audience."[29] Of course, in such a situation they more often play a journalistic role rather than a bureaucratic one. Nonofficial media and the Internet have sometimes also reported petitioning events, but petitioners have seldom addressed their claims to them. The data for this study does not sufficiently cover petitions to the media as such information has not always been sent to xinfang bureaus. So-called mass organizations (which are officially responsible for the advocacy of interests of various sectors), such as labor unions have also occasionally played a role in popular contention. Although there are some media reports about intellectuals and professionals involved in protest activities in China, there are few reports of this type in City Y.

Another type of third-party leverage comes from the public. The public in China, as in most other countries, consists of relatively powerless

---

[26] Jonathan Ocko, "I Will Take It All the Way to Beijing: Capital Appeals in the Qing," *Journal of Asian Studies* 47/2 (May, 1988), pp. 291–315.

[27] In this paper I mainly discuss media owned or run by the government. The commercialized print media have developed substantially in recent years, but their role in the process of grievance resolution is insignificant.

[28] Benjamin Liebman, "Watchdogs or Demagogues? The Media in the Chinese Legal System," *Columbia Law Review* (January 2005), p. 102.

[29] Kevin O'Brien, "Collective Action in the Chinese Countryside," *The China Journal* 48 (2002), p. 153.

individuals. Yet as an abstract and collective entity, the public possesses very strong normative power, as demonstrated by the "mass line" in China. It is no wonder that some petitioners would like to drag the public into the contentious arena. As Figure 6.1 shows, public petitioning can be combined with advocacy petitioning. Generating public sympathy can not only exert pressure on local officials directly, but also enhance the chance for elite advocates, such as upper authorities, to intervene. When a protest has generated enough publicity, it is more difficult for local officials to cover up the problem.

Because the media in China is generally forbidden from reporting about collective actions, at least when they take place or shortly thereafter, the general public – as readers of newspapers or as a TV or radio audience – can seldom be reached by petitioners. The development of the Internet has changed this situation to some extent in that some petitioners have learned to appeal to the public via the Internet, gaining impressive success in a few cases.[30] Yet because of increasingly stringent regulation of the Internet by the Chinese government, the public comprised of Internet users is still seldom available to many ordinary petitioners.

Petitioners in China therefore need to find other ways to appeal to the public. Usually, they need to contact bystanders directly. For this purpose, they must not only choose a public space to stage their actions, but also attract public attention by virtue of some form of action, symbol, or statement, such as displaying banners or distributing handbills. This makes it important for them to utilize specific publicity tactics.

PUBLICITY TACTICS

Publicity tactics have often been mistaken for disruptive tactics. From the perspective of local officials in particular, such activities as demonstrations or displaying banners with slogans are disturbing and disruptive. Upon close examination, however, most of such activities are not intended to disrupt social or government order. Such actions are powerful (and also disturbing to local officials) because they can catch the attention of the public. Of course, sometimes such tactics can be used for disruption. For example, a group of petitioners sitting in front of a government compound may also block the gate of the compound, and therefore disrupt

---

[30] Patricia Thornton, "Digital Contention and Political Divides: Popular Protest, State Repression and the Internet in Contemporary China," a paper presented to the APSA annual meeting in Chicago, 2004.

the operation of the government. Sometimes such tactics may also unintentionally cause disruption. Their main function, however, is usually to generate publicity rather than to interfere with the everyday affairs of the government or the public in a disruptive way.

In City Y, the most popular publicity tactic is the use of banners or placards with slogans. Petitioners usually employed this method around government buildings. In one particular case, however, petitioners displayed their banner on a highway to enhance the publicity. Hanging banners and placards with slogans can instantly reach a large audience. Because slogans have to be short, it is a challenge for petitioners to find catchy words to convey their core meaning to the public. In several such cases, people also shouted the slogans in addition to displaying the banners.

The second most popular method is the use of sit-ins.[31] Like marches, sit-ins are almost never legally authorized in China, but in practice organizers of sit-ins have seldom been punished. One advantage of sit-ins is that they are relatively easy to mobilize because they appear to be a natural outgrowth of permitted activities: Whenever petitioners who have peacefully reached the government feel dissatisfied with the government's response, they may sit in front of the government compounds or office buildings. As shown in Table 6.1, it is much more popular than marching because it is closer to authorized channels. Sit-ins can also reach a large public, but may not be as influential as marching.

Marching is a forceful tactic. Even though the Chinese constitution affords the public the right to march in protest, permission has almost never been granted to any group that has applied. Petitioners, however, sometimes still employ this tactic in violation of the law. As the table shows, nine marches were carried out, twelve were prepared but prevented, and in eleven cases petitioners threatened to march but ultimately did not do so. It is a very powerful tool, but because it usually requires extensive planning and mobilization, petitioners are more likely to threaten to march than to actually carry it out, as seen in Table 6.1.

Petitioners sometimes deliver their messages via handbills. Handbills can be distributed to the general public or to specific groups. In City Y, this tactic was used thirteen times from 1992 to 2002. It has the advantage

---

[31] Sit-in as a form of collective action is somewhat different from that in the United States. Chinese people usually sit outside government buildings or compounds. It more resembles a sit-out, which was invented in the 1960s on campuses of American universities. For a discussion of sit-out, see Sarah Soule, "The Diffusion of an Unsuccessful Innovation," *Annals of the American Academy of Political and Social Science* 655 (November 1999), pp. 120–131.

TABLE 6.1. *Incidence of Petitions with "Troublemaking" Tactics in City Y, 1992–2002*

Categories	Tactics	Carried out	Prepared	Threatened	Total
Publicity tactics N = 146	Banners or placards w/ slogans, shouting slogans	44	5	6	55
	Sit-ins	39	1	6	46
	Marches	9	12	11	32
	Handbills	8	1	4	13
Performing persuasive tactics N = 53	Kneeling in supplication	4	1	0	5
	Self-inflicted suffering	4	0	0	4
	Carrying victims	8	1	6	15
	Begging	1	1	6	8
	Costumes	6	0	0	6
	Revolutionary songs	4	0	0	4
	Official seals	7	0	2	9
	Honorary symbols	1	1	0	2
Disruption of social order N = 61	Blocking traffic	20	2	10	32
	Assaulting opponents	8	1	14	23
	Strikes	4	0	2	6
Disruption of government operation N = 236	Creating a commotion	126	0	0	126
	Damaging or destroying government property, offices, or buildings, or assaulting officials	38	2	4	44
	Staying over and/or carrying bedding rolls	34	2	0	36
	Blocking entrances/cars	29	1	0	30

Notes: The data includes 902 petitioning events. Petitioners may employ several tactics in one event. In some events, petitioners did not employ any "troublemaking" tactics.

Source: City Y Xinfang Bureau.

of delivering a larger volume of information, but usually cannot reach a large audience in a short time.

Overall, publicity tactics have been commonly employed. In the data set in City Y, there are 146 incidents with such tactics. In other words, such tactics can be found in about 16 percent of events in the data set.

PERFORMING PERSUASIVE TACTICS

Performing persuasive tactics refer to artful or symbolic activities used by petitioners to strengthen the signals in their petitions. Like publicity tactics, they are not disruptive by themselves, although they can potentially be used for the purpose of disruption. For example, kneeling in supplication can be used to block the gate of a government building but is not disruptive by itself. Even though some tactics such as self-immolation involve violence, such violence is not targeted at other people. Because such tactics are not disruptive, it is rare for a modern legal system to proscribe them. In China, such tactics as self-mutilation were sometimes forbidden in imperial times. In the Reform Era, local officials have often been wary of such activities, but only rarely have they actually outlawed them. One notable exception is Shenzhen City, which promulgated a local policy to explicitly outlaw fourteen types of "abnormal" petitioning activities in November 2009. Draping white cloth over one's shoulders, self-mutilation, and self-immolation are among those forbidden activities.[32]

In the City Y data set, symbolic tactics have only been recorded fifty-three times, a much smaller number than that of publicity or disruptive tactics. This is likely a result of a bias in the data set. Many symbolic tactics, especially the moderate ones, are less likely to be reported by local officials as compared to publicity or disruptive tactics.

Kneeling in Supplication

The tactic of kneeling down before an authority needs to be understood in the context of Chinese culture. In a sense, kneeling before other people is one form of self-inflicted suffering, albeit a form of spiritual rather than physical suffering. Anybody who is familiar with Chinese culture knows

---

[32] Duowei Xinwen, "Shenzhen Xianzhi 'Feizhengchang Shangfang' Xinzhengce Zao Piping" (Shenzhen City's New Policy to Restrain 'Abnormal Petitioning Activities' Was Criticized), www.dwnews.com, last visited on November 29, 2009.

that a person does not kneel before other people without serious reasons. Kneeling in supplication demonstrates an individual's willingness to relinquish his or her dignity and submit to another's authority. Forcing people to kneel down is a common way to shame them.

In fact, in imperial times, this could not serve as a particular protest tactic because every commoner was required to kneel in supplication when addressing their issues to the authorities. Such a requirement was not abolished until the early twentieth century. Paradoxically, now that it has become a very rare ritual, kneeling in supplication has begun to be regarded as a forceful gesture. An official who ignores kneeling petitioners tends to be regarded as too unsympathetic. In one telling case, a mayor in Liaoning Province who did not promptly respond to hundreds of kneeling petitioners was dismissed from his position for this very reason.[33]

One of the most famous performances within the 1989 student movement occurred when three student representatives knelt down before the People's Great Hall. Because kneeling down is a sign of sacrificing dignity, it was regarded by many students as inappropriate in such a "democratic movement." A student activist, Ma Shaofang, later recalled that moment:

> Faced with this scene, many people [who were students] shouted loudly: "No kneeling down, stand up, stand up!" ... Students on [Tiananmen] square requested that I call back the representatives who were kneeling down. On my way, I ran into Kaixi [a student leader], who looked very emotional, with tears on his face. He said, "I did not kneel down, I did not kneel down!" At that moment, I could feel his strong discontent with kneeling down as a way of petitioning.[34]

Ma also relates kneeling down with hunger strikes, which is a typical form of self-inflicted suffering: "If our petitioning with shouting does not work, we can still kneel down. If kneeling down does not work either, we can still petition with death (*sijian*)."[35]

---

[33] Xinhuanet, "Liaoning Zhuanghe Shizhang Bei Zeling Cizhi" (The Mayor of Zhuanghe City in Liaoning was Forced to Resign), www.news.xinhuanet.com/politics/2010-04/25/c_1254258.htm, last visited on April 25, 2010. Although the actual process might be more complicated than as reported by the media, the fact that the media commonly attributed the mayor's dismissal to his ignoring kneeling petitioners indicates a common perception in China of the power of kneeling in supplication, especially by such a large group of petitioners.

[34] Ma Shaofang 2004. "Lishi Zai Bianta Xianshi" (History Is Whipping the Reality), *Beijing Spring* 133 (June 2004), p. 8.

[35] Ibid. 8.

Despite the powerful symbolic meaning, kneeling before authority has not been a common strategy. There were only four such incidents recorded in the City Y data set.

Self-Inflicted Suffering

Self-inflicted suffering describes only immediate physical suffering and excludes spiritual, long-term, or psychological suffering. Perhaps the best examples of this tactic include self-immolation, self-mutilation, and hunger strikes.

Self-inflicted suffering has some advantages. As Michael Biggs argues, "Suffering lends salience."[36] This is especially important in China, where the attention of the government has often been the primary goal of petitioners. A good example can be found in the archives of the Hunan provincial government. In 1986, a worker from a state-owned farm in Yueyang City came to the National Xinfang Bureau with a kitchen knife hidden in his pocket. When he came to the reception area, he suddenly took out the knife and chopped off one of his fingers. He was immediately sent to the hospital, and the incident was reported to several central leaders. Some major central leaders, such as the Premier, instructed the government to handle the case seriously. Consequently, this very ordinary person's commonplace grievances were thoroughly redressed. In this case, the worker's decision to chop off his finger as a form of protest turned out to be a very effective strategy. By harming his body, he caught the attention and won sympathy from usually inaccessible central leaders.

Besides salience, self-inflicted suffering can also enhance the legitimacy of the protests and the credibility of the protesters. As Biggs points out, this is consistent with costly signaling theory, which was developed independently in biology and economics. In fact, it has been argued that "in order to be effective, signals have to be reliable; in order to be reliable, signals have to be costly."[37] As discussed in Chapter 4, in the xinfang system in China, the level of suffering that petitioners endure can also help the bureaucracy screen false claims from true ones.[38] Furthermore, self-inflicted suffering can signify determination and commitment.

[36] Michael Biggs, "When Costs Are Beneficial: Protest as Communicative Suffering," Sociology Working Papers, Number 2003–04, Department of Sociology at Oxford University.

[37] Amotz Zahavi and Avishag Zahavi, *The Handicap Principle: A Missing Piece of Darwin's Puzzle* (New York: Oxford University Press, 1997), p. xiv.

[38] Ying Xing, *Dahe Yimin Shangfang De Gushi* (The Story of the Petitioning of the Migrants in Dahe Town) (Beijing: Sanlian Press, 2002).

In City Y, these events were rare. There are four incidents, including two hunger strikes and two attempted suicides (one by slashing wrists and the other by eating poison).

Other Performing Persuasive Tactics

Like self-inflicted suffering, carrying and/or displaying corpses or wounded victims can create salience and signify petitioners' grief and deprivation. As shown in Table 6.1, this tactic has been used more frequently than kneeling down or enduring self-inflicted suffering in City Y. In eight cases, petitioners carried out this tactic, and in seven others, petitioners prepared or threatened to do so. Among the most dramatic events were efforts to take the bodies of the dead or wounded to the government and display them at the entrance of government buildings. The government often found it hard to bargain with the emotional relatives of the victim while hundreds, or even thousands, of people were watching.

Another way to signify the petitioners' grief is to use costumes. White cloth is the most common costume, because Chinese people usually drape it over their shoulders in funeral rites. Like carrying the bodies of victims, wearing white cloth or draping it around an object signifies the grief of the petitioners and creates a visually dramatic effect. In six cases in the data set, petitioners draped white cloth over their shoulders. In three of these cases, the petitioners wrote some characters on the white cloth. Usually Chinese petitioners write the character "*yuan*" (being wronged), and such cloth is often referred to as the "cloth of being wronged (*yuanyi*)."

A particular tactic used by petitioners to humiliate the local government is begging for food or money. When well-to-do people beg on streets, it is more humiliating for the government than for the petitioners because it signifies unjustified deprivation. Such action is only symbolic because the purpose of petitioners is not to get food or money but to protest. Like all the previously mentioned symbolic tactics, the central theme of these actions is grief and deprivation. Petitioners typically preferred begging for rice as opposed to money because rice signifies subsistence. In the eight cases of begging in the City Y data set, only one petitioner begged for money. It is worth noting that this tactic has primarily been used as a threat, with only one case in 1993 actually being carried out.

For those petitioners who claimed that the government was indebted to them because of their contribution to the regime, singing revolutionary songs is a sensible tactic. The City Y data set includes two cases of this tactic: one by retired cadres and workers and another by demobilized army officers. By singing revolutionary songs, petitioners tried to reach three audiences at once: the petitioners themselves, the public, and the state. For petitioners, revolutionary songs express their sentiment of nostalgia and can enhance their sense of solidarity. Singing songs can also remind both the public and the state that these petitioners have made their contribution to the country, and therefore deserve better treatment. This tactic highlights the contradiction between the CCP's proclaimed commitment to revolution and its acquiescence to social problems caused by a market economy.

Displaying honorary symbols in petitioning activities serves a similar function as singing revolutionary songs. This tactic signifies moral reciprocity even more directly. There are three cases of protesters displaying honorary symbols in the City Y data set. In one instance, retired and laid-off workers in a bankrupt enterprise carried to the city government an old certificate showing that the factory had contributed profits in excess of 3 million yuan to the government in one year. By displaying this symbol, the petitioners not only demanded economic security, but also protested the government's failure to manage the factory well. In two other cases, protesters displayed their medals of military merit.

Lastly, to prove the legitimacy and validity of the petitions, some petitioners managed to have their petitions stamped by official seals, usually by local governments. This strategy is straightforward, but the state is often averse to this tactic because it is a sign of alliance between state agencies and petitioners.

In sum, by taking advantage of traditional culture and contradictions in official ideology, Chinese petitioners have often tried to utilize artful or symbolic activities to press their claims. They count on the possibility that local officials' sympathy or sense of shame can prompt them to take action on the petitioners' behalf.

DISRUPTION OF SOCIAL ORDER

When petitioners decide to employ disruptive tactics, they can either disrupt social order or the government operations. Given that the government is responsible for social order, disruption of social order can indirectly impose costs on the government.

Among the tactics intended to disrupt social order, blocking traffic has become a favorite tactic of Chinese petitioners today. This tactic has several advantages. First, it is easy to carry out because national and provincial highways sprawl all over the country. People can block highways nearby without making too great an effort. Furthermore, most cities in Hunan Province are located across big rivers, where bridges connect different parts of the cities. In general, people can easily transition from peaceful action to the disruptive action of blocking a nearby road or bridge. In several cases in City Y, dozens to hundreds of depositors who went to the financial institutions to ask for their savings began to block the national highway nearby when they found out that they had no chance of receiving their savings in the near future.

Blocking traffic is usually very disruptive and can exert great pressure on the government to make concessions. Within minutes, hundreds or even thousands of vehicles can be forced to stop on the road. Because many of the roads in question are national or provincial highways, the impact of such protests often goes beyond the jurisdiction of the local government. Blocking bridges in the city can be even more disruptive because a considerable part of the busy social and economic activities in the city rely on uninterrupted bridge traffic.

Assaulting opponents is another tactic used to disrupt social order. By opponents, I mean the persons or institutions other than the government that petitioners complain, or protest, against. Examples include instances in which petitioners attacked managers or vandalized a factory to protest managers' corruption, depositors of banks attacked the institutions when they could not withdraw their savings in time to avoid a loss, and villagers attacked a factory to protest its pollution of the environment. As shown in Table 6.1, petitioners are more likely to threaten rather than actually use this tactic. There are fourteen events in the data set in which petitioners threatened to assault their opponents, but only eight events in which petitioners actually carried it out.

The third tactic in this category is to strike. Petitioners in City Y rarely used strikes, which are not allowed by law, to advance their interests. It is worth noting that among the four cases in which strikes were carried out, only one involved workers; the other three involved self-employed drivers. When the workers went on strike, the target of the protest was a government agency that intervened in the operation of the company, not the company managers themselves. Therefore, in City Y, strikes have been carried out not to impose costs on employers, but to exert pressure on the government.

As discussed earlier, Chinese petitioners tend to frame their "troublemaking" as a natural extension or escalation of moderate petitioning activities. However, compared to other "troublemaking" tactics, disruption of social order is relatively difficult to justify in this fashion. Consequently, petitioners often prefer to threaten to use such tactics rather than actually carry them out. As Table 6.1 shows, there are twenty-six incidents in which petitioners threatened to block traffic, assault their opponents, or go on strike. The ratio of threatened incidents to carried-out incidents is twenty-six to thirty-two. By comparison, such a ratio for disruption of government operation is 4 to 227; for performing persuasive tactics, the ratio is 14 to 35; and for publicity tactics, the ratio is 27 to 100.

DISRUPTION OF GOVERNMENT OPERATION

Compared to the incidence of disruption of social order (61), the incidence of disruptions of governmental operation (236) is considerably higher. This can be explained by two factors. First, disruption of government operation works more directly. Petitioners usually target the government, and the disruption of the government directly imposes costs on government officials. Second, it is closer to authorized channels, which is one of the main features of rightful resistance.[39] In cases where protesters do end up disrupting government operation, they usually begin with "civilized" forms of petitioning and only later shift to tactics that disrupt government function. For this reason, as noted earlier, it is very rare for petitioners to threaten to disrupt government operation. Such action is often simply carried out, as if unplanned.

Creating a commotion is the most common disruptive tactic used in petitioning. There are 126 incidents in this City Y data. This is hardly surprising, as anxious and impatient petitioners are quite likely to strengthen their voice by cursing, screaming, crying, and shouting. It requires little mobilization and is relatively moderate and tolerable. It has often been done indoors and is quite similar to "normal" petitions. The downside is that this tactic's tolerability often undermines its efficacy.

Petitioners have occasionally resorted to violence. They damaged or destroyed public properties and attacked or imprisoned officials. Such actions are disruptive in a very direct sense. There have been thirty-eight incidents in City Y in which petitioners resorted to violence. The often surprising leniency of the government has encouraged such actions. In the City Y data set, no more than a handful of assaults have been seriously punished.

A less violent tactic is staying over or carrying bedding rolls to government offices. When they are not satisfied with the response of government

---

[39] O'Brien and Li, *Rightful Resistance in Rural China*.

officials, petitioners may sometimes refuse to leave. They stay in the office or the government compound playing cards, chatting, shouting, or sleeping. In many cases this amounts to an occupation of the government office. Petitioners have sometimes deliberately demonstrated their determination to stay by bringing bedding rolls with them. This form of action is also relatively close to authorized activities, because petitioners only occupy space where they have access, such as reception areas in the bureaus of letters and visits or in government compounds. This is also a relatively common tactic. There are thirty-four incidents in the data set in which petitioners used it, and two other incidents in which petitioners prepared to use it.

The last main tactic in this category is blocking the gate of a government building or blocking the cars of government leaders. This is similar to the tactic of blocking traffic discussed earlier. Yet blocking the main entrance to the government compound or leaders' cars mainly aims at interrupting the operation of the government rather than disrupting the wider public. This is also a favorite strategy by petitioners in City Y. There are twenty-nine incidents of this tactic's use in the City Y data. Compared with blocking traffic, blocking entrances and cars are more likely to be tolerated by the government. It is regarded as less disruptive, even though government officials are often adversely affected. Blocking leaders' cars is related to a traditional tactic, called *yaochejia*, which refers to incidents in ancient China, when petitioners attempted to block the sedans of high-ranking officials to deliver petitions.

Having examined the routes and means of "troublemaking" tactics, I now want to take stock of the findings. The popularity of indirect routes of petitioning indicates that the political system offers a multitude of opportunities for petitioners to press their claims. In their struggle with the local government, ordinary people have identified a variety of potential advocates within the state structure. The system has also been sensitive to public opinion, which motivates petitioners to find ways to generate publicity. Consistent with the discussion in Chapter 5 on protest opportunism, evidence from City Y indicates that petitioners often did not want to frame their relationship with the local government as entirely antagonistic. They act as if there is mutual understanding between them and local officials, despite the tension in the relationship. They tried to make their cases with nondisruptive "troublemaking" tactics, hoping to win local officials' sympathy or shame them into action through public forms of persuasion. Of course, disruption is still a main form of "troublemaking." However, even when they employ disruptive tactics, they are often still very concerned about the justifiability of such activities. They therefore prefer those disruptive tactics that can be easily portrayed as a natural growth of moderate petitioning.

A STATISTICAL ANALYSIS OF PROTEST EFFICACY

"Troublemaking" tactics are often believed by petitioners to be effective in eliciting government response. The study of the xinfang system also suggests that such tactics can help petitioners overcome bureaucratic barriers. However, so far, no systematic empirical study has been conducted by China scholars to test this popular perception or to assess the effectiveness of various subtypes of "troublemaking" tactics. The data set from City Y provides us with a unique opportunity to conduct a statistical analysis on the effect of different types of "troublemaking" tactics.

The goal of this analysis is to test the efficacy of the four main types of "troublemaking tactics." The hypothesis is that *the presence of troublemaking tactics will increase the probability of substantial government responses.*

GOVERNMENT RESPONSES AS THE DEPENDENT VARIABLE

I only measure the short-term responses of the government; it is not feasible to measure long-term effects from the data. Short-term responses are a good indicator as to how much the government cares about complaints and protests. If a complaint or protest cannot catch the attention of the government in a short period of time, it is unlikely to get any substantial response afterward. Similarly, if a complaint or protest has received prompt attention, it is more likely to get a substantial response later. Of course, there are some exceptions. In some cases, the government was somewhat concerned about the complaints or protests when they first took place, but interest faded away and no substantial measures were taken afterward.

I distinguish government responses into two categories: substantial and nonsubstantial. I regard the following facts as indicative of substantial government responses: (1) major local leaders or department leaders dialogued with petitioners, or gave written instructions on how to deal with the petitions;[40] (2) the government set up a special work or investigative team, or convened a special meeting to discuss how to deal with the petitions; (3) the government met part or all of petitioners' demands.

---

[40] The term "major leaders" usually refers to all members of the standing committee of local party committees, heads and vice heads of government, and the secretary-general of both the party committee and the government.

When the government document only mentioned petitions and did not report any official measures, I assume that there was no substantial short-term response.[41] When no responses were reported, I exercise great caution in determining if it is because the government did not respond or because the officials who wrote the reports had no interest in mentioning the responses. If it was too hard to decide, I report it as missing data.

Of the 902 cases, there are 226 that lack information on government responses. Of the remaining cases, 449 are categorized as eliciting no substantial response and 227 as eliciting substantial responses. Because the dependent variable is dichotomous, a logit model is the most appropriate estimation technique.

"TROUBLEMAKING TACTICS" AS INDEPENDENT VARIABLES

I regard petitions delivered to provincial or national government officials as petitions with high-level targets. I use high-level petitions rather than skip-level petitions as an independent variable mainly because it is too difficult to measure skip-level petitions without sufficient information to judge which level of government is supposed to deal with each case. Because most cases in the City Y data set concerned the city government's response, it is reasonable to label petitions to provincial or central government officials as high-level petitions. I code any case in which people delivered their petitions to high-level government officials as 1, and all others as 0.

All three other independent variables are also dummy variables. I code cases in which petitioners used tactics of publicity, performing persuasion, or disruption as 1, and the others as 0.

CONTROL VARIABLES

The first control variable is the timing of protests or complaints. Petitioning at special times seems more likely to elicit substantial government response. For one thing, protesters can probably better catch the attention of the local leaders who often attend important local events

[41] It is necessary to note that, in general, many petitions have been completely ignored and received no response at all. Yet in my data set, every case has at least received a minimum level of government attention because they have been written into government reports. Therefore, in my data set, the cases without substantial government responses should be understood as "the cases that have been reported in government documents but have not received substantial responses."

such as festivals or important meetings. In addition, many of those events are political rituals that symbolize legitimacy and stability. Therefore, local governments usually make great efforts to avoid protests or dissolve them as quickly as they can. Among the 902 cases in the City Y data set, there are 161 petitioning events carried out, prepared, or threatened to be carried out on special occasions. The predominant choice is the "Two Conferences" (*lianghui*), which refers to the yearly conferences of People's Congresses and the People's Political Consultative Conferences. Other periods include other major political meetings, the three main holidays (New Year, Spring Festival, and National Day), and officially sponsored festivals or celebrations. In this dummy variable, I code any case in which people delivered their petitions in such special periods as 1, and all others as 0.

This study also considers the interaction effect between special timing and protest tactics. For instance, disruption might be substantially more effective during special periods when it can create a stronger impression of disorder on the public and higher level authorities.

The second control variable is the size of protests and complaints. The size of protests and complaints may significantly affect efficacy. This is partly because large-scale collective action facilitates disruption. As James Scott points out, large gatherings embolden participants and provide anonymity.[42] A large crowd is usually also more capable of disruption than a small one. More importantly, however, the number of participants has a significant symbolic value. A large turnout at a protest usually signifies more justifiable demands.

This five-category ordinal variable indicates the number of petitioners: very small (1–4), small (5–29), medium (30–99), large (100–499), and very large (over 500). In most cases I use the number of petitioners who deliver the petitions. When petitions have been mailed or telegraphed, and were not personally delivered, I use the number of signers of the letters or telegraphs. These categories are largely consistent with those used by xinfang bureaus. Xinfang bureaus define petitions with more than five participants as collective petitions, and regard petitions with more than thirty participants as relatively large. They are particularly alert to petitioning events with more than 100 participants, and have even specified some special procedures for handling such petitions.[43] Considering

[42] James Scott, *Domination and the Arts of Resistance: Hidden Transcripts* (New Haven, CT: Yale University Press, 1990), pp. 149–152.

[43] According to the Hunan provincial government's regulations, local governments need to report events with more than 100 participants more promptly.

that a few cases in which there are more than 500 participants might be handled differently from those cases with fewer participants, I further distinguish petitioning events with more than 500 participants from those whose participants' number between 100 and 499.

Another factor that may have significant impact on government response is the issues of the protests. It is possible that the government may be more responsive to issues that were perceived as urgent or important. Protest by peasants and urban pensioners have been two of the biggest concerns for the Chinese government. Accordingly, this study includes two dummy variables: villagers' and pensioners' protests.

RESULTS

Table 6.2 provides the result of the regression and includes two separate models, where Model 1 excludes the interaction terms that are included in Model 2. In general, the results conform to my expectations that the size of the protest, publicity petitioning, and disruptions all increase the likelihood of a substantial government response. In addition, there is modest evidence that skip-level petitioning slightly enhances protest efficacy.

In general, Model 1 provides a good fit to the data in that it correctly predicts government responses in 74.53 percent of the 644 filtered cases. After controlling for the size, timing, and issues of petitioning, and holding all other independent variables of tactics constant, the presence of publicity and disruptive petitioning tactics increases the probability of substantial government responses. The coefficients for these two dimensions of tactics are statistically significant and positive. The effectiveness of disruptive tactics is hardly surprising. More notable is the effect of publicity tactics, which indicates the government's concern about "social impact" even when no mass media carries the news.

The coefficients for performing persuasive tactics and elite-engaging tactics are small and statistically insignificant. Why do persuasive tactics not lead to substantive government response? One reason lies in the remarkable heterogeneity of this variable. It includes very intense forms such as self-immolation and quite moderate forms such as displaying honorary symbols. Indeed, an examination of those cases using highly intense tactics suggests that they have a strong impact. For example, all four cases of self-inflicted sufferings found substantive response. To examine this effect, I created a new dichotomous variable coded 1 for self-immolation and 0 for all else. I substitute it for the dummy variable of persuasive tactics. The coefficient for the new variable, however, is not

TABLE 6.2. *Logit Coefficients for Regression of the Presence of Substantial Government Responses to Petitioning Tactics in City Y, 1992–2002*

Independent Variable	Equation	
	(1)	(2)
Timing	−.096	−.137
	(.086)	(.103)
Size of protests or complaints	.316***	.312***
	(.093)	(.093)
Pensioners	−.064	−.008
	(.217)	(.219)
Villagers	−.983*	−.977
	(.499)	(.499)
Skip-level petitioning	.289	.294
	(.224)	(.224)
Publicity petitioning	1.071***	.805*
	(.290)	(.323)
Persuasive actions	.160	.330
	(.396)	(.428)
Disruptions	1.241***	1.283***
	(.233)	(.257)
Persuasive action * Timing	–	−.996
		(1.236)
Publicity * Timing	–	1.262
		(.739)
Disruption * Timing	–	−.012
		(.595)
Constant	−1.839***	−1.835***
	(.252)	(.253)
Log-likelihood	696.640	693.088
X^2	129.067	132.619
Degree of freedom	8	11
Number of cases	644	644

*p < .05; **p < .01; ***p < .001.

statistically significant even at the level of 0.1. This is likely due to the very small number of cases of self-immolation.

The insignificance of high-level petitioning is somewhat surprising considering that this tactic is generally perceived by petitioners as useful. It is possible that such a tactic can give petitioners some, but not a sufficient, advantage for eliciting a favorable response. To test this hypothesis, I create a new dependent variable: procedurally effective response. This variable is similar to substantial government response, but is measured by a lower standard. A substantial response is therefore necessarily a procedurally effective response. Yet there are three additional indicators for procedurally effective responses: (1) the report described the attitude of the government as "highly concerned;" (2) petitions have been put into a file;[44] and (3) petitions have been included in reports from upper-level government agencies distributed to lower-level government agencies so that the latter need to deal with them. Because this variable holds to a lower standard, there are more cases that fall into this category. Among 644 cases, there are 398 cases of procedurally effective response, in contrast with 227 cases of substantial government response. I substituted this variable for substantial government response and ran Model 1 again. Compared to the previous regression, the new one produces similar outcomes for all of the independent variables except for high-level petitioning. High-level petitioning turns out to be significant at the level of 0.001. The odds ratio is 13.8, which implies protests using this tactic are 13.8 times more likely than protests not using this tactic to obtain procedurally effective response. This confirms the hypothesis that high-level petitioning generates an advantage, albeit relatively weak, for the protesters.

Among the control variables, the size of protests or complaints is strongly correlated to the probability of substantial government response. The effect of size can possibly be mediated by disruption because disruption created by a large number of people tends to be more devastating. Yet this regression controls for the effect of disruption, so the effectiveness of large numbers lies mainly in its symbolic value. In other words, the government is more likely to give a larger-sized protest a substantive response because officials believe such protests have more legitimate and important claims.

Contrary to general expectations, the issues raised by protests seem to have little impact on government response. The issues raised by pensioners do not have a statistically significant effect. Similarly, the issues concerning villagers are barely significant in a statistical sense (at the level of 0.05). Of course, this result does not mean pensioners or villagers are not more successful, or even less successful than other groups. This study only uses the group identity as a control variable. It indicates that controlling for the size of protest and the use of disruption and other "troublemaking" tactics, peasants or pensioners are not more successful.

---

[44] Putting cases into file is a formal government procedure. When a case has been put into a file, specific officials or government agencies are required to handle the case and report the results when they have finished.

However, if in fact villagers or pensioners are more likely to engage in large-scale "troublemaking" tactics, they can potentially be more successful as a group because their successes will be reflected in the other variables that are included in the equation.

Another surprising finding is that the timing of protests or complaints does not correlate with the probability of substantial government response. To examine if the timing has an indirect effect, I conducted another logistic regression. In Model 2, the timing is treated as an interactive rather than an additive variable. Considering the possibility of multicollinearity, I conducted a joint significance test for timing and three other independent variables. These joint tests of significance show that the timing of protests has an interactive effect with disruption and publicity, but not with performing persuasive tactics. This indicates that although timing by itself does not help protesters elicit a substantial response, it can increase the effectiveness of disruptive and publicity tactics. The coefficients for all independent variables in Model 2 except the interactive ones are quite consistent with those in Model 1. This indicates that the coefficients in Model 1 are relatively robust.

CONCLUSION

Chinese petitioners have employed a variety of tactics to further their claims, many of which are "troublemaking" but not disruptive. The popularity of such "troublemaking" but ultimately nondisruptive tactics likely derives from the perception among petitioners that these tactics are in fact effective in achieving the protesters' desired outcomes. Whether their perceptions of protest efficacy are correct or not, such perceptions reflect protesters' understanding of their relationship with the authorities.

Although Chinese petitioners have employed a variety of "troublemaking" tactics during the period under review, their actions often involve one or more of the following four mechanisms: persuasion, disruption, publicity, and elite advocacy. The statistical study confirms that disruption, publicity, and event size all positively affect the likelihood of a substantial government response. Elite advocacy also gives some limited advantages to petitioners.

The fact that both the breadth of publicity and the number of participants have a significant influence on government response indicates that the government's action is not determined solely by negative inducements. The significance of publicity in determining official response indicates the government's concern about public opinion, even when it is highly unlikely that the public will be mobilized to engage in disruptive activities. Likewise, the presence of a large number of participants tends to imply more legitimate claims. Clearly, government officials also care about the symbolic aspects of protests and complaints.

When protesters choose persuasive tactics, they assume that their claims could potentially win sympathy from local officials. Protesters and local officials often share a cultural understanding about what can make a claim appear more important and legitimate. Protesters have also been astute at exploiting the contradictions within official ideology, as when they use symbols of revolution or socialism to protest their sufferings in a market economy. Although such tactics do not have a significant overall impact in a statistical sense, they still make a difference in specific cases. An examination of a few radical persuasive tactics such as self-immolation suggests that self-inflicted suffering is potentially quite efficacious, although the number of such cases is too small to produce statistical significance. Likewise, elite advocacy has had only a limited impact, mainly because skip-level petitions are so common. Skip-level petitioners can often gain some advantages, but still need to distinguish themselves from many others by other "troublemaking" tactics. The fact that so many protesters count on upper authorities indicates that the divisions among elites still offer them some hope.

This study of the range, variety, and efficacy of "troublemaking" tactics has not only deepened our understanding of the strategic orientation of social protests in China, but also confirmed the impact of changes in the political opportunity structure in China since the 1990s. Given the perceived, and often actual, effectiveness of a variety of "troublemaking" tactics, it is not difficult to understand how such activities have become so frequent in such a political environment.

PART IV

CONCLUSION

7

Reflections and Speculations

Even two decades ago, few people expected popular collective action to become common or even "normal" in China. A variety of social groups, including pensioners, laid-off workers, peasants, urban homeowners, demobilized army officers, and people with disabilities, have mounted collective protests to the government. Indeed, when such groups have strong claims to make to the government, they can seldom find a better way than through collective petitioning. From the early 1990s to present, such activities were not just common; many of them were actually a central part of protracted struggles with the government. Through forceful and often persistent collective action, many "disadvantaged" social groups have exerted considerable influence on local policies.

Contentious authoritarianism, wherein a strong authoritarian regime accommodates widespread and routinized collective protests, is a very rare phenomenon. Even in the long history of China, which witnessed numerous rebellions and occasional waves of protests and social movements, it is hard to find a relatively long period when collective protests were so common and routine. To be sure, protests movements have been substantially institutionalized and normalized in some liberal democracies, which are called "social movement societies." However, authoritarian regimes in general are still quite hostile to popular collective action, and the opening of political opportunity for mass mobilization in such societies tends to be very brief.

How can we account for the emergence of contentious authoritarianism in China in the 1990s? Even though widespread collective protests are probably the last thing that Chinese leaders want to see, they are a logical product of the Chinese political system. China is one of the few countries in today's world that still resolutely rejects liberal democracy as the best political model. Instead, it pursues a special version of "socialist democracy," in which the mass line ideology is an essential element. According to the mass line ideology, political power should be highly centralized, and only Party leaders can make important decisions. However, it also particularly values nonbinding political consultation and insists that policy making should be based on adequate ante- and post-decision consultation with the masses. Ordinary people are therefore invited to lodge complaints and submit petitions, and such (usually negative) "feedback" is considered indispensable for the Party to maintain responsiveness and to hold state agents accountable.

However, tensions between the centralized power structure and extensive nonbinding consultation have created abundant contradictions and ambiguities within the political system. In this power structure, ordinary people are tempted to address their issues directly to key leaders at various levels, and those leaders are also expected to personally handle at least some important complaints and petitions. Unsurprisingly, however, the volume of petitions far exceeds leaders' capacity for dealing with them, and therefore a vast majority of petitions cannot be adequately handled. This system therefore tends to frustrate moderate petitioners and ultimately motivates many of them to mount public and collective action with "troublemaking" tactics. Only in this way can they possibly overcome bureaucratic hurdles to elicit a government response. At the same time, to ensure adequate information flow via complaints and petitions, which act as a key instrument of political responsiveness and accountability in China, the xinfang system has been ambiguous toward, and thus provides a certain degree of legitimacy to, a variety of "troublemaking" activities such as collective, skip-level, overly persistent, and public petitioning. Upper authorities also tend to intensively supervise their subordinates, constraining their repression and assigning strong responsibility to them for handling petitions adequately and properly. This provides further security and bargaining power to petitioners.

Of course, by themselves, such contradictions and ambiguities cannot adequately account for the surge of collective protests. After all, there was no similar upsurge before the 1990s, even though such features have been present in the system for some time. Similarly, other socialist countries, such as the former Soviet Union, which maintained similar institutions for handling citizen complaints, did not witness comparable waves of collective protests.[1] Other aspects of the particular political structure of Reform-Era China have also played an essential role in bringing about the surge.

It should come as no surprise that contentious authoritarianism emerged in China only during the epochal transition to a market economy. This is not just because extensive economic transitions have engendered deep sufferings and grievances among large population sectors. More importantly, the way in which ordinary people are linked to the state has changed dramatically. With the abolition of the People's Communes in the countryside and the substantial decline of work units in urban areas, ordinary people have largely parted with the unit system, for good and for bad. They have lost most of the benefits and security associated with the old system, but they have also been freed from "organized dependence." For their basic needs and benefits they need to negotiate directly with the government rather than with state agents in their units. This transformation has dramatically changed the resources and mentalities of both state officials and ordinary people.

Economic reforms have also significantly transformed the state structure and increased divisions and functional differentiations among state agencies in both vertical and horizontal dimensions. Economic decentralization has created local interests that diverge considerably from central interests, and these changes have also weakened the central government's capacity to rein in local officials. At the same time, a variety of state and quasi-state agencies, such as the legislature, courts, official media, and mass organizations, have begun to develop somewhat distinctive identities, and may not always take a position consistent with other state agencies. The divisions in the state structure in vertical and horizontal dimensions have provided protesters with in-system advocates and protectors, and thus such divisions have further facilitated their efforts at collective protest.

[1] See Merle Fainsod, *Smolensk Under Soviet Rule* (New York: Vintage Books, 1979); James H. Oliver, "Citizen Demands and the Soviet Political System," *American Political Science Review* 63 (June 1969), pp. 465–475; Dietrich Rueschemeyer, "Planning without Markets: Knowledge and State Action in East German Housing Construction," *East European Politics and Societies* 4/3 (Fall 1990), pp. 557–579. Of course, there are some differences between the system in the former Soviet Union and Eastern European countries and the contemporary Chinese political system that help account for why contentious authoritarianism was unlikely to emerge in those former socialist regimes. For example, the system in those countries was not as centralized and did not value complaints and petitions as much as the system in Reform-Era China.

Even this particularly favorable institutional configuration does not automatically translate into widespread and routinized protests. When contradictions and ambiguities work as a key element of the political opportunity structure, petitioners have to take the initiative to exploit these opportunities. It is therefore especially important for Chinese petitioners to develop a strategic pattern of protest opportunism: They exert pressure on local officials with public and collective protests that utilize various "troublemaking" tactics, but also balance defiant activities with actions and statements that demonstrate their obedience. "Troublemaking" creates bargaining power, and obedience helps sustain the struggle. When an increasing number of people tried to appropriate existing institutions, such as the xinfang system, the Chinese government responded with a series of policy adjustments and institutional reforms aimed at containing collective petitioning. However, most of these adjustments and reforms have been futile or counterproductive because they merely strengthened local officials' responsibility and therefore paradoxically increased petitioners' bargaining power.

The examination of contentious authoritarianism in China presented in this book has several important theoretical implications. It calls for a reevaluation of the relationship between the state and popular contention, particularly in the context of authoritarianism. It underscores the oft-overlooked proactive role of the state and provides a concept of political opportunity structure that incorporates contradictions and ambiguities in state institutions and ideology, and can also integrate structural change with institutional and cultural continuity. However, this study does not only have theoretical significance; it also offers important insights on practical political concerns. As China has become the second-largest economy in the world, and risen to become a global superpower, political order in China is no longer merely a local concern. Political stability and the direction of China's political development have a profound impact on global political and economic affairs.[2] In particular, the China model, which combines a market economy with an authoritarian political system, has attracted enormous attention, especially from developing countries searching for an alternative to liberal democracy.[3] The book can shed light on an important but understudied aspect of this model – a contentious society – and help speculate on its future direction.

[2] Fareed Zakaria, *The Future of Freedom: Illiberal Democracy at Home and Abroad* (New York: W. W. Norton, 2003).
[3] For example, see Azar Gat, "The Return of Authoritarian Great Powers," *Foreign Affairs* 86/4 (July/August 2007), pp. 59–69.

A PROACTIVE STATE

To many people, the PRC is just a typical authoritarian regime intolerant of popular contention. The CCP's high-handed crackdown on the student movement of 1989 and Falungong demonstrations of 1999 shows its determination and capacity for dampening social movements. However, such harsh repression of social movements belies the regime's toleration and even facilitation of localized social protests on specific socioeconomic issues. The point is not that the Chinese government is unconcerned about rampant social protests. Rather, Chinese leaders have developed a strong sense of crisis and generally perceive social protests as a major threat to political stability. However, even though they have made many efforts to contain social protests, the regime has still often facilitated them.

When accounting for the puzzling emergence of contentious authoritarianism in China since the 1990s, this book focuses on the role of state toleration and facilitation. Although the presence of a proactive role on the part of the state might surprise many theorists, some astute scholars on China have observed it. Maoist China is famous for waves of political campaigns, in which the Party-state mobilized the masses extensively. What is especially puzzling is the Party-state's continuing role in seemingly spontaneous popular contention in the post-Mao era. In his study of the 1989 student movement, Andrew Walder wrote:

> I am arguing not simply that elite divisions and the loss of discipline within the Party-state apparatus combined to create an opening for protest; I am arguing that defecting members of the regime acted themselves to mobilize the general population into the streets, signaling to the populace that staged shows of support for hunger strikers were reasonable, even encouraged. Instead of an "additive" effect usually implied in studies inspired by resource mobilization theory or reasoning about historical conjunctures, I am arguing that the interaction of regime defectors with street protesters had a "multiplicative" effect that vastly expanded both the scale of the street protests and the paralysis of the government in a very short period of time.[4]

The role of state facilitation in the student movement of 1989 as described by Walder is not exactly the same as that in social protests discussed in this book. In the latter case, it is not regime defectors, but a converted

[4] Andrew Walder, "Collective Protest and the Waning of the Communist State in China," in Michael Hanagan, Leslie Page Moch, and Wayne te Brake (eds.), *Challenging Authority: The Historical Study of Contentious Politics* (Minneapolis: University of Minnesota Press, 1998), p. 71.

channel for interest articulation that provided incentives and favorable conditions for popular contention. Yet in both cases, the state provided very strong dynamics for mass mobilization.

A proactive role for an authoritarian state certainly poses challenges to our current understanding of contentious politics in the context of authoritarianism. Most theorists assume that authoritarian regimes are inherently repressive with regard to popular contention. Indeed, neglect of the proactive role of the state is not confined to studies of authoritarian regimes; state facilitation of spontaneous popular contention is seldom expected within any political system. Thus Elizabeth Perry remarks:

> The close relationship between state authorization and social move-
> ments in China raises some questions concerning the applicability of
> general theories of contentious politics, developed for the most part
> on the basis of European and American cases. Although these theories
> have certainly not ignored the role of the state, they have generally been
> content to suggest a negative correlation between state strength and
> politically threatening social movements ... but the Chinese experience
> argues for acknowledging a larger, more pro-active role for the state.[5]

The fact that contentious authoritarianism seems to be "unlikely" indicates the limits of current theories. An ability to comprehend how social protests can be tolerated and facilitated by authoritarian states can therefore expand our understanding of the complexity of authoritarian regimes and of the concept of political opportunity structures (POS) for mass mobilization.

LIMITS OF ELITE POWER

As McAdam suggests, theories of contentious politics always imply a more general model of institutionalized power.[6] Throughout the last four decades, the elite power model has undergirded the two dominant social movement theories: resource mobilization theory and political process theory. This model is sharply distinct from the previous pluralism model that assumes that no social group is powerful enough to exclude others from the political arena, even though the power may not be equal among them.[7] By contrast, this perspective assumes that wealth and power are

---

[5] Elizabeth J. Perry, *Challenging the Mandate of Heaven: Social Protest and State Power in China* (Armonk, NY: M.E. Sharpe, 2002), p. xxi.
[6] Doug McAdam, *Political Process and the Development of Black Insurgency, 1930–1970* (Chicago: University of Chicago Press, 1982), p. 36.
[7] Ibid, p. 5.

concentrated in the hands of a few groups, thus depriving most people of any real influence over the major decisions that affect their lives. Charles Tilly's polity model therefore distinguishes polity members who have regular and low-cost access to the policy-making process from challengers who are excluded.[8]

In most regimes, such categorical inequalities are not only systemic, but also durable. Tilly explains how such durable inequalities persist:

> Because exploitation and opportunity hoarding often involve an effective means of control over members of excluded and subordinated categories, because emulation neutralizes distinctions by making them ubiquitous, and because adaptation ties even exploited groups to the structure of exploitation, most categorical inequality stays in place without sustained, overt struggle.[9]

But when can the subordinate classes mount sustained and overt struggle? Given the huge advantages of the elite, subordinate classes' indigenous resources clearly are inadequate for sustaining an overt popular collective action. Scholars have thus put forth a variety of theories of political opportunity structures (POS). However, our current understanding of POS is at the same time too narrow and too general. It is too narrow because it leaves out some important elements of the political environment, which provide incentives and favorable conditions for popular contention. Let us examine one of the most authoritative formulas of POS:

1. The multiplicity of independent centers of power within it.
2. Its openness to new actors.
3. The instability of current political alignments.
4. The instability of influential allies or supporters for challengers.
5. The extent to which the regime represses or facilitates collective claim making.
6. Decisive changes in items 1 to 5.[10]

This formula heavily concentrates on divisions among elites. From the perspective of the whole regime, the multiplicity of independent centers of power, the instability of current political alignments, and the availability

[8] Charles Tilly, *From Mobilization to Revolution* (Reading, MA: Addison-Wesley, 1978), pp. 52–53.
[9] Charles Tilly, *Durable Inequality* (Berkeley: University of California Press, 1998), p. 225.
[10] Charles Tilly and Sidney Tarrow, *Contentious Politics* (Boulder, CO: Paradigm Publishers, 2007), p. 57.

of allies (items 1, 3, and 4) all essentially refer to divisions among elites, albeit from slightly different angles. Contradictions and ambiguities within state ideologies and institutions seem to have been left out of this formula.[11] If the formula includes state contradictions and ambiguities in items 2 and 5 by treating them as an aspect of regime openness or propensity for repression or facilitation, then these two items would look too general. Tarrow and McAdam warned that without precise specification, the concept of political opportunity may remain a grab bag of ad hoc residual categories, adduced whenever "deeper" structural factors cannot be identified.[12]

Although this study confirms the importance of elite divisions, it highlights another type of limit to elite power: the contradictions and ambiguities within state ideology and institutions. Like elite divisions, state contradictions and ambiguities can impose considerable constraints on elites' (or the state's) strategies for containing popular collective action. It is therefore reasonable to include them as an important aspect of POS.

Essentially, political opportunity for popular mobilization lies in the limits of elite power. Even though the elite enjoy a huge advantage in power, they may not always be able to take advantage of their superiority to outmaneuver challengers. Under some circumstances, not only can a relatively safe space be created, but the elite may even provide important resources for challengers. For example, the concession of British rulers to organized Protestant Dissenters in 1828 undermined their justifications for excluding organized Catholics in 1829.[13]

In many cases, the elite's facilitation of popular contention is not due to miscalculation, but to institutional or ideological constraints. Consequently their facilitation is systematic rather than haphazard. Elite divisions are certainly an important reason for some elites to offer their support to challengers, but state contradictions and ambiguities can often provide an equally strong, if not more important, impetus for popular contention.

James Scott casts doubt on the assumption that "dominant classes do, in fact, share a well-defined and coherent ideology" by pointing out that "such ideological coherence may be quite rare – perhaps even

---

[11] Ibid, p. 57.

[12] Sidney Tarrow, "States and Opportunities: The Political Structuring of Social Movements," in Doug McAdam, John D. McCarthy, Mayer N. Zald (eds.), *Comparative Perspectives on Social Movements: Political Opportunities, Mobilizing Structures, and Cultural Framings* (New York: Cambridge University Press, 1996), p. 54.

[13] Tilly, *Durable Inequality*, p. 225.

among intellectuals whose stock in trade is the formulation of systems of thought."[14] The conflicts and ambiguities within ideology can often provide opportunity for social appropriation by the underclass. As Scott remarks:

> The very process of attempting to legitimate a social order by idealizing it *always* provides its subjects with the means, the symbolic tools, the very ideas for a critique that operates entirely within the hegemony. ... The dominant ideology can be turned against its privileged beneficiaries not only because subordinate groups develop their own interpretations, understandings, and readings of its ambiguous terms, but also because of the promises that the dominant classes must make to propagate it in the first place.[15]

Like official ideology, law is notoriously double-edged. As illuminated by George Simmel, even in a legal relationship that suggests a purely unilateral situation, there is reciprocity between the rulers and the ruled. He explains, "If the absolute despot accompanies his orders by the threat of punishment or the promise of reward, this implies that he himself wishes to be bound by the decrees he issues. The subordinate is expected to have the right to request something of him; and by establishing the punishment, no matter how horrible, the despot commits himself not to impose a more severe one."[16] Scholars have also underscored a variety of other double-edged statements or practices, such as official rituals, that have significantly facilitated popular contention.[17]

A common source of contradictions and ambiguities in authoritarian regimes lies in their efforts to legitimate their rule. Except in some so-called sultanistic regimes, where rulers wield power in a highly personalistic and arbitrary fashion, most modern authoritarian rulers are concerned about legitimacy and have usually decorated their regime with "democratic" and "constitutional" institutions and ideologies.[18] Even the contemporary Arabian dynasties in the Middle East have maintained

---

[14] James Scott, *Weapons of the Weak* (New Haven, CT: Yale University Press, 1985), p. 341.

[15] Ibid, p. 338.

[16] George Simmel, *The Sociology of George Simmel* (New York: Free Press, 1950).

[17] Steven Pfaff and Guobin Yang, "Double-Edged Ritual and the Symbolic Resources of Collective Action: Political Commemorations and the Mobilization of Protest in 1989," *Theory and Society* 30 (2001), p. 550.

[18] Juan Linz and Alfred Stepan, *Problems of Democratic Transition and Consolidation: Southern Europe, South America and Post-Communist Europe* (Baltimore and London: The Johns Hopkins University Press, 1996), pp. 51–54.

so-called desert democracy, and rulers have routinely carried out political consultation with elites and ordinary people.[19]

Contradictions and ambiguities are particularly noticeable in communist regimes where political power has been highly centralized, yet the masses have been designated with an essential role in policy making and implementation. Such contradictions are different from those in so-called hybrid regimes, such as competitive authoritarian regimes.[20] In hybrid regimes, contradictions between democratic and authoritarian institutions are more apparent. By contrast, contradictions and ambiguities are more difficult to discern in full-blown authoritarian regimes such as China.

As the China case shows, under certain circumstances, it is possible for contradictions and ambiguities to be appropriated by ordinary people in their struggle with the government. For example, the xinfang system, an institution designed for controlled participation, has actually often been used by petitioners as an instrument for staging their protests. When Chinese leaders tried to reform the xinfang system to reduce collective petitioning, most of their efforts were often fruitless or counterproductive. This is because the contradictions and ambiguities in the system are based on entrenched principles of the mass line, which can hardly be altered or removed without substantial changes to the whole political system. Clearly, even this powerful authoritarian state became enmeshed in the contradictions and ambiguities that it created, and therefore the state often has difficulty in dealing with popular contention in its preferred way.

Of course, the stress on the weakness and limits of the state does not challenge the fundamental premises of the power structure suggested by elite power theory. No matter how routinized and efficacious their actions are, Chinese protesters do not enjoy regular and low-cost access to political arenas. Their mobilization is both stressful and somewhat risky. Even though state repression is generally restrained, specific activists still face the risk of being targeted for selective punishment. Moreover, even when they achieve a status of de facto pressure groups and can exert some influence on public policy through sustained protest, the gap in power between them and the elite remains significant.

---

[19] Michael Herb, *All in the Family: Absolutism, Revolution, and Democracy in the Middle Eastern Monarchies* (Albany: State University of New York Press, 1999).

[20] See Steven Levitsky and Lucan A. Way. *Competitive Authoritarianism: Hybrid Regimes after the Cold War* (New York: Cambridge University Press, 2010).

POLITICAL OPPORTUNITY STRUCTURES AS HISTORICAL JUNCTURES

As a core concept in the social movement field, POS has been extensively examined. Still, more attention is needed to identify and conceptualize processes and mechanisms through which opportunities open and close. In particular, theorists have long been aware of the importance of taking a dynamic approach to opportunities, but most studies still tend to treat elements of a POS either as stable or fast-shifting, while failing to examine how stable institutions can evolve and how a short-term change can take place in a stable structure. Along these lines, David Meyer has observed that most opportunity theories fall into two groups. One emphasizes the stable aspects of government, essentially holding opportunities constant for cross-sectional comparison. The other underscores the volatile aspects of opportunity, such as changing public policies and shifting political alignments.[21]

Indeed, each group can make a strong case for their views, but neither view is complete by itself. Some theorists have therefore called for a balanced view. Sidney Tarrow has argued that short-term changes are particularly important for explaining movement dynamics. He criticizes Tocqueville, who is often credited as the father of POS, for privileging long-term conditions and overlooking short-term changes. Tarrow remarks, "What strikes the observer from closer up is how often short-term changes in opportunity affect the propensity of social actors to engage in confrontational collective action."[22] Institutional evolution is, however, usually a mixture of continuity and change, and of stable and fast-moving elements. So Tarrow also points out that changing opportunities must be seen alongside more stable structural elements – like the strength or weakness of a state and the forms of repression it habitually employs.[23]

When discussing the collapse of regimes in Eastern Europe, Valerie Bunce also advocates for a balanced view. She points out two major

---

[21] David Meyer, "Protest and Political Opportunities," *Annual Review of Sociology* 30 (2004), pp. 134–135.

[22] Sidney Tarrow, "States and Opportunities: The Political Structuring of Social Movements," in Doug McAdam, John D. McCarthy, and Mayer N. Zald (eds.), *Comparative Perspectives on Social Movements: Political Opportunities, Mobilizing Structures, and Cultural Framing* (New York: Cambridge University Press, 1996), p. 57.

[23] Sidney Tarrow, *Power in Movement: Social Movements and Contentious Politics* (New York: Cambridge University Press, 1998), p. 5.

factors that account for the collapse of these states: "[O]ne is the institutional design of socialism and its long-term consequences for the regime,
the bloc, and the state. The other is the shorter-term effects of major
political and economic change throughout the 1980s. Why socialism and
the state collapsed in the eastern half of Europe from 1989 to 1992 was
in effect because both of these factors pushed in the same direction."[24]

Similarly, in his discussion of the dynamics of the student movement of
1989 in China, Dingxin Zhao analyzes how a stable condition – campus
ecology in Beijing – became a facilitative factor: "I stress how campus
ecology offset the weaknesses of movement organizations and otherwise
played a crucial role – but campus ecology was in turn a result of past state
designs, and it would not have been so effective for student mobilization
without a great decline of the student control system in universities."[25]

The proactive role of the xinfang system in popular contention in China
offers another example of a case when political opportunity structures
are created by a combination of stable features and short-term changes.
As a result of its inherent contradictions, the xinfang channel provides
a degree of legitimacy for popular collective action that utilizes troublemaking tactics and offers great advantages to "troublemakers" over
moderate petitioners. Such stable features can, to a large extent, account
for the current special interactive patterns between petitioners and the
government. However, by themselves they cannot explain the timing of
the rise of social protest in the 1990s. After all, popular collective action
was rare before the 1990s. Changes in state-society linkages in the 1990s,
especially the decline of the unit system, which has shifted the balance of
power and resources, made the xinfang channel work more frequently to
the advantages of petitioners.

All these studies suggest that in accounting for the dynamics of popular
contention, neither short-term nor long-term changes can be overlooked.
Without short-term changes, we cannot explain the timing of historical
processes. Without the long-term changes, we would miss an important
part of the incentive structure provided by the institutional framework.
Therefore the POS can best be understood as a configuration of stable
and fast-shifting conditions. This is what Tarrow called a "conjunctural"
concept of political opportunity.[26]

[24] Valerie Bunce, *Subversive Institutions: The Design and the Destruction of Socialism and
the State* (New York: Cambridge University Press, 1999), pp. 18–19.
[25] Dingxin Zhao, *The Power of Tiananmen* (Chicago: University of Chicago Press,
2001), p. 7.
[26] Sidney Tarrow, "States and Opportunities," p. 58.

On this issue, we can see how historical institutionalism can be effectively applied to the study of contentious politics. A weak conceptualization of continuity and change is not unique to the field of contentious politics. Ira Katznelson notes that historical-institutional theorists tend to unwisely draw overly sharp distinctions between "settled" and "unsettled" times.[27] Therefore, he advocates configurative explanations. This is an approach "focusing less on the causal importance of this or that variable contrasted with others but more on how variables are joined together in specific historical instances."[28] Such a configurative approach is exactly what we need to conceptualize the POS as a combination of continuity and change.

Of course, it is not sufficient to conceptualize the POS as solely the product of historical junctures. We need to explain how continuity and change can actually work together to create political opportunity. In fact, some theorists of historical institutionalism have rightly directed our attention to mechanisms and processes of social and institutional change. In particular, Kathleen Thelen calls for attention to specifying modes of change, such as institutional layering and institutional conversion.[29] Not incidentally, some leading theorists in contentious politics have also vigorously advocated the same approach.[30] Of course, in the field of contentious politics, as in historical-institutional studies in general, the mechanisms-based approach is still at an explorative stage. Nevertheless, it offers a promising alternative to the enduring structural biases of political process theory.

This study represents an effort in this vein. In accounting for the conversion of the xinfang system, the book confirms the importance of social appropriation as a mechanism for the formation of POS. For institutional contradictions and ambiguities to work as POS, protesters have to assume a particularly active role. They must take advantage

---

[27] Ira Katznelson, "Periodization and Preferences," in James Mahoney and Dietrich Rueschemeyer (eds.), *Comparative Historical Analysis in the Social Science* (Cambridge: Cambridge University Press, 2003), p. 277.

[28] Ira Katznelson, "Structures and Configuration," in Mark Lichbach and Alan S. Zuchkerman (eds.), *Comparative Politics: Rationality, Culture, and Structure* (Cambridge: Cambridge University Press, 1997), p. 99.

[29] Kathleen Thelen, "How Institutions Evolve: Insights from Comparative Historical Analysis," in James Mahoney and Dietrich Rueschemeyer (eds.), *Comparative Historical Analysis in the Social Science* (Cambridge: Cambridge University Press, 2003), pp. 224–225.

[30] Doug McAdam, Sidney Tarrow and Charles Tilly, *Dynamics of Contention* (New York: Cambridge University Press, 2001).

of the potential within the system and appropriate existing channels and institutions. In other words, opportunities have to be made. Of course, this study of the xinfang system has indicated that the process is more than social appropriation. In fact, appropriation is just part of the mechanism of appropriation-response. The response of the state has also significantly contributed to the conversion of the xinfang system. In response to the extensive popular struggles to appropriate the xinfang channel, the state has strengthened its control of local responses, exerted higher pressure on local officials to pacify petitioners with bargaining, and generally restrained local officials' use of force. The state responds in this way because it is constrained by the general ideological and institutional framework of mass line politics. Such efforts encourage further social appropriation, which in turn provokes state responses along the same lines.

AUTHORITARIAN STABILITY

As Andrew Nathan observes, authoritarian regimes are generally believed to be inherently unstable. Despite an extensive wave of democratization since the 1970s, however, authoritarianism is still remarkably resilient in today's world. China is one of the most striking examples. In 1989, when most other socialist regimes were undergoing democratic transitions, many China specialists and democracy theorists expected the PRC to fall to democratization's "third wave," too.[31] However, the regime has not only already survived the challenge for more than twenty years; in many aspects it has become more consolidated. This consolidation is especially remarkable considering two conditions: (1) most previous institutional foundations for maintaining communist political order have substantially declined;[32] and (2) Chinese society has become much more contentious since the 1990s, fraught as it is with popular collective action.

Some theorists have pointed out that some institutions of the Leninist regime in China actually survived and significantly contributed to the regime's stability. For example, Barry Naughton and Dali Yang have argued that the nomenclatural system of personnel management is the most important institution reinforcing national unity.[33] However,

---

[31] Andrew Nathan, "Authoritarian Resilience in China," *Journal of Democracy*, 14/1 (Jan. 2003), p. 6.

[32] Andrew Walder, "The Decline of Communist Power: Elements of a Theory of Institutional Change," *Theory and Society* 23 (1994), pp. 297–323.

[33] Barry J. Naughton and Dali Yang (eds.), *Holding China Together: Diversity and National Integration in the Post-Deng Era* (New York: Cambridge University Press, 2004), p. 9.

the dramatic decline of communist power triggered by economic reforms, such as the reduced capacity of the power center to monitor and sanction its subordinates and society at large, certainly posed formidable challenges to the survival of the state.

Perry has rightly pointed out that to a large extent, the regime's survival "rests upon its capacity to curb and channel potentially threatening social forces."[34] How can an authoritarian regime cope with such challenges from society? Przeworski has described their tool kit: terror, lies, and economic prosperity.[35] Given that socialist ideology is generally regarded as severely in decline in China, few people believed that the CCP could continue to rule mainly by lies.[36]

Governance by terror has been an enduring stereotype of communist regimes, and China, of course, is not an exception. The high-handed crackdown on the student movement in 1989 and the Falungong movement in 1999 have only reinforced such impressions. However, it is very dubious to argue that the CCP regime has maintained political order mainly by force. Their repression of the two aforementioned movements and some ethnic insurgencies has certainly been decisive and helped maintain their rule. Yet with regard to other forms of popular contention that have been more pervasive, state repression has been restrained overall.

Economic prosperity is not a sufficient explanation either. Despite the impressive economic development of the last two and half decades, the economic reforms have created hundreds of millions of "losers" whose living standards have relatively or even absolutely deteriorated. The well-being of their fellow citizens often signifies sharp inequality and can only aggravate rather than alleviate their grievances. Therefore, it is still unclear how social and political stability can be built on the discontent of large segments of the population, as is the case in China.

Among political scientists, an institutionalist approach in explaining political stability has been very influential in recent decades. One of the most famous arguments can be found in Samuel Huntington's formula: political participation / political institutionalization = social instability. In a changing society, as Huntington points out, "the political backwardness of the country in terms of political institutionalization … makes it

---

[34] Elizabeth Perry, "Studying Chinese Politics: Farewell to Revolution?" *China Journal* 57 (January 2007), pp. 1–22.

[35] See Adam Przeworski, *Democracy and the Market: Political and Economic Reforms in Eastern Europe and Latin America* (Cambridge: Cambridge University Press, 1991), pp. 58–59.

[36] See, for example, Andrew Nathan, "Authoritarian Resilience in China." He argues that in China "the social ideology has collapsed."

difficult if not impossible for the demands upon the government to be expressed through legitimate channels and to be moderated and aggregated within the political system. Hence a sharp increase in political participation gives rise to political instability."[37] Therefore, the solution to real or potential instability is the installation of new political institutions or the improvement of existing ones. In the case of China, as some scholars have emphasized, although there is little political liberalization and no democratization, creeping institutional evolution has worked as the main basis of the current political order.[38] For instance, Nathan argues that the institutionalization of the Chinese political system has contributed to "authoritarian resilience." More specifically, he remarks that the adjustments to various input institutions, such as local elections and the xinfang system, enable citizens to pursue grievances without creating the potential to threaten the regime as a whole.[39]

Such improvements of input institutions are certainly impressive considering how determined the Chinese political elite have been to resist changes in the political system. Yet such improvements are still manifestly inadequate to sustain a political order. For example, the xinfang system, as extensively analyzed in this work, is deeply flawed and severely inefficient in channeling interest articulation. Of course, Nathan is right that this channel has played a big role in sustaining political stability, but the reason does not lie in the improvements of the formal institutions. Instead, stability is mainly a consequence of the system's conversion into vehicles for contentious bargaining.

Institutional inadequacy is a typical feature for all authoritarian regimes. What differentiates them is often the elasticity of their system. Therefore, we must go beyond a focus on formal institutions and look to informal institutions and actual behavioral patterns to understand the political order in regimes like authoritarian China.[40] The role of toleration and facilitation in Chinese contention indicates the remarkable elasticity of its institutions.

---

[37] Samuel Huntington, *Political Order in Changing Societies* (New Haven, CT: Yale University Press, 1968), p. 55.

[38] Minxin Pei, "Creeping Democratization in China?" *Journal of Democracy* 6/4 (October 1995), pp. 65–79.

[39] Andrew Nathan, "Authoritarian Resilience in China," pp. 14–15.

[40] See Kellee S. Tsai, *Capitalism without Democracy: The Private Sector in Contemporary China* (Ithaca, NY: Cornell University Press, 2007); and Lily Tsai, *Accountability without Democracy: Solidarity Groups and Public Goods Provision in Rural China* (New York: Cambridge University Press, 2007).

By calling attention to popular contention instead of formal institutions in the perpetuation of political stability, this work raises some big questions about the relationship between popular contention and political stability. Popular contention's capacity for destabilizing authoritarian regimes is well understood. However, current theories on the positive impact of contention on political stability are still underdeveloped, despite the fact that many theories have been put forth. These theories not only need sorting out, but they also need to be substantiated and tested by empirical studies. This work is not intended to systematically test any such theory, but it can still offer some important insights on this issue.

Current theories of popular contention and political stability can be roughly divided into three schools. The first is the psychological valve theory. This theory assumes that popular contention can release psychological tensions and therefore contributes to political stability. Clearly, this theory derives from the classical model of social movements, which was especially influential until the 1960s. There are several variations of this model: mass society, collective behavior, status inconsistency, rising expectations, relative deprivation, and Davies' J-curve theory of revolution.[41] Yet they all assume that social movements are collective reactions to some form of disruptive system strain, and the motivation for movement participation is believed to be based not so much on the desire to attain political goals as on the need to manage the psychological tensions of a stressful social situation. Consequently, the social movement is effective not as political action but as therapy.[42]

The second school is associated with theories of hegemony. James Scott's works best represent this vein of explanations. According to Scott, ordinary people can employ "the weapons of the weak" and act according to "hidden transcripts" to resist the hegemony of the ruling class. In other words, through popular contention the underclass can unwittingly establish its own relatively autonomous political order, and therefore does not need to overthrow the whole political system.

The third school rests on the theory of contentious bargaining or, more generally, interest articulation. Because social protest provides a means for relatively powerless people to advance their interests in the political system, it can reduce the possibility for antisystem rebellions and revolutions. Unlike the first school, this vein of theories assumes that popular

[41] Doug McAdam, *Political Process and the Development of Black Insurgency, 1930–1970* (Chicago: University of Chicago Press, 1982), p. 6.
[42] Ibid, pp. 9–10.

contention represents rational efforts to attain some political goal. Unlike the second school, this group of theorists does not believe ordinary people have the capacity to establish their own political order. Instead, the subordinate classes are still subject to the domination of the ruling classes. Their resistance may partly change the existing political order, but it will never construct a political order of their own.

The role of popular contention as an important form of interest articulation was expounded by Almond and Powell in the 1960s. They contend, "One obvious means of articulating demands is through physical demonstrations and violence."[43] This point was well substantiated by an early study conducted by James Payne, who argued that in Peru in the 1950s–1960s, demonstrations and the threat of mass violence were integral parts of the political system itself. According to Payne, mass violence, when utilized in a rational and calculating fashion, becomes almost the equivalent of free elections in other political systems – the regularized means by which incumbent elites are threatened with loss of office if they do not accede to expressed demands of important groups in the populace.[44] Unfortunately, although Payne's book was lauded as "a landmark in the reassessment of the more ethnocentric views of possible roles of violence long held by Western political scientists,"[45] this vein of analysis has been picked up by very few theorists in political science.[46] Of course, outside the field of political science, some general studies of social history have supported this vein of theories. Notable examples include the works by E. P. Thompson and Eric Hobsbawm on "bargaining by riot."[47]

Findings in China clearly contradict the first school of theories. Most social protests in today's China are conspicuously rational and strategic, and therefore cannot be described as a simply psychological phenomenon. The findings here seem to offer some support to the second school, the hegemony theory, in that Chinese protesters have tried to appropriate

---

[43] Gabriel A. Almond and G. Bingham Powell, Jr., *Comparative Politics: A Developmental Approach* (Boston: Little, Brown & Co., 1966), p. 86.

[44] James L. Payne, *Labor and Politics in Peru* (New Haven, CT: Yale University Press, 1965).

[45] Gabriel A. Almond and G. Bingham Powell, Jr., *Comparative Politics*, p.11.

[46] James Payne's own methodological flaws, which were criticized by Albert Hirschman as "theorizing as an obstacle to understanding," may contribute to the lack of influence of his work. See Albert O. Hirschman, "The Search for Paradigms as a Hindrance to Our Understanding," *World Politics* 22/3 (1970), pp. 329–343.

[47] E. P. Thompson, "The Moral Economy of the English Crowd in the Eighteenth Century," *Past and Present* 50 (1971), pp. 76–136; E. J. Hobsbawm, "Peasants and Politics," *Journal of Peasant Studies* 1/13 (1973), pp. 3–22.

existing ideologies and institutions to establish a political order that is to their advantage. However, the effect of their appropriation cannot be exaggerated. In the process of institutional conversion, appropriation is only part of the mechanism of appropriation-response. In such strategic interactions between social protesters and the government, the government still enjoys the upper hand overall. Even though pervasive social protests are worrisome to Chinese leaders, the toleration and facilitation of social protests like the ones explored in this book are still consistent with the CCP's grand strategy of differentiated responses to various forms of popular contention.

Social protests in China can best be understood as contentious bargaining. Most of them are rational and strategic, and they are typically conducted in a give-and-take style. With social protests, many social groups have managed to exert pressure on the policy-making process, and therefore mitigated their disadvantages to some extent. When their claims are partly incorporated into the political system and when policy outcomes are more or less acceptable, the possibility for antisystem actions such as rebellions and revolutions becomes quite low.

This study has also suggested two additional ways in which contentious bargaining contributes to stability. The first is the effect of procrastination. From the perspective of the government, the most dangerous moments are those immediately after policies have been made or changed. If the government can absorb the first impact of popular discontent by skillful procrastination, the danger to political stability will decrease over time, because most people tend to resign themselves to the new reality. In handling social protests, the Chinese government has used procrastination extensively.

The second important way in which the accommodation of popular contention supports social stability is its molding effect on patterns of popular behavior. Through toleration and facilitation, the state promotes certain forms of popular contention with particular types of tactics. Thus the state creates a condition in which ordinary people are unlikely to engage in more threatening activities. Indeed, when protesters convert the xinfang system, the xinfang system is also converting them. Consequently, most Chinese protesters have confined their struggle to localized and materialist contention. Although we can find some exceptions, such exceptions tend to prove rather than disprove the rule. For example, in City Y, forty-seven enterprises formed a cross-sector coalition, which is quite striking given that typically most Chinese protesters deliberately avoid this kind of coalition building. However, closer examination indicates that this coalition of forty-seven is more symbolic that substantial. There was no collective action based on this broad coalition except for two jointly signed petition letters. The main objective of forming such a coalition was to show the government that its members were capable of doing so. Similarly, although protesters in China have sometimes talked about democracy or used other seemingly radical political terms, such inflammatory rhetoric is usually used to package their more substantial claims on specific socioeconomic issues. In this sense, those protesters who shout, "We demand democracy" are not different from the protesters shouting, "We don't want democracy; we want food!"

Economic struggles can be noisy, but they seldom threaten political stability. In *What Is to Be Done?*, Lenin thus slammed "economists" for confusing economic struggle with political struggle. With limited goals and narrow coalitions, economic struggles have no hope of substantially changing the system. On the contrary, they often contribute to the consolidation of the status quo.

AN ALTERNATIVE TO LIBERAL DEMOCRACY?

Despite occasional calls by mavericks within the Party for political reforms, the CCP leadership has adamantly rejected liberal democracy as a political model for China. The impressive political stability and remarkable economic growth in the Reform Era seem to have reinforced such a stance. For example, in March 2011, Wu Bangguo, Chairman of the National People's Congress, reiterated the Party's determination to maintain the present political system described as socialism with Chinese characteristics. He ruled out the possibility of political reforms toward separation of powers or "a system of multiple parties holding office in rotation." To justify such an assertion, he emphasized that "If we waver, the achievements gained thus far in development will be lost and it is possible the country could sink into the abyss of internal disorder."[48]

The political development in China has been closely watched by people around the world, especially rulers in other developing countries. China was once a beacon for illiberal forces around the world.[49] It comes as no surprise that some authoritarian rulers in other countries might again seek inspiration from the CCP, whose success in economic development and political control in the past three decades has been enviable.

---

[48] Bao Daozu (2011), "Top Legislator Warns of Chaos Unless Correct Path Is Taken," *China Daily*, March 11, 2011.

[49] Francis Fukuyama, "The End of History," *The National Interest* 16 (1989), pp. 3–18.

Can the CCP offer a feasible alternative to liberal democracy? So far, the political system in China has functioned well, but upon close examination, its institutions can hardly inspire confidence. Indeed, it would be a big mistake to credit political stability in the Reform Era to the political institutions in China. The study of contentious authoritarianism in this book not only highlights a remarkable advantage of the Chinese system – its flexibility – but also reveals serious weaknesses in the institutional design. The system is flexible enough to tolerate widespread popular collective action, and thus achieves a certain degree of political responsiveness. However, the regime's accommodation of popular contention is de facto, not de jure. In other words, most contentious government-citizen interactions took place outside laws and formal procedures. This is how the seemingly anachronistic political system manages to coexist with an increasingly mobile and assertive society.

The institutional weaknesses of the Chinese system are too evident to be ignored. One of the major advantages of liberal democracy is its institutions, which ensure a relatively high level of political responsiveness. By contrast, although the CCP has achieved a certain degree of political responsiveness through contentious bargaining, the regime is often either underresponsive or overresponsive. It is usually underresponsive because the government is insensitive to most ordinary claim makers, and responds to only a few privileged individuals and social groups or those with high capacity for "troublemaking." Paradoxically, the system is also sometimes overresponsive. It is not rare for Party leaders to intervene in a judicial process when a party in dispute mounted an effective social protest.[50] This tendency has, in turn, invited more litigants to challenge judicial decisions via petitioning and protests.

More importantly, contentious bargaining tends to be much costlier than institutionalized forms of interest articulation and conflict resolution. Indeed, this government-citizen interaction pattern is disliked by almost everyone for this reason. For the CCP leaders, this is a system that constantly produces and reproduces "troublemaking" activities, and the accommodation of widespread popular contention has become increasingly expensive. In 2011, the budget approved by the NPC included spending of 624 billion RMB ($95 billion) on items related to law and order, even exceeding military spending, which was 601.1 billion RMB.[51]

For local leaders, handling petitions and appeals has become a very burdensome task. It is not rare for them to rush to the xinfang bureau

---

[50] Personal communication with Benjamin Liebman.
[51] The Economist, "The Truncheon Budget," *The Economist* (March 12, 2011), pp. 48–49.

to dialogue with disgruntled petitioners at midnight. Moreover, many normal political and social activities that are supposed to be necessary and beneficial for national or local public interests are often disrupted.

Petitioners, including those "troublemakers," believe that they have paid too high a price for their basic demands. Not only is there the uncertainty of repression, but the efforts at even moderate mobilization seem too costly to most of them. To repeat a pensioner' words, "We old people cherish quietness. We cannot withstand noise even when we watch TV. Why should we like to make noise at the government?"[52] Troublemakers' aversion to troublemaking is certainly not confined to the elderly.

Even people who do not need to deliver or handle petitions dislike the system. The public has often been held hostage by collective protests. As discussed in Chapter 6, appealing to the public is one main "troublemaking" tactic. Yet, ironically enough, petitioners sometimes do not care about the interests or feelings of the public at all. They often try to catch the attention of the public, even if their action will not cause sympathy, but rather will actually annoy the public. As a protest in Shenzhen on October 6, 2005, indicates, many people whose normal life had been disrupted by petitioners felt quite annoyed. Because of petitioners' obstruction of the main road to protest their low salary, many passengers were stuck for more than four hours. Therefore, one of them complained, "If those employees [protesters] want to demand justice, they should bargain with their employers directly. They should not vent their grievances on the street to cause people unrelated to the dispute to suffer several hours."[53]

In spite of all the dissatisfaction with the current pattern of government-citizen interactions, so far there is no strong momentum for institutional reforms. Chapter 4 underscores the fact that minor institutional reforms cannot change the pattern deeply entrenched in Leninist mass line politics. Ultimately, as some Chinese scholars have pointed out, the pattern will not be changed unless the xinfang system is replaced by democratic representative institutions and the rule of law.[54] However, when the economy grows fast and as long as a variety of illegal or not-so-legal

---

[52] Interview in city Y, 2002.

[53] *The Southern Metropolitan Daily*, "Buman Xinshui Di Yungong Shangjie Dulu, Guanyuan Chumian Duihua Renqun (Discontent with Low Salaries, Employees Blocked the Road and Officials dialogued with the Crowd)," October 7, 2005.

[54] For example, see Yu Jianrong, "Zhongguo Xinfang Zhidu Pipan" (Critique of the Chinese Letters and Visits System), a speech at Beijing University in 2004, www.yannan.com, last visited on December 6, 2004.

petitioning and protest tactics are still tolerated, most people are not particularly concerned with fundamentally changing the institutions.

In fact, to a large degree, the success of reforms in China lies in the
regime's tolerance of extra-institutional behaviors. *The Economist*
rightly attributes the dynamic of economic growth in China to "bamboo
capitalism," in which private entrepreneurs have enjoyed booming success in a "laissez-faire bubble." Such entrepreneurs are allowed to "operate free not only of direct state management but also from many of the
laws tied to land ownership, labour relations, taxation, and licensing."
Similarly, the political order in the Reform Era to a large extent hinges
on the regime's toleration of "troublemaking" petitioners who may have
somehow violated laws and rules. Bamboo capitalism and contentious
authoritarianism are wonderfully flexible, but we cannot count on them
as long-term solutions to the economic and political problems in China.

Based on a survey study conducted in the late 1980s, Tianjian Shi
argued convincingly that ordinary people in urban China actively pur-
sued their private interests with a variety of activities. He contended that
the diversity and intensity of participatory activities in Beijing clearly
contradicted the claims made by many students of politics in communist societies, which described political participation either as the product
of regime-directed mobilization or window dressing used by leaders to
obtain a veneer of legitimacy.[55] However, of the activities under review,
most were confined to work units (*danwei*), which Shi described as a
traditional organization like family, kinship, and village. Consequently,
most such activities bore particularistic claims, and "the primary strategy
of interest articulation for the urban population in China is exclusion of,
rather than cooperation with, people with similar attributes." Therefore,
"group and party-based politics remains not only unnecessary but also
irrational for most participants."[56] When speculating on the possibility
for democratic transition in China, Shi thus counted on the dissolution
of the work unit system. He showed his optimism thus: "Such a change
would also make interest articulation at the policy implementation stage
through particularism become more and more difficult. The logic of politics in urban China today would gradually give way to a new one."[57]

Almost twenty years have passed since Shi concluded his research
trip. In a sense, his speculations have proven very astute – the decline of

---

[55] Tianjian Shi, *Political Participation in Beijing* (Cambridge, MA: Harvard University
Press, 1997), p. 269.
[56] Ibid, p. 279.
[57] Ibid, p. 281.

the work unit system has indeed brought about dramatic changes in the political landscape in China over the last two decades. As this book has repeatedly stressed, such a shift of state-society linkages from the unit system model to government-citizen model dramatically affected political participation and popular contention in two respects. First, instead of particularistic struggles by individuals within work units, we have begun to see the emergence of group struggles that directly targeted the government. Their claims are based on categorical identities, and therefore bear on citizenship rights. In addition, the shifts in state-society linkages also significantly changed the resources and incentives of both government officials and protesters. This has contributed to the rise and routinization of social protests.

However, the surge of group struggles has not met Shi's expectation of driving China toward democracy. Like individualized strategies, most group struggles still feature exclusion or competition more than cooperation and coalitions. Such cellular or divisive activism is, in a sense, an extension of the particularistic and individualized activities explored by Shi. They did not challenge the system. On the contrary, they helped maintain it.

It is difficult to foresee what kind of events will bring about a dramatic turn from the current path. It could be a horrendous economic setback, but no one knows for sure. When the day comes, Chinese people may suddenly find the political system, with all its long-term problems, no longer acceptable.

Appendix

I. MAIN SOURCES OF DATA FOR ANALYSIS

The Xinfang Bureau of Hunan Province (HNPXB)
The Xinfang Bureau of City Y, Hunan Province (CYXB)
The Xinfang Bureau of County H, Hunan Province (CHXB)
Diao Jiecheng, *Renmin Xinfang shilue* (A Brief History of People's Letters and Visits), (Beijing: Beijing Xueyuan Chubanshe, 1996) (RXS)
Henen Nianjian (*Provincial Yearbook of Henan*) (HNNJ)

II. CHARACTERISTICS OF THE INFORMANT POOL

In the fieldwork in Hunan Province, 2002, I conducted thirty-four formal interviews with fifty-five people. Interviewees can largely be classified into two types: government officials and petitioners.

Government officials: 14
    Provincial level: 3
    City level: 7
    County level: 4
Editors of an official newspaper: 3
Managers of SOEs: 1
Petitioners: 37
    College teachers: 2
    SOE workers or staff: 2
    SOE retirees: 13
    The laid-off from SOEs: 6
    The laid-off from collective enterprises: 4

    Self-employed: 6
    Unemployed: 1
    Elementary school teachers: 1
    Peasants: 2
Total: 55

III. DATA

For scholars who study popular contention in contemporary China, the difficulty of collecting reliable data has long been a problem. Although many protest and petitioning events in China have been reported by international and domestic media in recent years, and have sometimes also been available on the Internet, the strong sampling and reporting biases for these sources make them very difficult to serve as a basis for systematic studies.[1] I was lucky in getting access to government materials in Hunan Province, and have also supplemented them with in-depth interviews and on-site observations. Although the data are primarily from only one province, the analysis has, of course, been informed by available published materials on the whole country. More importantly, despite some regional variations, the basic patterns of government-citizen interactions and the political environment in which they occur are largely similar across most inland provinces.

There are four main types of sources I collected for this study:

Government Archival Materials

These include a variety of documents such as event reports, speeches, meeting minutes, and case files that could be found in xinfang bureaus. It should be noted that, as discussed in Chapter 2, although xinfang materials only cover petitions (letters and visits), the concept of petitioning in contemporary China is considerably broader than the concept of petitioning as it is commonly understood by non-Chinese common people. Such data actually cover a majority of protest events because even the most disruptive protests are often considered as "abnormal petitioning" by Chinese officials.

I visited four xinfang bureaus in Hunan Province and eventually compiled two event catalogs from government reports. I also used a variety of

---

[1] Still, there are some scholars who have effectively used such materials. A good example is Yongshun Cai's *Collective Resistance in China: Why Popular Protests Succeed or Fail* (Stanford, CA: Stanford University Press, 2010).

government statistics compiled by xinfang bureaus. Of course, one must be cautious when using such statistical data, which are biased to a certain degree. Moreover, official jargon used in such data has seldom been clearly defined, and therefore many categories in the statistical data are vague and sometimes overlapping. I have therefore sometimes rearranged the data to make them more sensible.[2]

In-depth Interviews

I conducted thirty-four formal and sixty informal interviews with both government officials and petitioners. The interviews with petitioners concentrated on the process of mobilization and their interactions with government officials, their understanding of their claims, and their personal histories. Interviews with government officials were focused on bureaucratic operations and the process of handling petitions.

On-site Observations

In each government office I visited, I often witnessed collective petitioning events, with the number of participants ranging from several to several hundred. Altogether I observed about twenty collective petitioning events. I usually avoided contacting petitioners on such occasions, because any involvement might complicate the situation, which was a bad lesson I learned from experience. The first event I observed was a collective petition staged by about forty people with disabilities. While they were waiting for a meeting with government officials in the xinfang bureau, I tried to ask one petitioner some questions, but very soon most of the petitioners began to gather around me. From this incident I learned that petitioners were highly sensitive to the presence of any outsider because they tended to suspect that such an outsider was either an undercover police agent or an official from upper authorities. If petitioners thought higher authorities had sent officials to observe their dialogue, they tended to become more assertive and would even be tempted to press for higher demands. After the incident I always kept my distance when observing petitioning events.

---

[2] More detailed discussion can be found in Xi Chen, "State-generated Data and the Study of Contentious Politics in China," in Allen Carlson, Mary Gallagher, Kenneth Lieberthal, and Melanie Manion (eds.), *Contemporary Chinese Politics: New Methods, Sources and Field strategies* (New York: Cambridge University Press, 2010), pp. 15–32.

Media Coverage and Secondary Materials

Although media coverage on collective action in China is insufficient for systematic research, it can be used to supplement my study in Hunan quite well. Some large-scale collective events have been covered in the media or examined by other studies (mainly in Chinese) in great detail. Provincial yearbooks have also included plenty of valuable information. Most provinces disclosed basic facts about petitions in their yearbooks since the 1980s. Comparisons between such information and what I collected in Hunan can expand the scope of my study and help generalize my findings and apply them to the whole country.

STATE-GENERATED ARCHIVAL DATA

Among the previously mentioned data, three parts are especially important for my research: an event catalog of 902 cases compiled from event reports in City Y, an event catalog of 125 cases compiled from case files in County H, and interviews with petitioners. More discussion is needed for these three types of data to better evaluate their validity and selective bias.

The Event Catalog in City Y

To better use the government reports, I compiled two event catalogs. One is derived primarily from one internal publication – Information Express (*xinxi kuaibao*) – published by the xinfang bureau of City Y. I have collected almost all of the editions of Information Express from January 1992 to July 2002. This publication was provided to local leaders with information on petitions. It not only reported on petitioners' actions and statements, but also often included descriptions of how the government handled them. Besides the reports in Information Express, I also used other documents including leaders' speeches, meeting records, and internal announcements. This dataset includes 902 petitioning events.

The Event Catalog in County H

Another catalog of 125 cases was compiled from case files in County H. These cases were investigated and handled between 1990 and 2001. It is reasonable to assume that this is an almost complete collection of all cases that have been seriously investigated by the county authorities. Although the county authorities formally put between 200 and 300 cases into files for investigation during this period, quite a few cases were not thoroughly investigated, and in the archives there was only a short note of explanation for such cases. These cases tended to be trivial cases, such as petitioners' requesting relief from personal economic difficulty.

For the aforementioned 125 cases, the archives included very rich information, including petition letters, leaders' instructions, investigation reports, meeting minutes, and so on. Therefore, this catalog is especially good for observing bureaucratic procedures in depth. Moreover, because petition letters are also included, they are useful for examining protesters' strategies for framing their claims as well.

Biases in State-generated Data

There are several significant biases in the data collected from xinfang bureaus. First, such data is biased toward events occurring in urban areas. This is mainly because xinfang bureaus are established at the county level and above, and their reports mainly cover petitions addressed to the county level and above, except for some very disruptive events that occurred in townships or villages. A larger number of petitioning activities, especially those staged by peasants, which took place at the township level, thus have not been included. Second, only petitions that caught the attention of the government are included in event reports and case files. Of course, every petition is included in the official statistics. Yet only a few petitions, which have been perceived as important, will be handled seriously. The government only produces event reports and case files for those petitions, and a vast majority of petitions will in fact eventually be thrown into trash bins. Third, the information about some petitions has possibly been hidden by low-level officials. Given that the frequency of petitions, especially those of a certain type, have sometimes been used as a negative criterion for evaluating local officials' performance, many officials tend to underreport the quantity of petitions they receive. Despite these issues, the problem of information hiding does not pose a serious challenge to data validity as long as government data are used cautiously.[3]

INTERVIEWS WITH PETITIONERS

The accessibility of petitioners was usually not a problem because most petitioners were very eager to find listeners. Among all the petitioners

[3] Ibid.

I contacted only one declined my request, for understandable reasons. This petitioner was involved in one of the most violent and persistent petitioning events in City Y in recent years, in which the government finally made important concessions to the protesters. He explained, "Since this matter is over, and our demands have been met, I don't want to touch on it in order to avoid any trouble."

None of the other petitioners I contacted had similar concerns. Most of them were still engaged in their struggle, and therefore they did not hesitate to talk about their stories. This is very understandable given that what bothered them most was a lack of attentive listeners. In addition, many petitioners today seem to have inherited a traditional myth about officials who travel incognito (*weifu sifang*). Petitioners often had the illusion that upper authorities would someday send officials down to take up their case. Such an illusion often made them particularly eager to talk to visitors, especially those from Beijing or provincial capitals.

Of course I always told them that I was not an official in disguise, and that what I was doing was academic research. However, many ordinary Chinese people have had little exposure to academic research. Therefore, I typically went into detail in explaining this point, and still was not quite sure in some cases if the interviewees were entirely convinced. If petitioners have mistaken researchers for officials in disguise, some bias might be generated for interviews. This study tried to reduce this source of bias, as well as to take this factor into account when evaluating the validity of interviews.

Another special attribute of interviewing collective petitioners is that individual interviews were likely to become collective ones. This is because the setting of interviews tended to be affected by interviewees' habits as developed through their collective struggle. Protesters habitually gathered together to talk to outsiders. Thus they sometimes organized our meeting in this way, and sometimes no arrangement was necessary because they seemed to always be in close contact with each other. When some outsiders came to visit one of the activists, the information would spread quickly in the neighborhood, and soon other petitioners would gather around.

Collective interviews are certainly different from individual interviews, and indeed collective interviews have some advantages. The information derived from these interviews can be more accurate and complete, because interviewees can supplement and verify each others' narratives. Yet they may also have some disadvantages. A collective interview creates a setting for public discourse, and interviewees might talk and behave differently than if they were alone. In such an environment, it is more difficult to probe into petitioners' personal motivations and understandings.

HUNAN AS A CASE

While I visited four cities in Hunan, I have registered little regional variation. Rather, Hunan has been treated as a single case. This is mainly due to two factors. First, available evidence suggests that the overall trends of petitioning activities, petitioners' repertoires, and government responses have been very similar across different regions. Of course, some local governments have paid more attention to handling petitions and invested more resources in the xinfang agencies than others. Yet overall patterns of government-citizen interactions have demonstrated little cross-regional variation. This is not surprising considering that the political structure and public policies relevant to presenting and handling petitions are all defined and well coordinated by the center. Second, data from the local bureaus that I visited were somewhat different from each other in some important aspects. As noted earlier, for example, County Z bureau kept a relatively complete selection of case files but few event reports. City Y bureau kept few case files but a relatively complete collection of event reports. On the other hand, City X bureau actually did a relatively poor job collecting either form of information. Therefore, the data from different areas can complement each other rather well, but are not suitable for cross-regional comparison.

The main reason I choose Hunan is that it is my home province, and therefore it is much more likely for local officials and petitioners to trust me. Although all government archival materials I reviewed were nonclassified, they could possibly be used for purposes conflicting with those government agencies' interests. For example, if such information were revealed to the media (especially the international media), overseas "hostile" organizations, or petitioners, local officials might get into trouble.

In China, Hunan is a province in the "middle." Geographically, it is located in the middle-south of China. In 2000, its population was 64.4 million, the sixth highest in the nation. Its GDP in 1999 was 332,675 million RMB, which ranked eleventh in the nation; its GDP per capita was 5,105 RMB, which ranked fifteenth. The proportion of rural residents in Hunan is slightly higher than the national average, and it has been regarded as a large agricultural province. The urban population accounted for 29.75 percent of the total population in 1999. The trajectory of

Economic Reform in Hunan has been very similar to those of most other provinces. Most of the social and economic problems associated with the progress of Economic Reform, such as pension arrears, peasant burdens, and so forth, occurred around the same time throughout the country. The administrative structure of Hunan Province is also very similar to most other inland provinces.

However, Hunan has a somewhat special history: Traditionally it is famous for popular collective action, especially in the Revolutionary Era. It is generally believed that Hunan has contributed more revolutionary leaders than other provinces. An examination of the composition of the first generation of PRC leaders will easily confirm this perception. A question relevant to this study is whether or not Hunan people are more defiant, and therefore more likely to engage in collective action than people from other provinces in the Reform Era.

A systematic comparison is not feasible, because data in many other provinces are inaccessible. I have therefore compared Hunan's situation with another province, Henan, which is not particularly famous for its rebellious or revolutionary history and where the data on petitioning activities is more accessible than most other provinces (see Chapter 2). The comparison finds that whereas both provinces have experienced a very similar rise in collective petitioning since the early 1990s, collective petitioning activities were actually more frequent in Henan Province, even after taking the differences among their respective populations into account. This comparison suggests that the revolutionary legacy of Hunan Province may not have much impact on the frequency of popular collective action.

Available evidence, most of which is anecdotal, suggests that there exists little systematic variation in petitioning strategies and government responses among most inland provinces.[4] Therefore, I venture to suggest that the findings in Hunan Province are largely applicable to at least most inland provinces of China, although readers should still be aware that some observations are mainly based on this particular province.

---

[4] Of course, there are always some cross-regional variations. For example, Lee compared protests in China's Rustbelt and Sunbelt in a very illuminating way. C. K. Lee, *Against the Law: Labor Protests in China's Rustbelt and Sunbelt* (Berkeley: University of California Press, 2007). William Hurst also tried to establish the cross-regional variation in government responses. See William Hurst, *The Chinese Worker after Socialism* (New York: Cambridge University Press, 2009).

Bibliography

Adams, Jan S. 1981. "Critical Letters to the Soviet Press: An Increasingly Important Forum." Pp. 108–36 in *Political Participation in Communist Systems* edited by D D Schulz and Jan S Adams. New York: Pergamon.

Alford, William. 1984. "Of Arsenic and Old Laws: Looking Anew at Criminal Justice in Late Imperial China." *California Law Review* 72:1180–255.

Amenta, Edwin, and et al. 1999. "The Strategies and Contexts of Social Protest: Political Mediation and the Impact of the Townsend Movement in California." *Mobilization* 4:1–23.

Amenta, Edwin, and Michael Young. 1999. "Making an Impact." Pp. 22–41 in *How Social Movements Matter*, edited by M Giugni, D McAdam, and C Tilly. Minneapolis, MN: University of Minnesota Press.

Andrews, Kenneth. 2001. "Social Movements and Policy Implementation: The Mississippi Civil Rights Movement and the War on Poverty, 1965 to 1971." *American Sociological Review* 66(1):71–95.

Baum, Richard 1994. *Burying Mao: Chinese Politics in the Age of Deng Xiaoping*. Princeton, NJ: Princeton University Press.

Baum, Richard, and Alexei Shevchenko. 1999. "The 'state of the state'." Pp. 333–60 in *The Paradox of China's Post-Mao Reforms* edited by Merle Goldman and Roderick MacFarquhar. Cambridge, MA: Harvard University Press.

Bendix, Reinhard. 1964. *Nation Building and Citizenship*. New York: John Wiley & Son.

Bernhardt, Kathryn. 1992. *Rents, Taxes and Peasant Resistance: The Lower Yangzi Region, 1840–1950* Stanford, CA: Stanford University Press.

Bernstein, Thomas, and Xiaobo Lü. 2000. "Taxation without Representation: Peasants, the Central and the Local States in Reform China." *China Quarterly* 163:742–63.

2003. *Taxation without Representation in Contemporary Rural China*. New York: Cambridge University Press.

Bernstein, Thomas P. 1999. "Farmer Discontent and Regime Responses." Pp. 197–219 in _The Paradox of China's Post-Mao Reforms_ edited by Merle Goldman and Roderick MacFarquhar. Cambridge, MA: Harvard University Press.

Bianco, Lucien 2001. _Peasants without the Party: Grass-roots Movements in Twentieth-Century China._ Armonk, NY: M.E.Sharpe.

Biggs, Michael. 2003. "When Costs are Beneficial: Protest as Communicative Suffering." Working paper at the Department of Sociology, University of Oxford.

Blecher, Marc J. 2002. "Hegemony and Workers' Politics in China." _China Quarterly_ 170:283–303.

Brubaker, Rogers. 1992. _Citizenship and Nationhood in France and Germany._ Cambridge, MA: Harvard University Press.

Burawoy, Michael. 1996. "The State and Economic Involution: Russia through a China Lens." _World Development_ 24(6):1105–17.

Burawoy, Michael, and Janos Lukacs. 1992. _The Radiant Past: Ideology and Reality in Hungary's Road to Capitalism._ Chicago: University of Chicago Press.

Cai, Yongshun. 2002. "The Resistance of Chinese Laid-off Workers in the Reform period." _China Quarterly_ 170:327–43.

2004. "Managed Participation in China." _Political Science Quarterly_ 119(3):425–51.

2010. _Collective Resistance in China: Why Popular Protests Succeed or Fail._ Stanford, CA: Stanford University Press.

Chang, Chung-li. 1955. _The Chinese Gentry: Studies on Their Role in Nineteenth Century Chinese Society._ Seattle: University of Washington Press.

Chen, Feng. 2000. "Subsistence Crises, Managerial Corruption and Labor Protests in China." _The China Journal_ 44:41–63.

Chen, Jinsheng. 2004. _Quntixing Shijian Yanjiu Baogao_ (Research Report on Mass Incidents). Beijing: Qunzhong Chubanshe.

Chen, Xi. 2009. "Power of Troublemaking: Chinese Petitioners' Tactics and Their Efficacy." _Comparative Politics_ 41(4):451–71.

2010. "State-generated Data and the Study of Contentious Politics in China." Pp. 15–32 in _Contemporary Chinese Politics: New Methods, Sources and Field Strategies_ edited by Allen Carlson and et al. New York: Cambridge University Press.

Chen, Xi, and Ping Xu. 2011. "From Resistance to Advocacy: Political Representation for Disabled People in China." _China Quarterly_ 207: pp. 649–67.

Cheng, Zhaoqi. 1998. "Chen Dong and Jingkang Student Movement." _Zhongguo Yanjiu (China Studies)_ 35.

Chong, Dennis. 1991. _Collective Action and the Civil Rights Movement._ Chicago: University of Chicago Press.

Colburn, Forrest 1989. _Everyday Forms of Peasant Resistance._ Armonk, NY: M.E. Sharpe.

Collier, Ruth Berins. 1999. _Paths toward Democracy: The Working Class and Elites in Western Europe and South America._ New York: Cambridge University Press.

Cress, Daniel, and David Snow. 2000. "The Outcomes of Homeless Mobilization: The Influence of Organization, Disruption, Political Mediation and Framing." _American Journal of Sociology_ 105:1063–104.

Daozu, Bao. 2011. "Top Legislator Warns of Chaos Unless Correct Path Is Taken." in *China Daily*.

Deng, Xiaoping 1994. *Dengxiaoping Wenxuan (Selected Works of Deng Xiaoping)*. Beijing: Renmin Chubanshe.

Diao, Jiecheng 1996. *Renmin Xinfang Shilue (A Brief History of People's Letters and Visits)*. Beijing: Beijing Xueyuan Chubanshe.

Douglas, Mary 1986. *How Institutions Think*. Syracuse, NY: Syracuse University Press.

Economist. 2011. "The Truncheon Budget." Pp. 48–49 in *The Economist* (March 12).

Economist. 2011. "Bamboo Capitalism." Pp. 13 in *The Economist* (March 12).

Edin, Maria. 2000. "Market Forces and Communist Power: Local Political Institutions and Economic Development in China." Dissertation at Uppsala University.

    2003. "State Capacity and Local Agent Control in China: CCP Cadre Management from a Township Perspective." *China Quarterly* 173:35–52.

    2007. "Taking an Aspirin: Implementing Fees and Tax Reforms at the Local Level." Paper presented in at the Grassroots Political Reform in China Conference October 29–31, 2004, Fairbank Center, Harvard University.

Eisinger, Peter K. 1973. "The Conditions of Protest Behavior in American Cities." *American Political Science Review* 67:11–28.

Elster, Jon 1999. "Accountability in Athenian Politics" Pp. 253–78 in *Democracy, Accountability, and Representation* edited by Adam Przeworski, Susan C Stokes, and Bernard Manin. New York: Cambridge University Press.

Esherick, Joseph, and Jeffrey Wasserstrom. 1990. "Acting out Democracy: Political Theater in Modern China." *The Journal of Asian Studies* 49(4):835–65.

Fainsod, Merle. 1979. *Smolensk Under Soviet Rule*. New York: Vintage Books.

Fang, Qiang. 2006. "A Hot Potato: The Chinese Complaint Systems from Early Times to the Present." Dissertation at the University of Buffalo.

Field, Daniel 1976. *Rebels in the Name of the Tsar*. Boston: Houghton Mifflin.

Fogelson, Robert M. 1968. "Violence as Protest." *Proceedings of the Academy of Political Science* 29(1):25–41.

Foucault, Michel. 1977. *Discipline and Punishment*. New York: Vintage Books.

Fox, Jonathan. 1994. "The Difficult Transition from Clientelism to Citizenship: Lessons from Mexico." *World Politics* 46:151–84.

Frakt, Phyllis M. 1979. "Mao's Concept of Representation." *American Journal of Political Science* 23(4):684–704.

French, Howard. 2005. "Land of 74,000 Protests (But Little Is Ever Fixed)." *New York Times*, August 24.

Fukuyama, Francis. 1989. "The End of History." *The National Interest* 16:3–18.

Gamson, William. 1975. *The Strategy of Social Protest*. Homewood, IL: The Dorsey Press.

Gao, Yang, and Qinglin Zhang. 1999. "Qunzhong Jiti Shangfang Chengwei Yingxiang Shoudu Wending de Tuchu Wenti (Mass Collective Visits Have Become a Prominent Problem Threatening Social Stability in the Capital)." *Beijing Renmin Jingcha Xueyuan Xuebao* 58(2):36–38.

Gat, Azar. 2007. "The Return of Authoritarian Great Powers." *Foreign Affairs* 86(4):59–69.

Geertz, Clifford. 1973. *The Interpretation of Cultures*. New York: Basic Books.

Giddens, Anthony. 1976. *New Rules of Sociological Method: A Positive Critique of Interpretative Sociologies*. London: Hutchinson.

Gilley, Bruce. 2003. "The Limits of Authoritarian Resilience." *Journal of Democracy* 14(1):18–26.

Giugni, Marco. 1998. "Was It Worth the Effort? The Outcomes and Consequences of Social Movements." *Annual Review of Sociology* 24:371–93.

1999. "How Social Movements Matter: Past Research, Present Problems, Future Developments." Pp. xiii–xxxiii in *How Social Movements Matter* edited by Marco Giugni, Doug McAdam, and Charles Tilly. Mineapolis: University of Minnesota Press.

Giugni, Marco, Doug McAdam, and Charles Tilly. 1999. *How Social Movements Matter*. Minneapolis: University of Minnesota Press.

Goldman, Merle. 2002. "The Reassertion of Political Citizenship in the Post-Mao Era: The Democracy Wall Movement" Pp. 159–86 in *Changing Meanings of Citizenship in Modern China* edited by Merle Goldman and Elizabeth Perry. Cambridge, MA: Harvard University Press.

Goldman, Merle, and Roderick MacFarquhar. 1999. "Dynamic Economy, Declining Party-State." Pp. 3–29 in *The Paradox of China's Post-Mao Reforms* edited by Merle Goldman and Roderick MacFarquhar. Cambridge, MA: Harvard University Press.

Granovetter, Mark. 1978. "Threshold Models of Collective Behavior." *American Journal of Sociology* 83:1420–43.

Gries, Peter Hayes, and Stanley Rosen. 2004. "Introduction: Popular Protest and State Legitimation in 21st-Century China." Pp. 1–23 in *State and Society in 21st-Century China: Crisis, Contention, and Legitimation* edited by Peter Hayes Gries and Stanley Rosen. London: Routledge.

Hanagan, Michael, Leslie Page Moch, and Wayne te Brake (Eds.). 1998. *Challenging Authority: The Historical Study of Contentious Politics*. Minneapolis: University of Minnesota Press.

Hanagan, Michael, and Charles Tilly. 1999. *Extending Citizenship, Reconfiguring States*. Lanham, MD: Rowman & Littlefield.

Havel, Vaclav. 1985. *The Power of the Powerless: Citizens against the State in Central Eastern Europe*. Armonk, NY: M.E. Sharpe.

Heilmann, Sebastian. 1995. "Grass-Roots Protest and the Counter-Cultural Revolution of the Seventies." Working paper at Hamburg.

Helmke, Gretchen, and Steven Levitsky. 2004. "Informal Institutions and Comparative Politics: A Research Agenda." *Perspectives on Politics* 2(4):725–40.

Herb, Michael. 1999. *All in the Family: Absolutism, Revolution, and Democracy in the Middle Eastern Monarchies*. Albany: State University of New York Press.

Hipsher, Patricia L. 1998. "Democratic Transitions as Protest Cycles: Social Movement Dynamics in Democratizing Latin America." Pp. 153–72 in *The Social Movement Society: Contentious Politics for a New Century* edited by David Meyer and Sidney Tarrow. Lanhan, MD: Rowman & Littlefield.

Hirschman, Albert O. 1970. "The Search for Paradigms as a Hindrance to Our Understanding," *World Politics* 22(3):329–343.

Hobsbawm, E. J. 1973. "Peasants and Politics." *Journal of Peasant Studies* 1(13):3–22.

Huang, Yasheng. 1995. "Administrative Monitoring in China." *China Quarterly* 143:834–35.

——— 2002. "Managing Chinese Bureaucrats: An Institutional Economic Perspective." *Political Studies* 50:278–95.

Huntington, Samuel. 1968. *Political Order in Changing Societies.* New Haven, CT: Yale University Press.

Hurst, William. 2004. "The Forgotten Player: Local State Strategies and the Dynamics of Laid-off Workers' Contention." Paper presented at the annual meeting of the American Political Science Association, Chicago.

——— 2009. *The Chinese Worker after Socialism.* New York: Cambridge University Press.

Hurst, William, and Kevin J. O'Brien. 2002. "Chinese Contentious Pensioners." *The China Quarterly* 170:345–58.

Jacobs, Andrew, and Jonathan Ansfield. 2011. "Well-Oiled Security Apparatus in China Stifles Calls for Change." *New York Times* February 28.

Jasper, James. 2002. "A Strategic Approach to Collective Action: Looking for Agency in Social Movement Choices." Paper presented at the *American Sociological Association* annual meeting, Chicago.

Jenkins, Joseph Craig, and Charles Perrow. 1977. "Insurgency of the Powerless: Farm Worker Movements (1946–1972)." *American Sociological Review* 42(2):249–68.

Jing, Jun. 2000. "Environmental Protests in Rural China." Pp. 143–60 in *Chinese Society: Change, Conflict and Resistance* edited by Elizabeth Perry and Mark Selden. London: Routledge.

Katznelson, Ira. 1997. "Structures and Configuration." Pp. 81–112 in *Comparative Politics: Rationality, Culture, and Structure* edited by Mark Lichbach and Alan S. Zuchkerman. Cambridge: Cambridge University Press.

——— 2003. "Periodization and Preferences." Pp. 270–301 in *Comparative Historical Analysis in the Social Science* edited by James Mahoney and Dietrich Rueschemeyer. Cambridge: Cambridge University Press.

Kahn, Joseph. 2006. "Pace and Scope of Protests in China Accelerated in '05." *New York Times* January 20.

Kinglun, Ngok. 1999. "New Collective Labor Relation Mechanisms in the Workplace: the Collective Contract System in Mainland China." *Issues and Studies* 35(6):119–43.

Kriesi, Hanspeter. 1995. *New Social Movements in Western Europe: A Comparative Analysis.* Mineapolis: University of Minnesota Press.

Lampert, Nicholas. 1985. *Whistle Blowing in the Soviet Union: Complaints and Abuses Under State Socialism.* London: MacMillan.

Landry, Pierre. 2009. *Decentralized Authoritarianism in China: The Communist Party's Control of Local Elites in the Post-Mao Era.* New York: Cambridge University Press.

Lee, Ching Kwan. 2000a. "From Organized Dependency to Disorganized Despotism." *China Quarterly* 157:44–71.

2000b. "Pathways of Labor Insurgency." Pp. 41–61 in *Chinese Society: Change, Conflict and Resistance* edited by Elizabeth Perry and Mark Selden. London: Routledge.

2000c. "The 'Revenge of History': Collective Memories and Labor Protests in Northeastern China." *Ethnography* 1(2):217–37.

2002. "From the Specter of Mao to the Spirit of the Law: Labor Insurgency in China." *Theory and Society* 31:189–228.

2007. *Against the Law: Labor Protests in China's Rustbelt and Sunbelt.* Berkeley: University of California Press.

Levitsky, Steven, and Lucan A Way. 2010. *Competitive Authoritarianism: Hybrid Regimes After the Cold War.* New York: Cambridge University Press.

Li, Guorong. 2007. *Qingchao Shida Kechang An (Ten Major Criminal Cases Related to the Imperial Exams).* Beijing: Renmin Chubanshe.

Li, Lianjiang, and Kevin O'Brien. 1996. "Villagers and Popular Resistance in Contemporary China." *Modern China* 22:40–55.

Lichbach, Mark, and Alan S Zuchkerman (Eds.). 1997. *Comparative Politics: Rationality, Culture, and Structure.* Cambridge: Cambridge University Press.

Lieberthal, Kenneth. 1995. *Governing China: From Revolution through Reform.* New York: W. W. Norton.

Lieberthal, Kenneth, and David Lampton. 1992. *Bureaucracy, Politics, and Decision Making in Post-Mao China.* Berkeley: University of California Press.

Liebman, Benjamin. 2005. "Watchdogs or Demagogues? The Media in the Chinese Legal System." *Columbia Law Review*: 1–157.

Lin, Yutang. 1936. *A History of the Press and Public Opinion in China.* Chicago: University of Chicago Press.

Lindblom, Charles. 1977. *Politics and Markets.* New York: Basic Books.

Linz, Juan. 2000. *Totalitarian and Authoritarian Regimes.* Boulder, CO: Lynn Rienner.

Linz, Juan, and Alfred Stepan. 1996. *Problems of Democratic Transition and Consolidation: Southern Europe, South America and Post-Communist Europe.* Baltimore and London: The Johns Hopkins University Press.

Lipsky, Michael. 1968. "Protest as a Political Resource." *The American Political Science Review* 62(4):1144–58.

Liu, Zhifeng. 1998. "Lun Qunzhong Luxian yu Qunzhong Canyu" (On the mass line and mass participation). *Kaifang Shidai* 2:14–20.

Lu, Xiaobo. 2000. "Booty Socialism, Bureau-preneurs, and the State in Transition: Organizational Corruption in China." *Comparative Politics* 32(3):273–94.

Lu, Xiaobo, and Elizabeth Perry. 1997. *Danwei: The Changing Chinese Workplace in Historical and Comparative Perspective.* Armonk, NY: M.E. Sharpe.

Lu, Xun 1980. *Huagai Ji Xu Bian.* Beijing: Renmin Wenxue Chubanshe.

Lubman, Stanley. 1999. *Bird in a Cage: Legal Reform in China after Mao.* Stanford, CA: Stanford University Press.

Luehrmann, Laura. 2000. "Officials Face the Masses: Citizen Contacting in Modern China." Dissertation at Ohio State University.

2003. "Facing Citizen Complaints in China, 1951–1996." *Asian Survey* 43(5): 845–66.

Ma, Shaofang. 2004. "Lishi zai Bianta Xianshi (History is Whipping the Reality)." *Beijing Spring* (133), available at http://beijingspring.com/bj2/2004/120/2004530230631.htm.

Magaloni, Beatriz, and Ruth Kricheli. 2010. "Political Order and One-Party Rule." *Annual Review of Political Science* 13:123–43.

Mainwaring, Scott. 1989. "Grassroots Popular Movements and the Struggle for Democracy: Nova Iguacu." Pp. 275–314 in *Democratizing Brazil: Problems of Transition and Consolidation* edited by Alfred Stepan. New York and Oxford: Oxford University Press.

Manin, Bernard, Adam Przeworski, and Susan C. Stokes (Eds.). 1999. *Democracy, Accountability, and Representation*. New York: Cambridge University Press.

Mann, Michael 1987. "Ruling Class Strategies and Citizenship." *Sociology* 21:339–54.

Mao, Zedong. 1969. "On the Mass Line." Pp. 315–17 in *The Political Thought of Mao Tse-tung* edited by Stuart R. Schram. New York: Praeger Publishers.

Markoff, John. 1996. *Waves of Democracy: Social Movements and Political Change*. Thousand Oaks, CA: Pine Forge.

Marshall, T. H. 1950. *Class, Citizenship, and Social Development*. Cambridge: Cambridge University Press.

McAdam, Doug. 1982. *Political Process and the Development of Black Insurgency, 1930–1970*. Chicago: University of Chicago Press.

  1996. "The Framing Function of Movement Tactics: Strategic Dramaturgy in the American Civil Rights Movement." Pp. 338–55 in *Comparative Perspectives on Social Movements: Political Opportunities, Mobilizing Structures, and Cultural Framings* edited by Doug McAdam, John D McCarthy, and Mayer N Zald. New York: Cambridge University Press.

McAdam, Doug, John D McCarthy, and Mayer N Zald. 1996. *Comparative Perspectives on Social Movements: Political Opportunities, Mobilizing Structures, and Cultural Framings*. New York: Cambridge University Press.

McAdam, Doug, Sidney Tarrow, and Charles Tilly. 2001. *Dynamics of Contention*. New York: Cambridge University Press.

McCann, Michael. 1994. *Rights at Work: Pay Equity Reform and the Politics of Legal Mobilization*. Chicago: University of Chicago Press.

McCarthy, John D, and Mayer N Zald. 1977. "Resource Mobilization and Social Movements: A Partial Theory." *American Journal of Sociology* 82(6):1212–41.

Meyer, David, and Sidney Tarrow (Eds.). 1998. *The Social Movement Society: Contentious Politics for a New Century*. Lanhan, MD: Rowman & Littlefield.

Minzner, Carl. 2006. "Xinfang: An Alternative to the Formal Chinese Legal System." *Stanford Journal of International Law* 42(1):103–79.

Morris, Aldon D. 1993. "Birmingham Confrontation Reconsidered: An Analysis of The Dynamics and Tactics of Mobilization." *American Sociological Review* 58:621–36.

Nathan, Andrew. 1997. *China's Transition*. New York: Columbia University Press.

  2003. "Authoritarian Resilience in China." *Journal of Democracy* 14(1):6–17.

Naughton, Barry. 1997. "Danwei: The Economic Foundations of a Unique Institution." Pp. 169–94 in *Danwei* edited by Xiaobo Lu and Elizabeth Perry. Armonk, NY: M.E. Sharpe.

Naughton, Barry J, and Dali Yang (Eds.). 2004. *Holding China Together: Diversity and National Integration in the Post-Deng Era.* New York: Cambridge University Press.

Nee, Victor. 1989. "A Theory of Market Transition: From Rědistribution to Markets in State Socialism." *American Sociological Review* 54(5):663–81.

Nee, Victor, and Rebecca Matthews. 1996. "Market Transition and Societal Transformation in Reforming State Socialism." *Annual Review of Sociology* 22:401–35.

Nubola, Cecilia. 2001. "Supplications between Politics and Justice: The Northern and Central Italian States in the Early Modern Age." *International Research of Social History* 46(Supplement):35–56.

O'Brien, Kevin. 1994. "Agents and Remonstrators: Role Accumulation by Chinese Congress Deputies." *China Quarterly* 138:359–80.

    1994. "Implementing Political Reform in China's Villages." *Australian Journal of Chinese Affairs* 32:33–59.

    1996. "Rightful Resistance." *World Politics* 49:31–56.

    1999. "Campaign Nostalgia in the Chinese Countryside." *Asia Survey* 39(3):375–93.

    2001. "Villagers, Elections, and Citizenship in Contemporary China." *Modern China* 27(4):407–35.

    2002. "Collective Action in the Chinese Countryside." *The China Journal* 48:139–54.

    2003. "Neither Transgressive nor Contained: Boundary-Spanning Contention in China." *Mobilization* 8(1):51–64.

    2005. "Popular Contention and Its Impact in Rural China." *Comparative Political Studies* 37(3):235–59.

O'Brien, Kevin, and Lianjiang Li. 1995. "The Politics of Lodging Complaints in Rural China." *The China Quarterly*:756–83.

    2006. *Rightful Resistance in Rural China.* New York: Cambridge University Press.

Ocko, Jonathan. 1988. "I Will Take It All the Way to Beijing: Capital Appeals in the Qing." *Journal of Asian Studies* 47(2):291–315.

Oi, Jean. 1985. "Communism and Clientelism: Rural Politics in China." *World Politics* 37(2):238–66.

    1989. *State and Peasant in Contemporary China: The Political Economy of Village Government.* Berkeley and Los Angeles: University of California Press.

    1999. *Rural China Takes Off: The Institutional Foundations of Economic Reform.* Berkeley: University of California Press.

Oliver, James H. 1969. "Citizen Demands and the Soviet Political System." *American Political Science Review* 63:465–75.

Olson, Mancur. 1993. "Democracy, Dictatorship, and Development." *American Political Science Review* 87(3):567–76.

Opp, Karl-Dieter. 1988. "Grievances and Participation in Social Movements." *American Sociological Review* 53(6):853–64.

Oxnam, Robert B. 1973. "Policies and Institutions of the Oboi Regency, 1661–1669." *Journal of Asian Studies* 32(2):279–80.

Pan, Philip. 2004. "A Study Group Is Crushed in China's Grip." *Washington Post*, April 23.

Parish, William. 1995. "Non-farm Work and Marketization of the Chinese Countryside." *China Quarterly* 143:697–730.

Payne, James L. 1965. *Labor and Politics in Peru.* New Haven, CT: Yale University Press.

Pei, Minxing. 2000. "Rights and Resistance: The Changing Contexts of the Dissident Movement." Pp. 20–40 in *Chinese Society: Change, Conflict, and Resistance* edited by Elizabeth Perry and Mark Selden. London and New York: Routledge.

2006. *China's Trapped Transition: The Limits of Developmental Autocracy.* Cambridge, MA: Harvard University Press.

Pereenboom, Randy. 2003. "A Government of Laws: Democracy, Rule of Law, and Administrative Law Reform in the PRC." *Journal of Contemporary China* 12:45–67.

Perry, Elizabeth. 1984. "Collective Violence in China 1880–1980." *Theory and Society* 13(3, Special issue on China):427–54.

1985. "Rural Violence in Socialist China." *China Quarterly* 103(September) : 414–40.

1993. *Shanghai on Strike: The Politics of Chinese Labor.* Stanford, CA: Stanford University Press.

1994. "Trends in the Study of Chinese Politics: State-Society Relations." *China Quarterly* 139:704–13.

1995. "To Rebel Is Justified: Maoist Influences on Popular Protest in Contemporary China." Paper in the Colloquium Series of the Program in Agrarian Studies at Yale University.

1997. "From Native Place to Workplace: Labor Origins and Outcomes of China's Danwei System." Pp. 42–59 in *Danwei: The Changing Chinese Workplace in Historical and Comparative Perspective* edited by Xiaobo Lu and Elizabeth Perry. Armonk, NY: M.E. Sharpe.

1999. "From Paris to the Paris of the East and Back: Workers as Citizens in Modern Shanghai." *Comparative Study of Society and History* 41(2):348–73.

2002. *Challenging the Mandate of Heaven: Social Protest and State Power in China.* Armonk: NY: M.E. Sharpe.

2007. "Studying Chinese Politics: Farewell to Revolution?" *China Journal* 57: 1–22.

2008. "Permanent Rebellion? Continuities and Discontinuities in Chinese Protest." Pp. 205–15 in *Popular Protest in China* edited by Kevin J O'Brien. Cambridge, MA: Harvard University Press.

Perry, Elizabeth, and Mark Selden (Eds.). 2000. *Chinese Society: Change Conflict and Resistance.* London: Routledge.

Pheffer, Richard M. 1972. "Serving the People and Continuing the Revolution." *The China Quarterly* 52:620–53.

Pieke, Frank. 2004. "Contours of an Anthropology of the Chinese State: Political Structure, Agency and Economic Development in Rural China." *Journal of Royal Anthropological Institute* 10:517–38.

Piven, Frances Fox, and Richard Cloward. 1977. *Poor People's Movements: Why They Succeed, How They Fail.* New York: Vintage Books.

Polanyi, Karl. 1957. *The Great Transformation: The Political and Economic Origins of Our Time.* Boston: Beacon Press.

Popkin, Samuel L. 1979. *The Rational Peasant: The Political Economy of Rural Society in Vietnam.* Berkeley and Los Angeles: University of California Press.

Potter, Pitman B. 1999. "The Chinese Legal System: Continuing Commitment to the Primacy of State Power." *The China Quarterly* 159:673–83.

Przeworski, Adam. 1991. *Democracy and the Market: Political and Economic Reforms in Eastern Europe and Latin America.* Cambridge: Cambridge University Press.

Przeworski, Adam, Susan C Stokes, and Bernard Manin. 1999. *Democracy, Accountability, and Representation.* New York: Cambridge University Press.

Qu, Tongzu. 2003. *Qingdai Difang Zhengfu (Local Governments in the Qing Dynasty).* Beijing: Falu Chubanshe.

Rankin, Mary Backus. 1982. "'Public Opinion' and Political Power: Qingyi in Late Nineteenth Century China." *Journal of Asian Studies* 41:453–84.

Rousseau, Jean-Jacques. 1983. *On the Social Contract.* Indianapolis, IN: Hackett.

Rueschemeyer, Dietrich. 1990. "Planning without Markets: Knowledge and State Action in East German Housing Construction." *East European Politics and Societies* 4(3):557–79.

Schneiberg, Marc, and Elisabeth Clemens. 2006. "The Typical Tool for the Job: Research Strategies in Institutional Analysis." *Sociological Theory* 24:195–227.

Schock, Kurt. 2005. *Unarmed Insurrections: People Power Movements in Nondemocracies.* Minneapolis: University of Minnesota Press.

Scott, James. 1976. *The Moral Economy of the Peasant.* New Haven, CT: Yale University Press.

   1985. *Weapons of the Weak.* New Haven, CT: Yale University Press.

   1990. *Domination and the Arts of Resistance: Hidden Transcripts.* New Haven, CT: Yale University Press.

   1998. *Seeing Like a State: How Certain Schemes to Improve the Human Condition Have Failed.* New Haven, CT: Yale University Press.

Selden, Mark. 1971. *The Yenan Way in Revolutionary China.* Cambridge, MA: Harvard University Press.

Sewell, William H. 2001. "Space in Contentious Politics." Pp. 51–88 in *Silence and Voice in the Study of Contentious Politics* edited by Ronald R Aminzade. New York: Cambridge University Press.

Shi, Tianjian. 1997. *Political Participation in Beijing.* Cambridge, MA: Harvard University Press.

Shue, Vivienne. 1988. *The Reach of the State.* Stanford, CA: Stanford University Press.

   2004. "Legitimacy Crisis in China?" Pp. 24–49 in *State and Society in 21st-Century China: Crisis, Contention, and Legitimation* edited by Peter Hayes Gries and Stanley Rosen. London: Routledge.

Simmel, George. 1950. *The Sociology of George Simmel*. New York: Free Press.

Skidmore, Thomas E. 1988. *The Politics of Military Rule in Brazil, 1964–85*. New York and Oxford: Oxford University Press.

Skocpol, Theda. 1985. "Bringing the State Back In: Strategies of Analysis in Current Research." Pp. 3–37 in *Bringing the State Back In* edited by Peter B Evans, Dietrich Rueschemeyer, and Theda Skocpol. New York: Cambridge University Press.

1999. "Association without Members." *American Prospect* 45:66–73.

Snow, David A, Daniel Cress, Liam Downey, and Andrew W Jones. 1998. "Disrupting the 'Quotidian': Re-conceptualizing the Relationship between Breakdown and the Emergence of Collective Action." *Mobilization* 3(1):9–14.

Snyder, David, and William R Kelly. 1976. "Industrial Violence in Italy, 1878–1903." *American Journal of Sociology* 82:131–62.

Solinger, Dorothy. 1999. *Contesting Citizenship in Urban China: Peasant Migrants, the State and the Logic of the Market*. Berkeley: University of California Press.

2004. "The New Crowd of the Dispossessed: The Shift of the Urban Proletariat from Master to Mendicant." Pp. 50–66 in *State and Society in 21st-Century China: Crisis, Contention, and Legitimation* edited by Peter Hayes Gries and Stanley Rosen. New York: Routledge.

Somers, Margaret. 1993. "Citizenship and the Place of the Public Sphere: Law, Community, and Political Culture in the Transition to Democracy." *American Sociological Review* 58:587–620.

1994. "Rights, Relationality, and Membership: Rethinking the Making and Meaning of Citizenship." *Law and Social Inquiry* 1:63–112.

Soule, Sarah. 1999. "The Diffusion of an Unsuccessful Innovation." *Annals of the American Academy of Political and Social Science* 655:120–31.

Steinberg, Marc. 1996. "'The Great End of All Government…': Working People's Construction of Citizenship Claims in Early Nineteenth-Century England and the Matter of Class." Pp. 19–50 in *Citizenship, Identity, and Social History* edited by Charles Tilly. Cambridge: Cambridge University Press.

Strand, David. 1990. "Protest in Beijing: Civil Society and Public Sphere in China." *Problems of Communism* 37:1–19.

Straughn, Jeremy B. 2005. "'Take the State at Its Word': The Arts of Consentful Contention in the German Democratic Republic." *American Journal of Sociology* 110(6):1598–650.

Sullivan, Lawrence R. 1990. "The Emergence of Civil Society in China, Spring 1989." Pp. 126–44 in *The Chinese People's Movement, Perspectives on Spring 1989* edited by Tony Saich. Armonk, NY: M.E. Sharpe.

Sun, Liping. 2004. *Shiheng: Duanlie Shehui de Yunzuo Luoji (Imbalance: the Logic of a Fractured Society)*. Beijing: Shehui wenxian chubanshe.

Szymanski, Ann-Marie. 2003. *Pathways to Prohibition: Radicals, Moderates and Social Movement Outcomes*. Durham, NC: Duke University Press.

Tanner, Murray Scott. 1999. "The National People's Congress." Pp. 100–28 in *The Paradox of China's Post-Mao Reforms* edited by Merle Goldman and Roderick MacFarquhar. Cambridge, MA: Harvard University Press.

2004. "China Rethinks Unrest." *Washington Quarterly* 27(3):137–56.

Tarrow, Sidney. 1994. *Power in Movement: Social Movements and Contentious Politics*. New York: Cambridge University Press.

1996. "States and Opportunities: The Political Structuring of Social Movements." Pp. 41–61 in *Comparative Perspectives on Social Movements: Political Opportunities, Mobilizing Structures, and Cultural Framings* edited by Doug McAdam, John D McCarthy, and Mayer N Zald. New York: Cambridge University Press.

Thelen, Kathleen. 2003. "How Institutions Evolve: Insights from Comparative Historical Analysis." Pp. 208–40 in *Comparative Historical Analysis in the Social Science* edited by James Mahoney and Dietrich Rueschemeyer. Cambridge: Cambridge University Press.

Thireau, Isabelle, and Linshan Hua. 2003. "The Moral Universe of Aggrieved Chinese Workers: Workers' Appeals to Arbitration Committees and Letters and Visits Offices." *China Journal* 50:83–103.

Thompson, E P. 1971. "The Moral Economy of the English Crowd in the Eighteenth Century." *Past and Present* 50:76–136.

1974. "Patrician Society, Plebian Culture." *Journal of Social History* 7(4):382–405.

1975. *Whigs and Hunters: The Origin of the Black Act*. London: Allen Lane.

Thornton, Patricia. 2004. "Digital Contention and Political Divides: Popular Protest, State Repression and the Internet in Contemporary China." Paper presented at the annual meeting of the Amecan Political Science Association. Chicago.

Tilly, Charles. 1978. *From Mobilization to Revolution*. Reading, MA: Addison-Wesley.

1984. *Big Structures, Large Processes, Huge Comparisons*. New York: Russell Sage Foundation.

1995. "Contentious Repertoires in Great Britain, 1758–1834." Pp. 15–42 in *Repertoires and Cycles of Collective Action* edited by Mark Traugott. Durham, NC: Duke University Press.

1998. *Durable Inequality*. Berkeley and Los Angeles: University of California Press.

1999. "From Interactions to Outcomes in Social Movements." Pp. 253–70 in *How Social Movements Matter* edited by Marco Giugni, Doug McAdam, and Charles Tilly. Minneapolis: University of Minnesota Press.

2004. *Contention and Democracy in Europe, 1650–2000*. New York: Cambridge University Press.

Tsai, Kellee S. 2007. *Capitalism without Democracy: The Private Sector in Contemporary China*. Ithaca, NY: Cornell University Press.

Tsai, Lily. 2007. *Accountability without Democracy: Solidarity Groups and Public Goods Provision in Rural China*. New York: Cambridge University Press.

Turner, Bryan. 1990. "Outline of a Theory of Citizenship." *Sociology* 24(2):189–217.

1993. *Citizenship and Social Theory*. London: Sage Publications.

Unger, Jonathan. 1989. "State and Peasant in Post-Revolution China." *Journal of Peasant Studies* 17:133–35.

Wakeman, Federick. 1975. "Introduction: The Evolution of Local Control in Late Imperial China." Pp. 1–25 in *Conflict and Control in Late Imperial China* edited by Federick Wakeman and Carolyn Grant. Berkeley and Los Angeles: University of California.

Wakeman, Federick, and Carolyn Grant. 1975. *Conflict and Control in Late Imperial China*. Berkeley and Los Angeles: University of California.

Walder, Andrew. 1986. *Communist Neo-Traditionalism: Work and Authority in Chinese Industry*. Berkeley and Los Angeles: University of California Press.

——— 1994. "The Decline of Communist Power: Elements of a Theory of Institutional Change." *Theory and Society* 23(2):297–323.

——— 1995. *The Waning of the Communist State: Economic Origins of Political Decline in China and Hungry*. Berkeley: University of California Press.

——— 1998. "Collective Protest and the Waning of the Communist State in China." Pp. 54–72 in *Challenging Authority: The Historical Study of Contentious Politics* edited by Michael Hanagan, Leslie Page Moch, and Wayne Te Brake. Minneapolis: University of Minnesota Press.

——— 2009. "Political Sociology and Social Movements." *Annual Review of Sociology* 35:393–412.

Wang, Shaoguang. 1995. "The Rise of the Regions: Fiscal Reform and the Decline of Central State Capacity in China." Pp. 87–113 in *The Waning of the Communist State: Economic Origins of Political Decline in China and Hungry* edited by Andrew Walder. Berkeley: University of California Press.

Weber, Max. 1946. *From Max Weber*. New York: Oxford University Press.

——— 1947. *The Theory of Social and Economic Organization*. New York: The Free Press.

Whyte, Martin King. 2010. *Myth of the Social Volcano: Perceptions of Inequality and Distributive Injustice in Contemporary China*. Stanford, CA: Stanford University Press.

Wilkinson, Steven I. 2009. "Riots." *Annual Review of Political Science* 12:329–43.

Wilson, James Q. 1961. "The Strategy of Protest: Problems of Negro Civic Action." *Journal of Conflict Resolution* 3:291–303.

Womack, Brantly. 1991. "Transfigured Community: Neo-Traditionalism and Work Unit Socialism in China." *China Quarterly* 126:313–32.

Wong, Bin R. 1997. *China Transformed: Historical Change and the Limits of European Experience*. Ithaca, NY: Cornell University Press.

——— 1998. "The Changing Horizons of Tax Resistance in Chinese History." Pp. 149–64 in *Challenging Authority: The Historical Study of Contentious Politics* edited by Michael Hanagan, Leslie Page Moch, and Wayne Te Brake. Minneapolis: University of Minnesota Press.

——— 1999. "Citizenship in Chinese History." Pp. 97–122 in *Extending Citizenship, Reconfiguring States* edited by Michael Hanagan and Charles Tilly. Lanham, MD: Rowman & Littlefield.

Wu, Zhong. 2010. "Beijing Hears Dissenting Voice on Unrest." *Asia Times Online* April 28, available at www.atimes.com.

Wurgler, Andreas. 2001. "Voices from among the 'Silent Masses': Humble Petitions and Social Conflicts in Early Modern Central Europe." *International Research of Social History* 46:11–34.

Yang, Dali. 1994. "Reform and the Restructuring of Central-Local Relations." Pp. 59–98 in *China Deconstructs: Politics, Trade, and Regionalism* edited by David S G Goodman and Gerald Segal. London: Routledge.

Yanlong, Zhao. 2003. "Xixia Xinfang Gongzuo Zhidu Tanwei (Exploration of the letters and visits system in Xixia)." *Ningxia Social Science* 119(4):50–53.

Ying, Xing. 2002. *Dahe Yimin Shangfang de Gushi (The Story of the Petitioning of the Migrants in Dahe Town).* Beijing: Sanlian Press.

———. 2004. "Zuowei Teshu Xingzheng Jiuji de Xinfang Jiuji" (The Xinfang Remedy: A Special Form of Administrative Relief)." *Faxue Yanjiu* 3:58–71.

Ying, Xing, and Jun Jing. 2000. "Jiti Shangfang Zhong de Wentihua Guocheng: Xinan Yige Shuidianzhan de Yimin de Guishi (The Process of Problemization in Collective Visits: A Story of Migration Caused by a Hydroelectric Plant in Southwest China)." *Qinghua Shehuixue Pinglun (Qinghua Sociological Journal)* (Special issue):80–109.

Young, Graham. 1984. "Control and Style: Discipline Inspection Commissions since the 11th Congress." *The China Quarterly* 97:24–52.

Yu, Jianrong. 2003. "Nongmin Youzuzhi Kangzheng Jiqi Zhengzhi Fengxian (Peasants' Organized Resistance and Its Political Risk)." *Zhanlue yu Guanli (Strategies and Management)* 3:1–16.

———. 2004. "Zhongguo Xinfang Zhidu Pipan (Critique of the Chinese Letters and Visits System)." A speech at Beijing University, available at www.yannan.com.

———. 2005. "Dangdai Zhongguo Nongmin Weiquan Zuzhi de Fayu yu Chengzhang: Jiyu Hengyang Nongmin Xiehui de Shizheng Yanjiu (Growth and Development of Peasants' Organizations of Rights Defense in Contemporary China: An Empirical Study of the Hengyang Peasant Associations)." *Zhongguo Nongcun Guancha (China Rural Survey)* 2:57–64.

Zahavi, Amotz, and Avishag Zahavi. 1997. *The Handicap Principle: A Missing Piece of Darwin's Puzzle.* New York and Oxford: Oxford University Press.

Zakaria, Fareed. 2003. *The Future of Freedom: Illiberal Democracy at Home and Abroad.* New York: W. W. Norton.

Zhang, Liang. 2001. *Liusi Zhenxiang (The Truth of June 4th).* Hong Kong: Mirror Publications.

Zhao, Dingxin. 1998. "Ecologies of Social Movements: Student Mobilization during the 1989 Prodemocarcy Movement in Beijing." *American Journal of Sociology* 103(6):1493–529.

———. 2000. "State-Society Relations and the Discourses and Activities of the 1989 Beijing Student Movement." *American Journal of Sociology* 105(5):1592–632.

———. 2001. *Power of Tiananmen.* Chicago: University of Chicago Press.

Zhou, Guangyuan. 1993. "Illusion and Reality in the Law of the Late Qing." *Modern China* 19(4):427–56.

Zhou, Xueguang. 1993. "Unorganized Interests and Collective Action in Communist China." *American Sociological Review* 58(1):54–73.

Zweig, David. 1987. "Law, Contracts, and Economic Modernization: Lessons from the Recent Chinese Rural Reforms." *Stanford Journal of International Law* 23:326–35.

Index

abnormal petitioning, 28, 214
accumulation, capital
  and legitimation, 11, 17
  local imperative for, 17
administrative reconsideration, 141
advocacy, 21, 25, 158, 160, 164, 165, 167,
  168, 185, 186
Alford, William, 105
All China Federation of Trade Unions
  (ACFTU), 16, 126, 127
alliance, cross-sector/region, 143, 147
Almond, Gabriel A., 206
anti-rightist campaign, 39
appropriation-response mechanism, 20, 21,
  22, 127, 130, 131, 202
Army Day, 69, 151
authoritarian regimes, 160, 163, 197
  competitive, 198
  the complexity of, 194
  full-blown, 198
  institutional inadequacy, 204
  and popular contention, 6, 26, 189,
    194, 205
  the stability in, 202
authoritarian resilience, 204

bamboo capitalism, 211
banners with slogans, 3, 168
bargaining by riot, 206
begging for food or money, 174
Beijing, 47, 69, 72, 129, 140
  campus ecology in, 200
  overflow of petitions to, 92

  participation in, 211
  petitioning to, 123, 129, 140, 141, 143,
    151, 155, 218
  retrieving petitioners from, 72
Bernstein, Thomas, 9, 72, 165
Bianco, Lucien, 13
Biggs, Michael, 173
black prisons, 73
blockade, of traffic, 3, 4, 36, 47, 71, 116,
  137, 139, 145, 148, 157, 161, 168,
  175, 176, 177, 178
Bunce, Valerie, 199, 200

capital, petitioning to, 19, 46, 167,
  See Beijing
capital, provincial, 122, *See* Changsha
cellular activism, 212
Central Xinfang Bureau. *See* National
  Xinfang Bureau
centralization
  of government, 90
  of power, 14, 90, 92
Chan, Anita, 127
Chang, Chungli, 52
Changsha, 43, 69
Chen Dong, 49, 50
China Disabled Persons Federation,
  131, 142
citizenship rights, 26, 212
civil affairs, bureaus (ministry) of, 129
civil society, 8, 9
Cloward, Richard, 161, 163
coercion, 75, 79

collective incidents, 27
collective petitioning, 4, 29, 55, 147, 189
    in the 1980s, 43
    in the 1990s, 101
    to Beijing, 129
    the concept of, 22
    containing, 14, 125, 192
    demands in, 38
    in imperial eras, 48
    and important periods, 123
    in the late Qing, 51
    multi-party game in, 9
    on national politics, 51
    official attitude toward, 115, 117
    on-site observations of, 215
    punishment for, 53
    required reports on, 122
    skip-level, 19
    and social protest, 22
    waves of, 40, 53
    xinfang system and, 88
collective visits, 32, 144, 149, *See* collective
    petitioning
communism, in China, 77
concessions, 19, 66, 74, 75, 76, 114, 218,
    See expedient concessions
contentious authoritarianism, 7, 8, 189,
    191, 192, 193, 194, 209, 211
    the definition of, 6, 189
contentious bargaining, 5, 21, 22, 88, 131,
    204, 205, 209
    social protests as, 207
    and stability, 207
contradictions among the people, 43, 71, 77
contradictions and ambiguities, 14, 16, 21,
    22, 24, 127, 135, 160, 190, 192,
    196, 197, 198
    appropriation of, 198
    of mass line politics, 128
    as POS, 201
corruption, 36, 37, 54, 82, 92, 109
costly signaling, 163, 173
costumes, petitioners', 174
court system, 32, 64, 65, 191
    as advocates, 72
    vs. xinfang system, 83, 119–121
Cultural Revolution, 39, 62, 74, 91, 95, 127

decentralization, 17, 63
    of economy, 191
demobilized army officers, 9, 36, 39, 43,
    138, 150, 151, 154, 175, 189

democratization, 26, 204
    the third wave of, 89, 202
demonstrations, 4, 51, 143, 161, 193, 206
Deng Pufang (Chairman of the China
        Disabled Persons Federation),
        64, 142
Deng Xiaoping
    on the mass line, 91
Department of Mass Work, 167
Diao Jiecheng, 41, 93, 129, 213
Ding, X. L., 16, 126, 130
direct petitioning, model of, 165
disabled people, i, 9, 64, 65, 72, 76, 81,
        139, 140, 141, 142
disadvantaged groups, 121
disputes, land, 75, 84
disputes, societal, 34, 37, 39, 43
    in Qing Dynasty, 47
disruptive tactics, 145, 162, 168
    effectiveness of, 182
    of government operation, 177
    influencing social order, 175–177
dissuasion stations, 129
divisions
    between central and local government, 13
    between hard-liners and soft-liners, 6
    horizontal, 16, 63, 65, 72, 191
    in the state structure, 14, 15, 24, 60, 62,
        86, 130, 137, 158, 160, 191, 195
    vertical, 63, 70, 72
Dongxiang County, 51
drum of remonstration, 46

Eastern Europe, 89, 199
Economist, 211
efficacy, protest, 5, 40, 160, 164
    perception of, 185
    vs. safety, 136, 155
    a statistical analysis of, 179
elections, local, 204
    interference with, 43
elections, village
    irregularities in, 36
    petitions about, 5, 36
England, Victorian, 78
enterprise restructuring, 33, 34, 37
everyday forms of resistance, 136
expedient concessions, 24, 59, 75, 76, 86,
        110, 138

facilitation of popular contention, 13, 44,
        54, 193, 196

Falungong movement, 82, 193
feedback, negative, 190
food rationing system, 21, 38, 39,
    128, 129
Foucault, 68
Frakt, Phyllis M., 90
framing, 5, 17

Gamson, William, 161
Gengsheng reforms, 43
Great Leap Forward (GLF), 17, 40
grievance-centered analysis, 8
Gu Yanwu, 53
Gurr, Ted, 8

handbills, 139, 168, 169
Henan, 29, 213, 220
    vs. Hunan, 29, 31, 32
historical institutionalism, 201
Hobsbawm, Eric, 206
house demolition, 34, 35, 39
Hu Jintao, 89
Hu Yaobang, 120
hukou, 43
Hunan, 103, 113, 116, 124
    blockade of bridges, 176
    as a case, 220
    a document on long-term petitioners, 114
    a case of self-inflicted sufferings, 173
    collective petitioning events, 3, 29
    collective petitioning events in
        1985–1986, 44
    demands in collective petitioning events
        in, 33, 34
    disabled people, 140
    government archival materials, 214
    peasant activists, 156
    policy on reports on collective
        petitioning events, 122
    policy on the use of force, 71
    a provincial leader, 43, 112
    provincial xinfang bureau, 73, 97,
        102, 123
    reforms on the xinfang system, 117
    and savings crises, 85
    three forms of claim-making
        activities, 31
    training manual in the xinfang
        system, 101
    the trends in, 29
    xinfang bureaus in, 214
    xinfang bureaus in 1957, 94

Hunan Teachers' College, 43
Hundred Flowers Campaign, 41, 43
hunger strikes, 172, 173, 174
Huntington, Samuel, 203
Hurst, William, 9, 11

ideology
    mass line, 18, 190
    socialist, 78, 89, 118, 203
    the strength of, 79, 80
    taking advantage of, 175
individual petitions, 32, 33, 54, 124, 151
individual visits, vi, 30, 31, 32, 44,
        See individual petitions
informal institutions, 204
institutional amphibiousness, 126, 131
institutional configuration, 14, 20, 88, 130
institutional conversion, 24, 126, 127,
        131, 201
    the definition of, 88
intellectuals, 52, 197
    as advocates for protesters, 167
Internet, 167, 168, 214

Jiahe County, 70, 83
Jiang Zemin, 81, 89
Jiangsu Province, 51, 159
Jin Dynasties, 46
Jin Shengtan, 51
jobs and placements, 36

Kang Youwei, 50
Katznelson, Ira, 201
King, Martin Luther, Jr., 161
kneeling in supplication, 171, 172

laid-off workers, 33, 39
Lampert, Nicolas, 111
land expropriation, 5, 35, 38
laohu, 84, 113, 114, 123
Late Han, 48, 49
Law on Marches and Demonstrations, 146
Lee, C. K., 9, 17, 63, 118
legal education, 82
legal reform, 17, 118, 138
legitimation, 11, 17, 63
Lenin, V. I., 208
letters and visits. *See* xinfang
Li, Lianjiang, 15, 136, 137
Liang Qichao, 50
Liangshan, 45
Liaoning Province, 68, 156

liberal democracy, 89, 190, 192
    an advantage of, 209
    an alternative to, 208, 209
Liebman, Benjamin, 12, 18, 167, 209
Lin Biao, 41
Lin Yutang, 48, 49
Lindblom, Charles, 76, 78, 79
Linz, Juan, 6
Lipsky, Michael, 163
litigation, 28, 30, 55
    civil, 12
Liu Shaoqi, 89, 91
long-term petitioners. See *laohu*
Lu Xun, 51
Lü, Xiaobo, 9, 227
lung stone, 46

Ma Shaofang, 172
managed participation, 87
mandate of heaven, 45
Mao Zedong
    anticipated petitioning activities, 111
    Deng Xiaoping's comments on, 92
    dissolving the labor unions, 127
    encouraging protests, 43
    instruction on the xinfang system, 93
    and mass line politics, 89, 91
    on persuasion, 77
Mao Zedong Thought, 149, 150, 154
marching, 157, 169
market economy, 10, 39, 175, 186, 191
market socialism, 10
mass campaigns, 39, 89, 91, *See* political
        campaigns
    initiated by Mao, 91
mass line, 14, 15, 21, 22, 128, 137,
        168, 210
    definition of, 89
    and the designing the xinfang
        system, 92
    dilemma of, 99
    and institutions, 90
    inherent tensions of, 18, 88
    institutional approaches to, 91
    vs. liberal democracy, 89
    Mao's definition of, 90
    and mass campaigns, 89, 91
    principles of, 90
mass organizations, 16, 64, 72, 131,
        165, 191
May 4th movement, 51

McAdam, Doug, 128, 135, 162, 163,
        194, 196
McCarthy, John, 7
McPhail, Clark, 7
mediation, 32, 55
    labor, 131
Meyer, David, 7, 199
mobilizing structure, 8, 9, 15
    explanations based on, 8
modernization theories, 10

Nathan, Andrew, 20, 60, 202, 204
National People's Congress (NPC), 72, 208.
        See also People's congresses
National Xinfang Bureau, 82, 103
Naughton, Barry, 202
negative inducements, 161, 163, 185
networks, 9
    communal, 9
    as mobilizing structure, 8
    patron-client, 61
Northern Song, 49

O'Brien, Kevin, 9, 11, 15, 131, 136,
        137, 167
Ocko, Jonathan, 47
official media, 64, 98, 131
    amphibious, 126
    as elite advocates, 167, 191
Oi, Jean, 60
opportunistic troublemaking, 24
organization-centered analysis, 9
organized dependence, 14, 21, 128, 191
organized migration, 35, 38
Orwell, George, 78
over-taxation, 51, 97

particularism, 60, 70, 75, 211, 212
Payne, James, 206
peasant burden, 36, 37, 75, 80, 84,
        85, 220
Pei, Minxin, 11
pension arrears, 3, 34, 75, 81, 84, 220
pensioners, 3, 12, 34, 71, 110, 143,
        182, 189
    association of, 9
    and workers, 11
people's communes, 20, 60, 129, 191
People's congresses, 16, 35, 64, 67, 69, 96,
        98, 165, 181
people's mediation committees, 12, 32

People's Political Consultative Conference, 69, 98, 165, 181
performing persuasive tactics, 170, 174, 177, 182, 185
  definition of, 171
Perry, Elizabeth, 4, 9, 15, 43, 44, 45, 194, 203
persuasion
  ideological, 78, 80
  practical, 24, 59, 78, 79, 80, 85
  as a state strategy, 66
Peru, 206
Piven, Frances Fox, 161, 163
pluralist model
  vs. power elite model, 163
political campaigns, 13, 23, 39, 40, 42, 43, 54, 89, 119, 193
political consultation, 18, 99, 122, 190, 198
  in mass line politics, 14
  non-binding direct, 18
political opportunities, 6, 13, 88
political opportunity structures, 13, 15, 21, 39, 60, 88, 135, 138, 186, 192, 194, 200
  explanations based on, 12
  historical construction of, 19
  as historical junctures, 199
  perception of, 165
  state-centered, 8, 13, 15
  theories of, 195
political participation, 20, 84, 85, 203, 204, 211, 212
  prescribed, 5
political process theory, 8, 12, 16, 194
  structural biases of, 201
polity model, 163, 195
Powell, Bingham, 206
preceptoral system, 77
pressure groups, 157
  de facto, 5, 198
proactive role of the state, 15, 22, 192, 193
procrastination, 65, 83, 84, 85, 138, 207
  as a state strategy, 59, 66
protest opportunism, 137, 150, 153, 158, 159, 178, 192
  the concept of, 136
  consequences of, 157
Przeworski, Adam, 6, 203
public petitioning, 168, 190

Public Security, Ministry of, 27, 29, 129
publicity, 21, 25, 153, 156, 160, 163, 178
  effect of, 182, 185
  tactics, 165, 168, 169, 171, 177, 182
punishment, 154
  arbitrary, 116, 138
  in imperial eras, 53
  of officials, 36
  of petitioners, 47, 53, 68, 73, 115
  resulted from disruption, 53
  selective, 198
  selective and exemplary, 116, 138
  threat of, 197

Qin Dynasty, 46
Qing Dynasty, 46, 47, 50, 51, 53, 92, 105, 109

railway system, 21, 128
  for social control, 129
rebellions, 9, 44, 54, 189, 205, 207
  ancient, 45
  attempting, 53
rectification campaign, 41
Regulations on Letters and Visits, 124
Regulations on Public Security Management, 146
repertoire of contention, 46, 52, 219
  imperial-era, 53
repetitive petitioning, 112, 113, *See laohu*
repression, 7, 65, 76, 121, 136, 138, 154, 196, 198
  capacity for, 59
  of petitions, 51
  preventive, 85
  restrained, 68, 72, 86
  as a state strategy, 60, 66
  uncertainty of, 158, 210
resource mobilization theory, 8, 194
responsibility, local officials', 18, 96, 109, 121, 124, 125, 190, 192
responsiveness, government, 90, 190, 209
  inadequate or excessive, 209
revolutionary songs, 151, 174, 175
revolutions, 54, 205, 207
rightful resistance, 15, 131, 177
  the concept of, 136
  vs. protest opportunism, 137
riots, 49
rule by men, 118
rule of law, 18, 118, 210

Schock, Kurt, 162
Scott, James, 136, 181, 196, 197, 205
Selden, Mark, 4, 89
self-immolation, 157, 163, 171, 173, 182, 186
self-inflicted sufferings, 47, 182
Sewell, William, 135
shangfang. *See* xinfang
Shenzhen, 171, 210
Shi, Tianjian, 20, 211, 212
Shun, 46
Sichuan Province, 41, 51, 67, 68
Simmel, George, 197
sit-ins, 157, 169
skip-level petitioning, 112, 113, 122, 182
Skocpol, Theda, 165
social appropriation, 15, 22, 126, 128, 130, 131, 197, 201, 202
social movement industry, 10
social movement organizations (SMO), 8
social movement society, 7
social movements
    theories, 160, 194
social networks. *See* networks
social stability, 78, 82, 207
Solinger, Dorothy, 154
Southern Song, 49
Soviet Union, 89, 93, 105, 190
specialized petitioners, 114
Stalin, Joseph, 127
state, a dialectical view of, 17
State Council, 41, 42, 70, 94, 97, 129, 153
state strategies, 22, 59, 65, 84, 86
    changes in, 138
    repertoire of, 24, 65
state-owned enterprises, 33, 37, 61, 62, 96, 147, 213
state-society linkages, 68, 74
    changes in, 59, 62, 200
    in the unit system, 80
strikes, 43, 172, 176
    in Shanghai, 43
    waves of, 6
student movements
    in 1989, 6, 9, 10, 17, 68, 82, 126, 127, 172, 193, 200
    in imperial eras, 48
Su, Yang, 162
suicide, 47, 137, 174
Sun Zhigang, victim of police abuse, 129
system of custody and repatriation, 21, 128, 129, 130

Tanner, Murray Scot, 67, 71
Tarrow, Sidney, 6, 7, 46, 196, 199, 200
Thelen, Kathleen, 88, 201
Thompson, E. P., 206
Tian Jiyun, 120
Tilly, Charles, 110, 163, 195
Tocqueville, Alexis de, 90, 199
toleration, 44, 193, 204, 207, 211
    of extra-institutional behaviors, 211
totalitarian systems, 77
troublemaking tactics, 99, 122, 144, 154, 156, 165, 200
    effect of, 179, 180
trust
    in higher authorities, 166
    in the Party, 153
    in the state, 165
tutelary system, 77

Unger, Jonathan, 127
unit system, 20, 21, 68, 70, 74, 85, 211
    the authority in, 75
    the concept of, 60
    the decline of, 88, 128, 200
    the model of, 60, 61
    the transition from, 78, 137, 158
unrest
    labor, 68
    social, 119, 161
urban affairs management, 35

veterans. *See* demobilized army officers
violence, 171, 177, 206
    courting, 163
    decline in, 8
    vs. disruption, 162

Walder, Andrew, 60, 63, 74, 77, 193
Wang, Shaoguang, 63
Water Margin, 45
Wen Jiabao, 120
Western Zhou Dynasty, 46
Wilson, James, 161, 163
work units. *See* unit system
workers' welfare, 33, 37, 39
Wuxian County, 51

Xiangtan, 43
xinfang
    big, 96
    small, 96
xinfang system, 88, 109

appropriation of, 5
conversion of, 202
vs. court system, 83, 120
designing, 92
reforms of, 118, 119, 122, 124
structures of, 95

Yang, Dali, 130, 202
Yang Shangkun, 100
Yao, 46

Ying Xing, 9, 40, 120
Yu, 46
Yu Jianrong, 129, 156

Zhao, Dingxin, 10, 15, 200
Zhejiang Province, 105
Zhou Guangyuan, 51, 52, 109
Zhou, Xueguang, 10
Zhu Rongji, 14, 70, 77, 81, 100, 104, 120